'Race', Gender, Social Welfare

For my Mum, for whom dreaming was both a necessity and an impossibility, and for Simon, Bianca and Kyle, that their dreams are easier to hold.

'Race', Gender, Social Welfare

Encounters in a Postcolonial Society

Gail Lewis

Polity Press

First published in 2000 by Polity Press in association with Blackwell Publishers Ltd

Editorial office:
Polity Press
65 Bridge Street
Cambridge CB2 1UR, UK

Marketing and production:
Blackwell Publishers Ltd
108 Cowley Road
Oxford OX4 1JF, UK

Published in the USA by
Blackwell Publishers Inc.
Commerce Place
350 Main Street
Malden, MA 02148, USA

ISBN 0-7456-2284-4
ISBN 0-7456-2285-2 (pbk)

A catalogue record for this book is available from the British Library and has been applied for from the Library of Congress.

Typeset in 10 on 12 pt Times New Roman
by Best-set Typesetter Ltd., Hong Kong
Printed in Great Britain by MPG Books Ltd, Bodmin, Cornwall

This book is printed on acid-free paper.

Contents

Conclusion

Acknowledgements

There are of course numerous people who have helped, encouraged and held me during this book's long gestation period. From its original incarnation as a Ph.D. thesis, through to its more refined version here, none of it would have been possible without the support, encouragement, argument and above all interest of the following people: Liliane Landor, Catherine Hall, Ann Phoenix, Avtar Brah, Mary Hickman, Jacqui Alexander, Esther Saraga, Aisha Phoenix, John Clarke, Allan Cochrane and my Ph.D. examiners, Margaret Wetherell and Fiona Williams. Pauline Hetherington, Sue Lacey and Doreen Pendlebury have been invaluable, and are as inscribed in these pages as the people above. Also thanks to Rebecca Harkin, who restores my faith in publishers, and to Doreen Massey for suggesting me to Polity. Chapter 7 was previously published in *Feminist Review*, and I thank the editorial collective of that time for their support, especially Annie Whitehead. I am grateful for permission to publish an extract from Toni Morrison, *Playing in the Dark*, pp. 9–10, reprinted by permission of International Creative Management, Inc. © 1992 Harvard University Press. Finally two further heartfelt thanks. First to all those women and men in the social services departments who gave so generously of their time and understandings of what was going on. And to my beloved Nan, and my teacher Mr Jones, whose combined efforts to teach me to read at age 10 pointed me in this direction.

List of Abbreviations

ABSWAP	Association of Black Social Workers and Allied Professionals
ADSS	Association of Directors of Social Services
BASW	British Association of Social Workers
CBI	Confederation of British Industry
CCETSW	Central Council for Education and Training in Social Work
CQSW	Certificate of Qualifying Social Work
CRC	Community Relations Council
CRE	Commission for Racial Equality
DES	Department of Education and Science
DipSW	Diploma in Social Work
DS	*Difendere la società*, M. Foucault (1990)
FSU	Family Service Unit
GLC	Greater London Council
HC	House of Commons
HMSO	Her Majesty's Stationery Office (now The Stationery Office)
ICP	Inner City Partnership
IEA	Institute of Economic Affairs
IMF	International Monetary Fund
JCWI	Joint Council for the Welfare of Immigrants
NCVO	National Council of Voluntary Organizations
NCWP	New Commonwealth and Pakistan
NHS	National Health Service
PAU	Positive Action Unit
PSI	Policy Studies Institute

REU	Race Equality Unit
RRA	Race Relations Act
SBS	Southall Black Sisters
SRB	Single Regeneration Budget
SSD	Social Services Department
SSI	Social Services Inspectorate
TUC	Trades Union Congress

Preface

This book explores the relationships among 'race', gender and social welfare in late twentieth-century Britain. Its specific focus is the entry of women of African-Caribbean, African and south Asian origin and descent into professional social work during the 1980s and early 1990s but the argument and general approach extend into other fields of social welfare. The book is empirically based, drawing on primary data from three sources. First, is material from *Hansard* parliamentary reports. Reports of the main House of Commons debates on proposed legislation dealing with inner cities policy, local government powers, race relations, and social services work with children and adults provided the first layer of primary material. The period covered ranged from 1966 when the Local Government Act introduced section 11 monies to 1995 when this source of funds was coming to an end in its original form. The legislation considered was: the Local Government Act 1966; the Local Government Grants (Social Need) Act 1969; the Inner Urban Areas Act 1978; the Race Relations Act 1976; the Children Act 1989; and the National Health Service and Community Care Act 1990.

These statutes, and the debates accompanying their passage through Parliament, formed the framework of successive central government policies. These in turn provided part of the legal and financial context for the employment of black women (and men) in qualified social work positions in local authority social services departments. These parliamentary debates played a key part in the constitution of the racialized populations from which black and Asian women social workers were drawn and amongst whom they were expected to work. In providing for local authority action in specific geographical and policy areas, a framework was established that enabled recruitment of black women (and men) to social services employment on racialized terms. In this book I consider the discursive associations made between specific policy agendas, the characterization of certain geographical areas and the presence of black and Asian populations in these areas.

If central policy agendas and debates helped form part of the legal, financial and discursive fields through which black women (and men) were recruited to local authority social services departments, the specifics of their employment were established in the local policy arena. The second source of primary data is that derived from policies in two social services departments, one a London borough authority, the other a city authority. For purposes of anonymity these are called respectively 'Coolville' and 'Inland City'. These authorities were selected on the basis of two criteria: that at least 10 per cent of their population be classified as 'ethnic minority' for the purposes of the 1991 Census; and that they had a record of, or commitment to, active recruitment of 'ethnic minority' staff to qualified social work positions.

I analysed a large number of reports presented to the social services committees in the two authorities (and where relevant a small number from other committees such as Finance and General Purposes or Equal Opportunities). I was concerned to analyse how black and Asian recruitment to qualified social work positions was achieved; what issues such recruitment was seen to address; and what subject positions were being textually constituted by these policies. As with the *Hansard* papers, many more were collected and read than are explicitly quoted. All those dealing directly or indirectly with the employment of black and Asian social workers in qualified positions or with the delivery of services to 'ethnic minority' service users were considered. In the borough authority this covered the years from 1982 to 1995. For the city authority the period ranged from 1985 to 1995. The earlier dates mark the point when the authority began explicitly to address the issue of its work with a multi-racial/multi-ethnic population. Those policy documents that most clearly illustrated the general direction and tenor of the policy, and the discourses inscribed within them, are referred to in the chapters that follow. Those not directly cited provide part of the general background for my argument.

Third, is data from thirty-three interviews I conducted between 1994 and 1995.[1] Twenty-two of the interviews were with women social workers up to and including team manager level and from African-Caribbean, African or south Asian ethnic backgrounds. Eight were with area office managers, four of whom were women defined as ethnic minority; the other four being two white women and two white men, all of English ethnicity. Two interview participants, one woman and one man, were assistant directors of social services, both white and with uncertain ethnic background. The final interview was with a woman of Caribbean descent who had worked in a specialist unit in the City authority. Most of the extracts from the interviews appear in Part II and these extracts are referred to as 'accounts'. In keeping with the post-structuralist framing of the book, language is conceived as an active process in which those discursive repertoires that are available are deployed in an attempt to construct a position in and from which to make sense of the world. Accounts, then, are social in three aspects. First, the discursive repertoires that are available to an individual are socially produced. Second, the ways that individuals use these resources are social in an iterative or citational sense in that people draw upon and deploy meanings that pre-exist them. Third, they are social in an inter-actional sense in that they are the mechanisms through which individuals connect with others. The 'selves' and 'others' produced in and by accounts are contingent subjects and here I use the accounts to explore the moments at and methods by which discourses of 'race' and gender were used to give meaning to the social relations of the social services department.

These data form the basis of the argument developed in the book. My argument is that the entry of black and Asian women into professional social work in this period occurred as part of a moment of racial for-mation and social regulation in which specific racialized populations were managed through a regime of governmentality in which 'new black subjects' were formed. These 'new black subjects' were reconstituted as 'ethnic minorities' out of an earlier form of social being as 'immigrants'. Central to this process of reconstitution was a discourse of black and Asian family forms as pathological and yet governable through the inter-vention of state welfare agencies. Social work as a specific form of state-organized intervention was articulated to discourses of 'race' and black and Asian family formations. This articulation suggested that the man-agement of those racialized families who could be defined as pathologi-cal or 'in need' required specific 'ethnic' knowledge and in this way the creation of a space for the entry of black and Asian women into quali-fied social work occurred. This process intersected with a spate of riotous protests in many cities and towns and a moment of municipal socialism that had seen the assimilation into the policies of numerous town halls the demands of diverse social movements for greater social equality. This made it incumbent on those authorities to implement equality of oppor-tunity within their directorates. Whilst the discourses of 'race'/ethnicity and gender equality provided some of the impetus for the entry of black and Asian women into professional social work, these women's under-standing and experience of this employment was mediated through a sense of organizational exclusion and a set of oppositional discourses. These understandings provided the substance through which the women negotiated their position within social services.

The structure of the book follows the tiers of the argument as it unfolds using data from central and local policies and debates, and interview material. The introduction lays out the intellectual and political antecedents of the research project. Part I comprises chapters 1–4 and maps processes of racial formation at national and local levels. It begins by using the Foucauldian notion of 'governmentality' to examine the processes of formation of ethnic minority populations and how specific welfare institutions were centrally involved in the constitution of these new racial subjects. Social work was just one of these welfare agencies but its place as the agency dealing with 'the family' – albeit specific families – assigned it a special place in the process of bringing racialized 'others' into new forms of regulation. Chapters 2 and 3 respectively discuss the central and local government policies that were used in, or developed for, the recruitment of black and Asian women to professional social work. These chapters do more than just outline the relevant policies. By analysing parliamentary debates in *Hansard* and local authority committee reports, I explore two intersecting processes: on the one hand, the connections between the discursive frameworks embedded within these debates and policies and processes of racial formation; on the other, the mutually constitutive relation between policy formation and racialized and gendered 'othering'. Significantly, racial and gender formations emerge out of the struggle between hegemonic ideologies and practices and challenges to such ideologies and practices. Chapter 4, then, focuses on the discourses of 'race' and ethnicity that, under the influence of the Association of Black Social Workers and Allied Professionals, began to circulate within the profession of social work in the late 1980s and early 1990s.

Part II, consisting of chapters 5, 6 and 7, narrows the lens of analysis and focuses on interview participants' accounts. These accounts are used to stage a kind of encounter between the understandings of the dynamic between social welfare and 'race' and gender conveyed in central, local and professional policies and statements, and the meanings given to this dynamic by black and Asian women social workers. The accounts are used to unfold an argument about the contexts in which, and the processes by which, the racialized and gendered category 'black woman social worker' is constructed and given meaning in a specific institutional setting. Thus, my argument is extended to the ways that 'race', gender and ethnicity structure and saturate the everyday world of social services departments.

Finally, the concluding chapter provides a brief summary of the argument and indicates areas of further investigation.

Introduction

How was it that in the 1980s women of African-Caribbean, African and south Asian origin and descent were afforded the opportunity to enter professional social work grades in local authority social services departments? How did women from these groups understand the creation of this relatively new employment opportunity and how did they interpret their experience of the job of social work? These are the questions this book addresses. Temporally located in the 1980s and early 1990s, it focuses on the links between social work as a specific state welfare practice and the discursive production of racialized knowledges, social locations and categories of belonging. As a story about a particular employment opportunity, the book eschews more usual approaches to the employment patterns and experiences of women and racialized populations of colour.[1] Such approaches have tended to cluster around the development and operation of segmented labour markets; theories of a reserve army of labour; or the racially and sexually disadvantaging effects of the behavioural patterns of employers in the private and public sectors. Similarly, as a story about the production and satisfaction of particularized welfare needs, the book also rejects the orthodox approaches to the relation between welfare agencies and Britain's racialized populations of colour. In their stead an argument is developed which seeks to connect the 'social' and 'work' of 'social work' with the construction and regulation of populations of people racialized as 'ethnic minorities'. The argument is built through the use of concepts and categories of analysis drawn from areas of sociological enquiry and theoretical frameworks usually thought of as discrete and/or of little relevance to an understanding of employment creation and welfare inequalities. These are: analyses of the ways in which black populations are constructed and represented in official and popular discourse; the location of black and 'ethnic minority' populations within the social relations of welfare; the emergence of self-organized, self-defined organizations under the sign 'black', especially within black feminism and black cultural productions; and, finally, analysis of narrative accounts of everyday experience. Individually, each of these fields of enquiry offers some understanding of the social and discursive locations occupied by racialized populations of colour and the processes which determine both these locations and the very forms of their racialization. These literatures also help understanding of mechanisms and forms of destabilization and resistance to patterns of discrimination, disadvantage and racialization. However, despite the contributions they make to an understanding of the social relations of 'race', their limitations reside in the way in which they separate the material from the cultural and structure from agency. Equally problematic for the issues considered in this book is the tendency within these literatures to separate 'race' from gender or, at best, to privilege one of these axes of differentiation and subordination. This book attempts to build on the insights into the social relations of 'race' contained in the existing literatures by using perspectives and categories of analysis contained in recent developments in social and cultural theory. In particular I use categories of analysis drawn from post-structuralist and postcolonial perspectives to develop an argument about the creation of a particular employment opportunity for a specific segment of the population.

Intellectual and political roots

My route into the questions which lie at the heart of this book, and the theoretical frameworks I employ in the attempt to answer them, emerge directly from the political movements of which I had been part. These antecedents were concerned with the constitution of new forms of belonging, new positions from which to speak, new 'imagined communities' organized around, and articulated through, particularity and difference. In short, the struggles and debates with which I had been connected, and the political and intellectual projects with which I was concerned, had been preoccupied with effecting a decentring of the old grand-narratives and their attendant political subjects (including that of Marxism). Collectively, and often fractiously, we sought to substitute new locations and codes through which to articulate other subjects and constituencies who might be harnessed to a hegemonic project of democratic transformation. These collective concerns were to disrupt the old certainties and to introduce the idea of new political constituencies which had emerged from the margins, but whose existence embodied and represented the anxieties and fears of difference and the 'other', which, paradoxically, had partially produced the old certainties and universal subjects. It was not that the 'new social movements' (Touraine, 1981) and other constituencies of struggle were unambiguously divorced from Marxism and class-based politics. A particularly clear example of this was that provided by the anti-colonial and national liberation struggles in parts of the 'third world', and indeed in the black trade union organizations and struggles within Britain. Rather, it was that this disparate range of contestatory sites to dominant political, economic, social and cultural relations attempted to articulate their oppositional practices around and through the formation of political actors outside of the proletarian/bourgeois binary at the heart of Marxism. What links there were between the class subject and the gendered, 'raced', colonial or sexual subject became the object of much agonized, heated and at times antagonistic debate as activists in these diverse movements sought to construct economies of sign and practice which would have the effect of reconfiguring the boundaries of diverse belongings.

For me, chief among these new political projects was what was to become known as black feminism as it emerged in Britain from the mid-1970s. As with any of the new political constituencies, black feminism was not singular or unitary in its approaches. Yet it is possible to identify a set of concerns which indicate a commonality of political project. In its earliest incarnation black feminism had at its heart a critique of black masculinist and white feminist ways of storytelling, both of which erased and silenced black women. In constructing their narratives of 'race'/racism and gender these two political constituencies failed to include the possibility that 'race' needed to be gendered and gender needed to be 'raced'. In contrast, black feminism was concerned to struggle for a politics which was both grounded in the 'experiences' of black women and which theorized those experiences. In addition, many black feminists focused their political activity on the relationship between black women and the welfare state, both as a site of employment and as a provider of services. Bryan, Dadzie and Scafe's *Heart of the Race* (1985) was an early example of this focus and its importance lies in its identification of welfare institutions as sites of professional practice which served to reproduce black women's gendered and 'raced' subordination as both employees and service users. Since that time, black feminist texts have proliferated and, in carving out a speaking position within and against the dominant narratives of class, 'race' and gender, they have served to deconstruct the myth of black or gender homogeneity.

Black feminists, then, had squarely placed the 'caring' professions of the welfare state on the political and intellectual agenda. As I show in chapter 4, by the 1980s, social work had come to occupy a special place in the struggles of black people for improved welfare services. Moreover, the challenge to the racism of service provision occurred in the context of a history in which the state welfare sector had been a major employer of black and other racialized groups (including Irish women) since the Second World War. To a large extent this employment has been in numerous occupations in the National Health Service – as nurses, doctors, cleaners and cooks. There has, then, been some post-war continuity in employment in state welfare.

Social services departments were not, however, traditional areas of employment for black women, particularly as qualified practitioners in the professional occupations. It has only been since the 1980s that there has been an increase in the numbers of qualified black social workers, and this only in some specific local authority departments. To a large extent the opening of this sector of the occupation to 'ethnic minority' women resulted from the pressure for, and adoption of, equal opportunities policies across the local authority sector. In social services departments the pressure to promote and increase the employment of black social workers was also linked to a recognition of the increasingly multi-ethnic and multi-faith character of the population, especially in large metropolitan cities. This increased diversity impacted on social services departments in a number of ways. Since the majority of clients of social services are drawn from the economically poorer sections of the population and because there is an over-representation of black people amongst the economically poor, ethnic diversity reconfigures as inequality and reflects itself amongst social work client groups. In addition, the impact of racist discourses and practices resulted in the pathologization of black clients and their forms of familial and community life. As a result, they have more easily been positioned as potential clients of social services. In the 1980s, these trends converged with a growing concern for 'ethnic sensitivity' and, together with the professional discourse of 'care', resulted in the demand for the staff profile of social service departments to reflect the populations they serve. This led to an increase in the numbers of 'ethnic minority' social workers employed by some departments. Thus, as both employers and service providers, welfare agencies were incorporated into the political sights of black feminists.

The emergence of black feminist positions within Britain intersected with the rise of black cultural criticism, which, in engaging in a war of position over representations of 'race', was also challenging the myth of internal homogeneity amongst the diverse racialized populations of colour in Britain. Central to this war of position was the question of who could be included in the 'imagined community' of England/Britain.[2] The 1980s and early 1990s saw the emergence of dominant narratives of post-imperial Britain which sought to produce a 'little Englandism' through a nostalgic reconstruction of imperial greatness. In cultural productions this manifested itself in the fascination with the Raj, as exemplified

in the TV series *The Jewel in the Crown* or the expressions of anxiety
and uncertainty contained in the numerous Merchant–Ivory films (for
example, *A Room With a View*; *Howard's End*; *The Remains of the Day*).
Expressions of national anxiety also appeared in the tabloid newspapers
and often explicitly evoked 'race' and nation. For example, Alfred
Sherman, writing in the *Daily Telegraph* in 1979, stated:

> The imposition of mass immigration from backward alien cultures is just
> one symptom of this self-destructive urge reflected in the assault on patri-
> otism, the family – both as conjugal and economic unit – the Christian reli-
> gion in public life and schools, traditional morality, in matters of sex,
> honesty, public display, and respect for the law – in short, all that is English
> and wholesome.   (9 September, 'Britain's urge to self-destruction')

In contrast to sentiments such as these, black cultural producers (for
example, the films of the Black Audio and Visual Collective and Sankofa;
the paintings of Sonia Boyce or Chaila Burman; and the photography
of Ingrid Pollard, Sunil Gupta and David A. Bailey) sought to challenge
and interrogate the boundaries and meanings of national belonging
expressed in statements like that of Sherman.

Black cultural productions of this kind raised two issues which are
particularly pertinent to the concerns of this book. On the one hand is
the attempt to disarticulate forms of, and claims to, national belonging
from notions of 'race' and ethnicity. This involves at least two interconnected processes. It requires a rejection of the idea that only particular
'racial' or ethnic groups have a legitimate claim to national belonging or
identity. For example, that only white Anglo-Saxons can be fully British.
This implies a rejection of the idea that national belonging/identity must
be tied to *any* 'racial' categorizations, even if this is in the form of numerous 'racial' or ethnic groups. For example, disclaiming the idea that an
enlightened understanding of the connections between 'race'/ethnicity
and nationhood is about increasing the range of ethnicities which
provide the basis of a legitimate claim. As such, the work of several black
cultural producers and critics constituted a vastly counter-hegemonic
project aimed at addressing the difficult tasks of building alliances among
an array of political subjects and constituencies organized around multiple identities without privileging any of these. Second is a point rarely
noticed and which marks the framework adopted here as distinctive.
This is that the disarticulation of forms of representation from processes
of 'othering' offered social policy tools of critique and analysis which
could challenge and disrupt understandings of 'race' and ethnicity as
fixed and essentialized categories. Thus, in so far as policies embody and
produce representations as much as they provide the frame within which
professional practices are enacted, cultural production which unsettles

established ways of seeing can offer much to the development of a critical social policy.

These projects of re-articulation were developed within the context of what the authors of *The Empire Strikes Back* (Centre for Contemporary Cultural Studies, 1982) termed an 'organic crisis'. To suggest that the crisis which Britain has faced from the mid-1970s is organic means 'that it is the result of the combined effect of economic, political, ideological and cultural processes' (p. 11). Moreover, 'race' played a central role in articulating the deep anxieties which accompanied the crisis and increasingly became 'one of the means through which hegemonic relations [were] secured in a period of structural crisis management' (p. 11). The ideological response by sections of the establishment to this organic crisis was to construct a chain of association connecting a series of social changes with what was seen by some as a decline in traditional values and authority relations. Alfred Sherman's statement is an eloquent expression of this ideological position. This view was especially, though not exclusively (see, for example, Halsey, 1992), expounded by what became known as the New Right, who focused their attention on issues of law and order, family values, the 'threat' posed by Europe to British sovereignty, and the 'loony left' – i.e. all those areas which were identified as the 'natural' province of conservatism, respectability and indeed 'greatness'. Increasingly, the welfare state became central to this ideological and policy onslaught as successive Conservative governments sought to alter both the criteria of eligibility for numerous welfare benefits and services, and the balance of rights and responsibilities between state and citizen, and between state and 'asylum seeker' or refugee (Hughes and Lewis, eds, 1998; JCWI, 1999). The rhetorical turn to the terrain of family values carried with it a profound anxiety about, and attack upon, the changes in gender and sexual relations which had emerged since the 1960s. Thus, single-motherhood, other forms of non-traditional household, and homosexuality were at best constructed as cause for concern, at worst blatantly vilified or outlawed (as in the Local Government Act of 1988) at the same time that the rights, and responsibilities, of heterosexual, married parents were promoted and reinforced (as in the 1989 Children Act, and the 1988 Education Reform Act).

What 'law and order' and 'family values' carried with them were racialized representations and codes which helped to configure the crisis in a binary split between Englishness/Britishness and its 'aliens within'. Thus, the then Secretary of State for Education, Mark Carlisle, could state in 1981 that the spate of riotous protest which had spread throughout many of Britain's inner cities over the preceding year was a result of 'a breakdown in the stabilizing forces of society: the nation, patriotism, the family and the whole community' (*The Times*, 18 July). Explicit racialization was left to John Brown, one of the architects of community policing. Brown did not, however, racialize those of Asian and Caribbean origin or descent in the same ways. 'Beyond the contextual forces', he wrote,

> lie what seems to me the most primary force of all: that of 'culture', by which I mean the characteristic ways of life, relationships and values of people of different regions and countries. This may be clearly seen in the microcosm of Handsworth, for example, where it is of utmost pertinence to compare the capacity for care and order [including crime control] of Asian groups, with their strong communal traditions and value system, with those of Caribbean groups, with their relatively weak communal traditions framed within a dependent culture. (1981, p. 8)

Mercer (1994) has made the point that this ideological ground had been prefigured some twelve to fifteen years earlier in Enoch Powell's speeches about the black presence in Britain, which he made in the late 1960s. Mercer writes:

> The 'conspiracy theory' expressed [by Powell] . . . already acknowledges the populist rupture created by the April 'rivers of blood' speech: moreover, the splitting which Powell reveals is not the antagonism between whites and blacks but the antagonism between 'the people' as silent majority, against the media and the 'establishment' which thus represent 'the state'. Through this bipolar division, Powell's discourse set in motion a system of equivalences predicated on a textual strategy of binary reversal, which culminated in his 'enemies within' speech on the eve of the 1970 General Election.
>
> This text marked a crucial turning point in the popularization of a New Right perspective in British politics. In it, Powell depicts the nation under attack from a series of enemies, thereby linking the 'anarchy' of student demonstrations, the 'civil war' in Northern Ireland, and the racially coded image of the 'United States engulfed in fire and fighting'. The signifying chain is underpinned by the central issue in the conspiracy: 'The exploitation of what is called "race" is a common factor which links the operations of the enemy on several different fronts'. It is through this equivalence that Powell's conspiracy theory posits the reversibility of racial metaphor as the liminal site of a crisis of national identity. (p. 306)

In this analysis, Powell had already set the terms within which the New Right, under the helm of Mrs Thatcher, was to set about its radical restructuring of Britain. Racialized 'others' were among those defined as the 'enemies within' as early as the late 1960s/early 1970s.

If 'race' was central from early on in the attempt to reinvigorate and relegitimate traditional authority relations as hegemonic, the introduction of 'the family' opened the possibility for both articulating 'race' to gender relations and for the 'caring' institutions of the welfare state to be incorporated into this project. Education had long been a central site upon which the struggle was to be fought (see Rattansi, 1992; and Lewis, 1998). This is clear both from the centrality of this sector in issues about immigration and nationhood and from the fact that Keith Joseph, a key architect of Thatcherite strategy, had placed education at the fore in the 1970s. However, as the post-war welfare consensus crumbled under the onslaught of economic, political and ideological attack from the New Right think-tanks and politicians, the way was set for the inclusion of a wider circuit of welfare state agencies in the project of hegemonic restructuring. In this way, social work, as a specific set of institutional practices, became a location from which to attempt to re-authorize forms of family formation and practice, in general, and to negotiate crisis management of racialized populations, in particular.

'Necessary bread' – a new cadre of social workers

The New Right, and fellow travellers, were not, however, alone in identifying social work as a potential site for the resolution of racial tensions. Thus, in 1986 Ahmed, Cheetham and Small published an edited collection of essays entitled *Social Work with Black Children and their Families*. In their introduction they identified a number of thematic and practical issues which, in their view, needed to be addressed by social services departments if they were to better meet the needs of black children and families. Thematically there was a need for change in three areas. First, the existing propensity for social workers and other welfare practitioners to pathologize black families should be replaced by a perspective in which the strengths of such families was valued. Second, diversity of perspective and opinion between, and within, different 'ethnic minority' groups should be welcomed as evidence of the heterogeneity of Britain's black populations. Recognition of this heterogeneity was the necessary starting point if the racist tendency towards homogenization of 'ethnic minority' communities was to be disrupted. However, whilst it was important to recognize the diversity of opinion within black populations, Ahmed et al. cautioned against taking this to mean that strategies which aimed at identifying and meeting the needs of black children and families were redundant. Heterogeneity of view among black communities should not be a premise for the avoidance of responsibility on the part of white practitioners. Finally, the authors argued for acceptance '. . . of the positive changes in the experience of black people which can flow from social work practice which tries to combat racism and to reflect Britain's multi-racial society' (p. 4).

These thematic issues were followed by a number of practical recommendations for local authority social services departments (SSDs).

First, positive action policies should be devised and implemented, including recruitment of black families as foster and adoptive carers, and the location of community-based measures in areas where black children and families live. Second, staff in SSDs needed to recognize the special needs of 'ethnic minority' groups and develop systems for the delivery of relevant information and services to these client groups. Third, SSDs should devise measures to recruit black social workers to their staff teams. 'Because of the problems of communicating across cultures, and the consequent dangers of wrong assessment and decisions,' they argued, 'special efforts must be made to recruit and train ethnic minority social workers who will enlarge their agencies' understanding, make their approach more appropriate and their staffing more representative of a multi-racial society' (p. 17).

While professionals and trainers were arguing the case for the recruitment of qualified black social workers, the Central Council for Education and Training in Social Work (CCETSW) was promoting recruitment of black students to social work qualifying courses. CCETSW was also attempting to ensure that the content of the courses it accredited promoted anti-oppressive practice. Figures from CCETSW show that, in 1993, 14.3 per cent of all those entering either a diploma in social work course (DipSW) or a certificate course (CQSW) were classified as black in the Council's ethnic monitoring categories. This figure had fallen from a peak of 16.9 per cent in 1992, but was still above the 1991 figure of 13.6 per cent. The Ahmed, Cheetham and Small collection and the CCETSW initiatives are indicative of the increasing demand for social services departments to recognize the inadequacy – even racism – of their existing provision and to devise strategies able to redress these inadequacies (Cheetham, 1982; Dominelli, 1988; Pearson, 1988; Ahmed, 1990; Dutt, ed., 1990; Patel, ed., 1991).

Clearly, then, the 1980s represented a moment in which 'ethnic minorities' were identified as having particularistic welfare needs which welfare agencies in general, and social services departments in particular, were not able to recognize or adequately cater for. Faced with this inadequacy, one way forward was increasingly taken to be the employment of staff from racialized populations of colour.

A poverty of theory – established approaches to 'race', gender, welfare and employment

This development placed big practical and theoretical questions on the agenda of diverse constituencies as the impact produced by the encounter between social changes, activism on the part of new political constituencies, welfare reform and crisis management was felt more deeply. What was required was a new analytical framework through which to comprehend both the 'racial' antagonisms and conceptual convergences which the call for a cadre of black social workers represented. Such a framework was not, however, to be found in the established approaches either to the intersection of 'race', gender and employment or to that of 'race', gender and welfare.

'Race', gender and employment

Established approaches to the employment profiles and experiences of racialized populations of colour and women tend towards an analytic separation of 'race' and gender. Predominant approaches are situated within a neo-liberal economic, Marxist and/or feminist perspective. In the former, patterns of inequality tend to be analysed as the effects of imperfect labour markets, themselves caused by the irrational and prejudicial behaviour of employers (see, for example, Stewart, 1983). In the latter, patterns of 'racial' or sexual inequality in employment opportunity, patterns and experiences are seen as stemming from the internal logics of the capitalist accumulation and labour process. Thus, women, immigrants, migrants and 'ethnic minority' workers function either as sources of reserve army of labour or as a means by which to intensify and/or capitalize the labour process (see, for example, Cohen and Jenner, 1968/9; Castles and Kosack, 1972, 1973; Braham, Rhodes and Pearn, 1981; Phizacklea and Miles, 1980; Sivanandan, 1982).

Feminist analyses have sought to map the empirical contours of, and shifts in, women's employment patterns and experiences and to theorize these patterns in terms of the dynamic intersections of capitalist and patriarchal relations, both within the workplace and in the relation between the domestic world of unpaid work and that of paid work (see, for example, Beechey, 1987; Crompton and Sanderson, 1990; Pringle, 1988; Adkins, 1995). Though largely ignoring questions of 'race', ethnicity or racism in all but the most cursory of ways, a few texts by (mainly white) feminists have attempted to construct their analyses around the intersections of class, domestic/familial, migrant and/or 'racial' or ethnic formations (Phizacklea, 1983; Glucksmann, as Cavendish, 1982, 1990; Bryan, Dadzie and Scafe, 1985; Doyal, Hunt and Mellor, 1981; Lewis, 1993). However, none of these has yet sought a systematic analysis of the creation and experience of a specific employment opportunity for women from 'ethnic minority' groups in ways which foreground social, political and cultural relations. The existing literatures, then, fail to provide an adequate conceptual framework through which to analyse how 'racial', ethnic and gender formations intersect to mediate black women's employment positions and experiences. In my view, this failure is itself part of the process of racialization of populations of colour since in relation to an homogeneous entity called women, (white) feminists have indeed attempted to explore women's employment in terms of the dynamics of the *social* as much as the (narrowly defined) economic, as is demonstrated by the work of Pringle (1988); Cockburn (1983, 1991); and Adkins (1995). However, in relation to women from racialized populations of colour, the social and discursive connections to the experience and opportunity of labour market participation disappear. Alternatively, where any social aspect is referenced it tends to take the form of the assumed constraints of 'cultural' factors, understood as ways of life and values internal to the racialized group, and not part of the wider social formation in which women of all ethnicities, including those of white groups, are imbricated. (For a critique of such racializing approaches and alternative conceptualization, see Brah's work on the labour market participation of Muslim women, 1996, chapters 3 and 6.) This privileging of 'the economic' in relation to black women's employment has retained the theoretical separation between black people's role in the economy and their position in other aspects of the social formation. As a result, developments in social and cultural theory – including those offered by black cultural criticism and feminism, where some of the best work on processes of racialization has occurred – have not been used to explore aspects of black employment. This reduces greatly their theoretical and political utility, since they are unable to conceptualize the link between the changing employment profiles found amongst racialized populations of colour and changes in their position more generally. As such, continuities and discontinuities in the racial formation of Britain cannot be charted, nor can its articulation with other aspects of the social formation. Given these limitations I am concerned to explore the ways in which the *discursive and social* (as opposed to economic) location of black populations made possible their spatially concentrated entry into qualified social work.

'Race', gender and welfare

Predominant approaches to the relationship between state organized, regulated and delivered welfare policies and services and the social relations of 'race' and gender can be divided into three main categories. First, there is what might be characterized as the orthodoxy, represented in works by, for example, Glennerster (1991); Mishra (1984); George and Wilding (1976); Glennerster and Hills, eds (1998). Texts such as these are notable for (at least) two main reasons: first, their empirical and analytical separation of issues of gender from those of 'race' and class; and second, because they either virtually ignore questions of 'race' and racism, or, in keeping with the empiricist roots of social policy (or more precisely in this context, social administration), treat 'race' and/or ethnicity as one more (new) dimension of inequality to be quantified and categorized. In addition, in this literature, ethnicity and/or 'race' are conceptualized as if they are pre-social, static and externally generated qualities or conditions belonging to 'minority' groups relatively newly arrived in Britain. The pre-social and static quality afforded to 'race' emerges from its conceptualization as a biological fact rather than a social relation. Similarly, the term 'minority' is understood numerically rather than as indicating social location and social process. Even 'ethnicity', with its referencing of 'culture', tends to be treated as a static condition belonging to groups of people with a relatively recent presence in the UK. Thus, in the 1998 edition of Glennerster and Hills's *The State of Welfare*, Glennerster can use terminology such as the following in his chapter on education: 'We saw that the attainments of black children and those of *new British citizens more generally . . .*' and 'More striking, through secondary school those from *the ethnic groups* went on catching up' (pp. 57 and 59, my emphases). Ethnicity, in this view, then, is a characteristic belonging to all but the white population, and, moreover, is something arrived in Britain from the outside. A similar approach to these dimensions of the social formation is embedded in some recent government policies, for example, the White and Green papers on health published in 1998 (The Stationery Office).

The construction of matters of 'race' and ethnicity as being externally generated has, as we see in chapter 2, a long history and is closely interwoven with the denial of the UK as a racial formation. This denial is premised upon an active process of 'forgetting' from which a series of overlapping amnesias result:

- 'forgetting' the long history of policy and politics centred on the Irish, and Irish-descent, population resident in Britain and articulated through a discourse of 'race' (see, for example, Hickman, 1995);
- 'forgetting' an equally long and ambivalent history of policy and politics centred on the Jewish population in Britain, including medieval expulsions from cities and towns, and, of course, the 1905 Aliens Act (Cesarani, 1996). This Act was in many ways the precursor to the wave of immigration and nationality legislation, instituted from 1962 and aimed at controlling the migration and settlement of people from the New Commonwealth and Pakistan – i.e. those groups of people who are now constituted as 'ethnic minorities' or 'the ethnic communities' (Lewis, 1998a);
- 'forgetting' that successive British monarchs and governments had long been concerned to 'manage' black/white race relations, from

Elizabeth I's declaration that there were too many blackamoors in the realm (Walvin, 1973; the Sierra Leone project of 1786–91 (Braidwood, 1994); through the legislation instituted after the First World War, restricting the rights of 'coloured seamen' (Ramdin, 1987); to the vast administrative and political structures and practices of colonial administration (Fryer, 1984).

Amnesias such as these both reflect and produce the construction of the UK as only recently multi-ethnic and diverse, and its heterogeneity (and the differentiation which accompanies it), as the product of externally introduced dimensions of the social formation.

In opposition to the tendency towards marginalization of 'race' and racism in social policy, a second literature has developed which has sought to analyse the ways in which racial inequalities produce specific welfare profiles and needs, and the way welfare policies and practices help to reproduce racial inequalities. This body of literature (much of it by black people working as welfare professionals or social policy analysts) has turned its attention to mapping the racial and ethnic patterning of welfare need and inequality (for example, Cheetham, 1972 and 1982; Ben-Tovim et al., 1986; Patel, 1990; Stubbs, 1985; Solomos and Singh, 1990; Ousley, 1984; Connelly, 1985; Nasir, 1996; Walker and Ahmed, 1994). In its concern with empirical descriptions, there are some parallels between work within this genre and that already outlined. Similarly, this second body of work also tends to analytically separate gender and 'race', though Nasir's work is a notable exception. However, in other ways it differs quite significantly in that rather than constructing questions of 'race' and ethnicity as externally generated factors recently introduced into the national formation, it sees these as key terms in the social relations of welfare. Thus, 'racial' and ethnic inequalities in patterns of welfare need, and the distribution of access to welfare benefits and services, are seen as being constituted by, and constitutive of, the welfare regime. 'Race', racism and welfare are, then, seen as standing in a relationship of contradiction, such that in the absence or retrenchment of a wide-ranging welfare state, racial disadvantage and inequality would deepen; whilst welfare policies and practices have also fostered such disadvantage and inequality (Ginsburg, 1992). Moreover, and this may be the most significant point of distinction with orthodox social policy, some of this work has also sought to critique the dominant *conceptualizations* of both the categories of 'race' and ethnicity and their links to the social relations of welfare more generally. Ginsburg again illustrates the distinction in approach when he writes of 'race', 'the concept "race" is used here as a political and sociological category, whose meaning is established in concrete historical and political circumstances, and is therefore subject to change. Racial differences are not a constant or objective phenomenon' (1992, p. 5). Ginsburg's conceptualization draws on the work of social and cultural critics often located outside of the discipline of social policy (for example, Hall et al., 1978; Hall, 1990 and 1992a; Gilroy, 1987). Such an approach is still relatively rare, although, as this book demonstrates, it is growing. (For an argument about the analytic utility for social policy offered by Hall's work, see Lewis, 2000. For a slightly different view, see Denney, 1995.)

However, within social policy, the first major shift in the conceptualization and analysis of the place of 'race' within the welfare regime was provided by Fiona Williams's *Social Policy: A Critical Introduction* (1989). The distinctive rupture which this book marked was that Williams sought to construct an analysis in which class, 'race' and gender were understood as intersecting articulations of power, each of which stood at the very heart of the British welfare state. Her project was eloquently summarized on the last page of the book, where she writes that she has

> . . . argued for the need for gender and 'race' to be taken to the heart of an analysis of the welfare state within capitalism. [And] shown how work on women and welfare and on 'race' and welfare raises new and important dimensions for welfare analysis and strategy, and, at the same time, throws new light on existing social policy issues. [The book begins] the construction of an analytical framework, . . . which is able to generate an account of the ways in which the welfare experiences and welfare needs of women and Black people are both specific *and* central to welfare analysis and welfare strategy.   (p. 213, emphasis in the original)

The central terms of this new framework of analysis were 'work' and 'family' and 'nation', which signalled class, gender and 'race' (though the two sets of terms are not directly commensurable) and whose configurations within the social relations of welfare were the object of enquiry. It was this which marked the new departure represented by the book, since it insisted, for the first time in post-war social policy, that 'nation' was a category referencing a set of relations that had to be analysed rather than assumed. Feminists had already established the same for 'family', as had Marxists for class. The insistence on 'nation' as a category of equal status and importance was, however, to mark a difference.

In recent years, these two literatures have been joined by a third, emergent field of writing which seeks either to develop what might be called a post-structuralist social policy or to engage, in a social policy/social welfare context, with some of the issues and debates raised by post-structuralism (for example, Carabine, 1998; Carter, ed., 1998; Hillyard and Watson, 1996; Hughes and Lewis, eds., 1998; Leonard, 1997; O'Brien and Penna, 1998; Saraga, ed., 1998; Williams, 1992). These new perspectives have widened the terms of debate and enquiry within the discipline of social policy, beyond a focus on issues of the production, distribution and administration of welfare resources; the patterns of access or participation of particular groups; or the degree of correspondence between the shape and character of the social formation more generally, and that of the system of social welfare. The rise of post-structuralist perspectives in the social sciences generally, and their incorporation into the discipline of social policy, has meant that new questions, objects of enquiry, and dimensions of analysis have emerged. Whilst retaining a concern with the dynamics of power, embedded within and (re)produced by the system of social welfare, post-structuralist approaches shift attention away from a sole focus on the state, the logics of capital or patterns of material inequality. Power remains a concept central to any post-structuralist understanding of the social practices of welfare, but in new and multifarious ways. This is, of course, especially true of those working within a Foucauldian, or Foucault-influenced, framework, but the idea of power is also central to those using, for example, a Derridean approach. One way of expressing the new dimensions added by post-structuralist approaches is captured by O'Brien and Penna, when they write,

> social welfare can [also] be conceptualised as a discourse . . . a 'discourse of social welfare' comprises an organisation or matrix of knowledges – a culturally constructed and politically sanctioned framework defining experience and for realising definitions in practice. A discourse of social welfare gives definition to the world in both the conceptual and material senses of this term.   (1998, p. 8)

The effect of this has been to call into question – draw into a field of interrogation – the categories and assumptions standing at the very heart of social policy, understood here as both discipline and practice. In raising the question of 'knowledge' as a socially constituted category, through which power is manifested and deployed, post-structuralist approaches destabilize the notion of a universal human subject whose needs can be known through the application of rational, bureaucratic procedures – i.e. the subject who is the target of social welfare. This means that not only does the ontological status of 'the subject' of welfare become open to deconstructive scrutiny, but so too do the methods by which this subject is categorized and described. Similarly, the status of the welfare professional as a 'rational actor' standing at the heart of the bureau-professional machine has been destabilized. Post-structuralism's positive effect has been to place the issue of difference, identity, particularity and the subjective of historical experience squarely onto the social policy (and wider) agenda.

Difference, discourse, subject position – a new social policy approach

The deployment of post-structuralist perspectives has facilitated disruptions of both the meta-narratives inscribed within traditional social policy (as both discipline and policy) and the ontological status of its subjects. As such this approach potentially offers social policy analysts the tools to further the work begun by Williams in her introduction to social policy, especially her insistence on the articulation of 'race', gender and class in the social relations of welfare. This is achieved not only by the post-structuralist disruption of the old grand-narratives and certainties but also by its insistence on exploration of categories, practices and relations previously assumed. This has a number of methodological implications but two are particularly relevant to the concerns of this book. These are processes of subject formation and the refusal to treat social differences as pre-social or essential characteristics of particular groups or individuals. By highlighting the social, fragmentation and diversity become reconfigured as 'difference', and 'difference' is understood as inscribed in and through the operation of power. Thus, both 'race' and gender difference become objects of analysis in the attempt to explicate their processes of constitution, as does their relation to that which is simultaneously (if silently) constructed as the norm. Of course these categories of 'difference' are peopled by a series of 'subjects', discursively constituted in the very operations of power by which difference is produced. Thus, these positions of difference and the subjects who inhabit them are also central to post-structuralist analyses. These points mean that for social policy analysts working within post-structuralist perspectives, difference matters not just because of the way it mediates inequalities of access to welfare resources but also because it draws attention to processes by which meaning is constructed. Thus, the sociality of difference is both material and discursive and in this way is central to the construction of categories of belonging and entitlement. As both material and discursive location, 'difference' signals a series of self/other, 'us/them', which are 'known' and given meaning through the organizational and professional practices of those working in welfare agencies.

This is the starting point for the approach adopted in this book. The general argument I make is that the recruitment of 'ethnic minority' social workers to SSDs took place at a time when the structural location and discursive positioning of racialized populations was being challenged from a number of directions. These include the rise of the equal opportunities agenda; the economic and organizational restructuring of welfare; and the development of critiques of current social work at both policy and practice level by black professionals within the field. These emerged in an environment of intense ideological struggle over the boundaries of 'the nation' and the forms of legitimate relation between 'people' and state. From this, I argue that social work became articulated to a project of management of racialized populations of colour, who were themselves undergoing a process of discursive reconstruction from 'immigrant' to 'ethnic minority'. Thus, I develop a three-tiered analysis of the entry of black women into professional social work grades. I begin with an argument about the reconstitution of racialized populations of colour from 'immigrants' to 'ethnic minorities' and the pathologization of their family forms. This is followed by analysis and discussion of the legislative framework established by central government, and the policy environment developed in two local authorities. I then move on to a discussion of narrative accounts contained in interviews with black women social workers. In this way I hope to offer an analysis of a specific moment in the articulation of 'race', gender and welfare and to indicate a methodological and conceptual approach more able to capture the complexities of this field of articulation. Changes over the past decade in the shape, practices and modes of co-ordination of the welfare regime, and the 'racial' and gender formations which are both constituted by, and constitutive of it, suggest that just such a shift is urgently needed.

Part I

Governing Racial Formation

1

Configuring the Terrain: Governmentality, Racialized Population and Social Work

Introduction

> It is a racism that a society will practice against itself, against its own elements, against its own products; it is an internal racism . . . which will be one of the fundamental dimensions of social normalization.
>
> *(Foucault, 1990: cited in Stoler, 1995, p. 67)*

In the introduction I indicated the limitations of established approaches to racialized employment patterns and racialized welfare needs and access to services. In this chapter I want to begin to outline an alternative theoretical framework by focusing on the constitution of 'ethnic minority populations'. I argue that the Foucaldian notion of 'governmentality' provides a more incisive analytical frame through which to comprehend the connections between formation of population, the generation of welfare needs and the creation of specific employment opportunities. In particular, I argue that the notion of governmentality enables us to contextualize the opening up of the 'professionalized' sector of the occupation of social work within the dynamics of the official recognition of, and resistance to, the re-formation of Britain as a multi-racial/multi-ethnic society.

Governmentality

By governmentality I refer to the processes by which there was an attempt to imbricate black populations within the English/British as ethnic minorities. This suggests that the term 'ethnic minorities' does not refer to ontologically stable categories of people, but rather to socially constituted groups who occupy specific locations within the bio-politics of power. Governmentality refers to the encompassing of these populations within the net of the nation at the level of 'the social'. Family relations and household practices occupied a central role in this process of incorporation and subjectivization. As such, the term also refers to a set of simultaneous processes and practices which, though in many senses in tension with each other, functioned to cast these same 'ethnic minority' populations outside the 'nation'. Paradoxically, these latter processes often also centred on the family, most starkly in the form of immigration legislation, rules and practices, but also in other state practices and institutions, for example policing and education.

My use of the concept of governmentality derives from the work of Foucault (1991) and Donzelot (1980). Foucault argues that the problematic of 'government' had preoccupied western powers from the sixteenth century onwards as they searched for a means of extending new forms of social relations throughout civil society.

> The art of government . . . is essentially concerned with answering the question of how to introduce economy – that is to say the correct manner of managing individuals, goods and wealth within the family . . . and of making the family fortunes prosper – how to introduce this meticulous attention of the father towards his family into the management of the state. (1991, p. 92)

Three notions are embedded in this idea of governmentality. The first is the idea that the modern state in western society strengthened itself by the adoption of numerous techniques which were not solely premised on the threat or use of force, especially force applied directly to the body. The second is the way that the family occupies a central place in techniques of government. Initially this was because of the close association between the idea of economy and the assumed beneficent and responsible social relations found within the patriarchal family. Indeed this is what the term 'economy' originally meant. Later – that is, by the mid-eighteenth century – the word 'economy' became restricted to its contemporary meaning concerned with the production, distribution and consumption of goods and services. Whilst this meant a corresponding narrowing of the place of the family in the idea of government, the family still retained a central role. The family was no longer the model of government but rather it was to be 'considered as an element internal to population, and as a fundamental instrument in its government. No longer a model but a segment. Nevertheless . . . a privileged segment' (pp. 99–100).

The family retains its privileged place because it is the instrument through which information on population is received. In this way we are led to the third notion: that of population. This is a key term in Foucault's idea of governmentality for two reasons. First, it is the demographic changes that occurred in the seventeenth and eighteenth centuries in Europe which facilitated the break with family as a model for government. It also gave rise to a new set of knowledges about the dynamics, regularities and contours of population. Second, 'population' is key because it became the aim or end of government: it is this which must be taken account of in the practice of government.

The term 'population' needs some elaboration. In discussing the switch from sovereign power to that of 'governmental' power, Foucault attempts to elaborate the sets of relations with which power and authority are now concerned. The issue of land and territory are no longer the primary aim or concern of government; rather, with the rise of governmentality, a 'plurality of specific aims' arises which centres on the 'complex of men [*sic*] and things'. Physical property is one element in this ensemble but increasingly in conjunction with the social and psychoemotive elements. In other words, these latter elements are of equal importance in the newly evolving regimes of truth and power.

> The things with which in this sense government is to be concerned are in fact men, but men in their relations, their links, their imbrication with those other things which are wealth, resources, means of subsistence, the territory with its specific qualities, climate, irrigation, fertility, etc.; men in their relation to . . . customs, habits, ways of acting and thinking, etc.; lastly, men in their relation to that other kind of things, accidents and misfortunes such as famine, epidemics, death, etc.   (p. 93)

The elicitation of issues of culture, patterns of behaviour and thought alongside those of demography foregrounds the key areas which were covered by the new terrain of 'the social'. Moreover, Foucault conjures up the family again as a homology of governmentality.

> Governing a household, a family, does not essentially mean safeguarding the family property; what concerns it is the individuals that compose the family, their wealth and prosperity. It means to reckon with all the possible events that may intervene, such as births and deaths, and with all the things that can be done, such as possible alliances with other families; it is this general form of management that is characteristic of government. (p. 94)

If this formulation of the concerns and scope of government was begun in the sixteenth-century debates about how to rule, with the rise of the bourgeois order such a definition of 'government' was to become dominant. It is in this era that the two aspects of governmentality which concern me are brought to the fore. It is important to note that Foucault's discussion is based on Catholic France. In Protestant England the development of a normalized family and conceptions of the self were powerfully inflected with Puritan notions of self-regulation which were deeply embedded in the reformulation of class and gender relations.

Here there is an alignment of the sexual/emotional with the social, which the image of the family contains within it. Embedded within this are notions of discipline, which in turn are linked to the idea of the self-reliant subject. For as Hall et al. (1978) have argued:

> . . . in English culture the preferred forms of discipline are all *internalised*: they are forms of *self*-discipline, *self*-control. They depend on all those institutions and processes which establish the internal self-regulating mechanisms of control: guilt, conscience, obedience and super-ego. The exercise of self-discipline within this perspective has as much to do with *emotional* control (and thus with sexual repression, the taboo on pleasure, the regulation of the feelings) as it does with *social* control (the taking over of the 'morale' of society, the preparation for work and the productive life, the postponement of gratifications in the service of thrift and accumulation). It follows that the three social image clusters . . . *respectability*, *work* and *discipline* – are inextricably connected with the fourth image: that of the *family*. (p. 144, their emphases)

In the late eighteenth and nineteenth centuries it was precisely the boundaries between and relations amongst these four images that were being refigured. In the process, a 'subject' and a 'people' were being simultaneously constituted and it is on this terrain that the idea of governmentality carries a second level of relevance to my concerns. This is the aspect of governmentality which considers the transformation of a mass of 'population' (here considered as a group of human beings with particular patterns and rates of marriage, fecundity, legitimacy, illegitimacy, health, disease, death and so on) into a 'people' with national, gendered, classed and even 'raced' specificities. That issues of the 'self' should emerge to take centre stage in the context of questions of individual and social discipline is illustrative of the point. But so too is the nineteenth-century obsession with all those diverse aspects of demography and public hygiene. This concern was expressed not only in the enumeration, distribution and categorization of the population, but also in the more sociological concerns expressed in enquiries into the hygiene, nutrition, education, household management, fecundity, fertility, health, mortality, immiseration and delinquency to be found amongst the working or 'lower' classes. As I discuss later, the exploration and resolution of these issues was to become a heavily gendered, nay feminized, social space. Such a consideration of the rise of 'the social' cannot adequately be undertaken outside an analysis of a reconfiguration of gender relations amongst the emerging middle classes and the rise of a transformed sociological category 'women'. Thus, 'population', and its dynamics, both facilitate the move to governmentality as the means through which regulation is achieved (and away from sovereignty) and in so doing become the object of government. The 'art of government' found fresh outlets through the emergence of the 'problem of population': 'there occurred a subtle process . . . through which the science of government, the recentring of the theme of economy on a different plane from that of family, and the problem of population are all inter-connected' (Foucault, 1991, p. 99).

'Government', then, has a plurality of aims and encompasses a range of intersecting sets of social relations, all of which are concerned with ordering, mediating and regulating relations between a multifarious complex of 'things'. Such ordering, mediation and regulation also involve the constitution of a 'people' who, whilst being defined in relation to some racial, ethnic, religious or psychological criteria, also understand themselves individually, and as an imagined community, to be self-reliant and 'free'. They become inscribed in a multiplicity of knowledges, practices, techniques and observations to which they are subjected and of which they are the subject. Indeed it is precisely the dynamic tension between technologies of 'population' and 'people' that provides one vector for the operation of disciplinary power, with its strategy of normalization, to operate. The ability to sustain such inscriptions and subjectivities whilst simultaneously depoliticizing the processes by which they are maintained is the aim of government. However, the methods and channels through which to exercise powers of definition, description, classification and subjection had to be created and continually reconstituted in the interplay of power and resistance. For if the object of government is the creation of stable and domesticated subjects and subject positions, its achievement is a much more uncertain and dangerous thing.

Goldberg (1993) has made the point that the business of 'population' was also concerned with the development of racial taxonomies. Thus, in the eighteenth century when science began to occupy the discursive position of 'truth',

> The neutrality and objectifying distantiation of the rational scientist created the theoretical space for a view to develop of *subjectless* bodies. Once objectified, these bodies could be analysed, categorised, classified, and ordered with the cold gaze of scientific distance. (1993, p. 50, my emphasis)

Thus, whilst some populations were being constituted as a people of subjects, others were being constituted as objectified populations. It is in this (often invisible) relation of differentiation and 'othering' that 'race' can be said to occupy a central place in the development of governmentality as a regime of power.

Indeed, it was to the relation between a discourse of 'race' and the emergence of a 'society of normalization' that Foucault turned his attention in the mid-1970s in a series of lectures delivered at the Collège de France. For those limited to working in the English language we have Ann Stoler's scholarly and fascinating *Race and the Education of Desire* (1995) to thank for making the content of these lectures available. In a close textual reading of these lectures, Stoler is concerned to trace the convergences and divergences between Foucault's concerns in the *History of Sexuality* and in these lectures. In particular she

> examine[s] what the lectures say about the discursive production of unsuitable participants in the body politic, and how the maintenance of such internal exclusions were codified as necessary and noble pursuits to ensure the well-being and very survival of the social body by a protective state. (Stoler, p. 62)

Moreover she does this by cross-reading his analysis of the emergences of 'racisms of the state' (the concerns of the lectures) through her own work on the 'cultivation of whiteness' in the colonial East Indies. She therefore brings the lens of the process of production of external – colonial – 'others' to the production of internal 'others' that are the concern of Foucault.

Clearly, then, Stoler's interest in the lectures (hereafter referenced as DS, after the title *Difendere la Società*, given in the Italian publication of the lectures) is beyond the scope of the concerns of this book. However, I do want to use her reading of the lectures for what they tell us about Foucault's understanding of the link between 'governmentality' and 'race'.[1] Foucault situates the emergence of a 'discourse of race' within the development of a critique of sovereign right and the rise of bio-power and a society regulated through a regime of normalization. Indeed, the production of 'population' and 'people', with their technologies of enumeration, classification and categorizations, is central to this strategy of normalization. Linked to the emergence of bio-power is the rise of a bifurcated imagery of society in which bifurcation through a discourse of 'race' and biology is a key element. Understanding, categorization and valorization of the elements of the social body now occur through a binary grammar – a grammar in which 'there are always two groups, two categories of individuals, two armies confronting one another' (DS, p. 45, cited in Stoler, 1995, p. 65). The linguistic imagery is that of war, and in the seventeenth century it is a war of races which prevails as the dominant imagery, and which provides a 'matrix within which all the forms of social war will be sought afterwards' (DS, p. 54; Stoler, p. 66). But while this binary vision of a war of races becomes the main vector through which to conceptualize the tensions within the social body, by the nineteenth century it will be reinscribed in such a way as to 'tend to erase all the traces of the conflict of races and redefine them as class struggle' (DS, p. 54; Stoler, p. 66).

In the chapter which follows we will see an echo of this reinscription of 'race' into class when I discuss some of the ways in which the presence of black populations has been debated in the House of Commons. Here, though, Foucault argues that prior to this nineteenth-century class 'transcription' was another biological transcription in which 'biologico-social racism' (DS, p. 54; Stoler, p. 66) emerged. In this context the state is central and state racism is a tactic of power constitutive of the binary division of the social body. Moreover,

> The other race is neither one arrived from somewhere else, nor one which at a certain moment triumphed and dominated, but instead, one with a permanent presence, that incessantly infiltrates the social body – that reproduces itself uninterruptedly within . . . the social fabric.   (DS, p. 54; Stoler, p. 66)

The Collège de France lectures, then, clearly indicate the connection between a discourse of 'race' and the emergence of a bio-politics of normalization. Moreover, the concept of governmentality is useful because it brings to the centre of analysis the reconstitution of a population into a nation of people who occupy new subject positions and articulate a range of new categories of social belonging. It thus makes us aware of the binary division of the social body in which a racial metaphor is centred, even if subtextual. The constitution of these emergent positions and subjects takes place within specific institutional and social spaces which provide the fields upon and through which regimes of truth operate. Power then, as in all of Foucault's work, is a central component of governmentality as a social practice. McNay (1994) argues that in his later work (including that on governmentality) Foucault overcame some of the tensions and contradictions which existed in his earlier explorations of the play of power. Certainly the link between a Foucauldian concept of power and his theory of governmentality, especially as presented in the Collège de France lectures, admits that models of power, other than those which conceptualize it as residing in one class and/or the state, enter into a theory of social regulation (McNay, 1994). 'Governmentality' maintains the analytical distinction between power based on coercive relations and other more positive modes of power. In so doing it facilitates a grasp of the complexity of power relations which, in their diverse modalities, intersect in multifarious and contradictory ways. 'That is to say that social control is not always achieved through a monotonous logic of domination but is often realised indirectly through a convergence of different social practices' (McNay, 1994, pp. 124–5).

That subjects are constituted through the play of power and that this is a productive as well as repressive process is indeed one of the most important contributions made by Foucault to social scientific understanding. Moreover, in the Collège de France lectures, Foucault clarifies the relationship between sovereign and disciplinary power and suggests that these are not temporally distinct forms of social domination. Rather, disciplinary power becomes superimposed upon sovereign power and articulated in a 'society of normalization' through a reinscription of the language of rights. Thus, whilst the language of rights associated with sovereign power transmutes into a system of 'truth claims' and normalization, disciplinary power 'is not . . . a discourse that detaches itself from the language of rights; on the contrary, its truth claims are made to specific rights and by specific holders of them; the rights of a family (to property), of a class (to privilege); of a race (to rule)' (Stoler, 1995, p. 65).

This formulation is helpful because, whilst holding the analytic distinction between productive and repressive power, it allows us to see the embeddedness of the one in the other, an embeddedness centred on the potential coercive force of juridico-political 'rights'. For example, the emergence of a form of policing called 'community policing' was based on a strategy aimed at the minimal use of repressive force *through* the creation of citizens/subjects who were articulated to the project of policing. The point then is not to postulate a mutually exclusive divide between repressive and productive power but rather to see how the one can work through the other. This necessarily entails an examination of the terrains on which new social subjects are constituted.

One such terrain which emerged in the context of a move from a regime of sovereign power to that of governmental power was a space which has become known as 'the social'. This new conceptual space was to play a central role in the emerging fields of social relations which accompanied the rise of governmentality as the dominant mode of ruling. Centred on the points of demarcation between social 'types' and the intersections amongst the family, the state and the market, 'the social' had the institutional practices and knowledges of charity, philanthropy and (later) forms of social work at its core.

'The social'

If Foucault's concept of governmentality offers the beginnings of an understanding of how power operates in the constitution of 'population', 'people' and 'subjects', the work of Donzelot facilitates the application of this approach to the specific set of discourses and institutional practices associated with what was to become social work.

Donzelot (1980) was concerned to analyse the transformations which occurred in the relations between the state and the realm of the family as a result of the demise of feudal forms of social organization and control. This transformation led to the emergence of a new set of discourses and practices in the area of familial and household relations structured as they were in and through the accompanying refigured relations of gender and age. In this a new conceptual and institutional space opened up, a space which Donzelot refers to as 'the social'.

'The family' was a key figure in this new space not least because it was at the centre of the intense struggle occurring in political discourses of the Right and Left over the definition and parameters of the state. The family occupied a central place along the range of political positions. Indeed, it was partly in relation to their respective views of the family that political discourses were defined as of the Left or Right. Left was equated with statist/anti-family, and Right was equated with a circumscribed state, private property and a sacrosanct, self-reliant family.

However, if this was part of the terrain on which 'the family' was conceptualized, it is not enough to explain

either the present configuration of the family or the nature of the attachment that individuals of liberal societies have conceived for it. It does not explain why this fondness for the family is associated with a feeling for liberty and how defence of the family can be effectively undertaken in the name of safeguarding people's sphere of autonomy. (Donzelot, 1980, p. 52)

Donzelot thus reformulates Foucault's object of enquiry into one which asks how a transformed 'family' is both articulated to a liberal definition of the state and yet ideologically separated from the realm of politics and class domination and antagonism. He then seeks to analyse this process in clear Foucauldian terms. The issue at hand, he suggests, was

how was it possible to ensure the development of practices of preservation and formulation of the population while at the same time detaching it from any direct political role and yet applying to it a mission of domination, pacification and social integration? The answer: By means of philanthropy. *Philanthropy in this case . . . must be considered as a deliberately depoliticising strategy for establishing public services and facilities at a sensitive point midway between private initiative and the state.* (p. 55, my emphasis)

The midway point was 'the social'. This hybrid complex of discursive and institutional activity reformulated relations between the fields of law, medicine, administration, education, psychiatry and the family. However, in re-articulating relations between these fields, an ideological separation between 'the family' (as private) and the state or 'high politics' (as public) had to be achieved whilst simultaneously according to the state the authority to set the parameters of the relations between private and public. The object of political demands for 'rights' to livelihoods, standards of living, etc. – all those aspects of 'population' – had to be deflected from the state. Philanthropy was thus organized around two opposing poles with the aim of transforming 'a question of political right into a question of economic morality' (p. 55).

So not a question of right to assistance from the state but rather a transmission of '. . . the means to be self-sufficient by teaching you the virtues of saving' (p. 56) in return for which the tutors of such virtues would have the right to gaze, to subject their tutees 'to a disapproving scrutiny of the demands for aid that you (the immiserised) might still put forward, since they would constitute a flagrant indication of a breach of morality' (p. 56).

The suggestion of a differentiation between the 'tutees' and the 'tutors' indicates a division between the form of relation specific categories of family had with the state, in what Donzelot calls the 'tutelary complex'.

Such a tutelary complex was itself organized around the twin tasks of moralization and normalization. Reserved for the 'deserving' poor, 'moralization' refers to the use of financial and other means of material assistance with the aim of lifting such families out of their immiseration. They were seen as redeemable and the assistance was meant to prevent their falling into the habits of 'immorality' associated with the 'undeserving' poor. This category were regarded as being in poverty as a result of moral ineptitude and degeneracy. Moralization, then, was also a discursive differentiation between those whose circumstances were the result of factors beyond their control and those who had only themselves to blame. To achieve such differentiations, poor families were subjected to close scrutiny via the casework interview during which all their 'habits' and conditions were meticulously recorded. The gaze of their 'moral betters' was therefore achieved via the application of a whole set of techniques of questioning, recording, coding and tutoring.

Attempts to inculcate specific norms of living – especially in relation to gender relations within the family, marriage, parental responsibilities and associated behaviours such as temperance and gainful employment – are referred to as 'normalization'. Philanthropic intervention was not the sole means by which such normalization was to occur, but philanthropy was a central practice in this sphere not least because it was the main way in which direct access to the household, and especially the women of these households, was gained. Again, as the statutory rights and duties of social work increased throughout the twentieth century, such access assumed even greater tutelary authority. We can see an example of this in the increasing professionalization of those involved in the personal social services which accompanied the Curtis Report of 1946. As Hopkins (1996) has pointed out, with the sharpening of focus in social work training 'a new profession of child care emerged at the behest of the Curtis Committee. Their report marks a significant rise in the influence of the "hands-on" practitioner within the framework of a statutory service' (p. 26).

In analysing the creation of a new field of social relations centred on a nexus of contacts between the family and philanthropy, Donzelot's work offers a major contribution to understanding the interplay between forms of power and the constitution of subject positions through which 'difference' is organized and normalized. Importantly he shows that 'the social' is both a conceptual space and a set of practices which are embedded in class relations but not reducible to them. One of Donzelot's aims was to take issue with a form of Marxist interpretation which rendered the family no more than a key role in the reproduction of the bourgeois order (1980, p. xx). In the Marxist version of events the family, an inherently bourgeois form, suffered a crisis, reflective of the internal contradictions of capital *per se*, as a result of the developments in the nineteenth century. In contrast, Donzelot seeks to show both that the family was a key institution in the socio-political ensemble of the *ancien régime*, and that the transformations in the family which resulted from the rise and modification of family law and of the discourses of medicine and education served to suture the family firmly 'within a new form of sociality, of which it appears to be both queen and prisoner' (1980, p. xxii).

If this is the strength of Donzelot's work, its weakness lies in the way in which gender relations (a central element in 'the family') are missing from the core of his analysis. For a more detailed analysis of the place of gender and the sociological category 'women' in the major transformations which occurred in nineteenth-century Britain (and other parts of western Europe) we have to turn to the work of feminist historians. Such work facilitates insights into the highly gendered nature of 'the social' and the ways in which this category also emerged in the context of the upheavals and anxieties provoked by the major transformations of which 'the social' (and its link to governmentality) was a symbol. Thus, in Britain the re-articulation of 'the public and the private' in the late eighteenth and early nineteenth centuries was spearheaded by the emerging middle classes as part of their claim for legitimacy and power in a society which had been dominated by land. The creation of a private space of the home guarded by women was to provide an antidote to the anxieties generated by a market economy. Women had a critical role as moralizers of men and children, both within their own classes and later as moralizers of the working class[2] (Davidoff and Hall, 1987).

In *Am I that Name?*, Denise Riley (1988) develops some of these themes by specifically considering the relation between the category 'women' and the major transformations which were occurring in the late eighteenth and early nineteenth centuries. Philanthropy in the nineteenth century and social work in the twentieth came to occupy the position as the forms of social practice with the set of knowledges and methods deemed most suited to the task of managing the tensions between the bourgeois market, a re-articulated realm of the private, and an 'all-encompassing state' (Donzelot, 1979). It should be clear from the earlier discussion of both Foucault's and Donzelot's ideas of governmentality that the reference to an 'all-encompassing state' is not to suggest that the state had actually assumed such proportions. On the contrary, the liberal democracies, which had come to characterize western nation states, were committed to the prevention of such a state arising. However, the conundrum this posed for them was how to ensure the governability of the population in the wake of the erosion of older forms of integration. This erosion was accompanied by the demise of pre-existing family forms and responsibilities which had served to anchor individuals into class, authority and gender relations.

In this context two issues presented themselves. First, there was the problem of how to encourage new family forms, especially amongst the working classes, through which to hook and anchor men, women and children into new subjectivities and private and public responsibilities. Second, there was the issue of how to do this within liberalism with its complex and ambivalent relation to the individual liberties of those who were deemed not yet fully inculcated in the civilities of bourgeois society.

'The social' came to occupy the space between private families living in households and the public domain of the market and the state. Its role was to refigure or re-articulate the boundaries between the public and the private whilst allowing for the entry of the one into the other. This in its turn presented further difficulties. On the one hand, the ideological boundary between the public and the private had to be maintained because this was central to both the creation of a liberal state and the recomposition of gender relations. On the other hand, the private was not to be so autonomous as to construct a space outside of the field of governmentality. One way in which this tension was held and managed was via the constitution of new 'free and autonomous subjects', who in part knew themselves by the constitution of the 'abnormal' and 'deviant'. In the field of philanthropy and charity, deviancy and abnormality were constituted in the discursive frame of the family. The representations of particular family forms, dynamics and relations operated as the marker between the 'good' and the 'normal' and their opposites. And those who were cast outside the 'normal' were then subjected to a whole range of tutelary discourses and practices aimed at reconstituting them as subjects within governmentality. One way of achieving such a reconstitution of the 'abnormal' was through the rights of 'social betters' to enter and make judgement upon particular families.

By the twentieth century such rights of gaze, judgement and intervention became increasingly the rights of state agencies as philanthropy transmuted into social work and as this became increasingly controlled and legitimated through state regulation and rules of professional practice. In the 1908 Children Act, for example, it is possible to see the transference of philanthropic activities into social work. With the rise of statutory regulation, social work became the main agency through which the older institutions of law and medicine were brought to bear on 'the family'. Social work increasingly became established as one of the dividing practices which served to demarcate the boundaries between the normal family and those defined as abnormal families. This half of the binary was then subject to another, internal differentiation which centred on the deprived/depraved split. As the institution whose main area of responsibility was children and families this dual process of differentiation was a replay of the moralization/normalization split.

Up to this point I have outlined the chain of connections between 'population' and the constitution of an internally differentiated 'national people' occupying new subject positions which articulate refigured social relations including those between the public and the private. This general process Foucault has termed 'governmentality'. The specifics of the re-articulation of the public/private has been conceptualized as occurring on the terrain of 'the social'.

Racialized population in late twentieth-century Britain

How might these ways of thinking about governmentality and 'the social' be utilized in a discussion of late twentieth-century professionalization of black or Asian social workers? Here the crucial issue is that of the reconstitution of one form of racialized subject – the 'immigrant' – into another form – the 'ethnic minority'. To introduce these social categories requires expanding the category of 'the social' as conceptualized by Donzelot and Riley. Their respective expositions of the rise of the social may be full of subjects but in the main these subjects are not explicitly 'raced'. Their specificity as white European or English subjects – of whatever class or gender – is unspoken, is implicit. As such they are inevitably cast as universal, their historicity only temporal and not spatial, racial or national. This expansion of the concept of the social can then be mapped onto Foucault's conceptualization of population, and its link to governmentality and a regime of normalization. What I want to argue is that in the post-Second-World-War period, when the erstwhile 'objects' of taxonomic classification came 'home', it increasingly came to be seen as necessary to reconstitute 'them' progressively as 'coloured', then 'immigrant' and more recently 'ethnic' subjects. The issue of governmentality thus reposes itself in a sharply and visibly 'raced' way and it is in this that we can begin to explicate the forces which were to open up the professionalized parts of the occupation of social work to black women (and men) in the 1980s.

The idea of governmentality can be appropriated to open up a way of thinking about and interpreting the entry of black women (and men) into qualified social work in particular localities. Rather than seeing this as only a function of the geographical concentration of black populations in any simple sense, or as only an outcome of the application of equal opportunities policies at local government level, or even as a result of the outcome of processes of 'integration' of 'immigrant' communities, I would suggest that we need to understand this entry in terms of wider processes of population and social regulation. The dynamics within and across these sites served to structure the experience of racialized populations of colour in Britain and provides part of the context in which access to employment in new occupations was gained. Moreover, they served to demarcate the black family as a central site through which to bring 'outside' black populations within the field of social regulation and as sites through which to interpellate black and Asian people as specific kinds of racial subject – i.e. as 'ethnic minorities'.

Such reconstitution of racial subjects has been referred to as 'racial formation' (Winant, 1994; Omi and Winant, 1994). 'Racial formation' theory holds together three indissoluble elements. First, it insists that the meaning of 'race', as a concept signifying conflicts and interests in reference to human beings organized into distinct categories on the basis of phenotypic variation, pervades social life. Second, it argues that there has been an intensification and expansion of racial phenomena in the late twentieth-century world. Third, the theory embodies a conception of 'racial time', itself understood as consisting of two dimensions. These are the genealogical time of 'race', which refers to the emergence of 'race' as an organizer of social relations within and across nations and peoples at the time of the European conquests, African enslavement, colonial subjugation and capitalist domination; that is, the long march from the Renaissance to modernity in which racial classifications and hierarchies structured and legitimated economic, political and social relations and also discursively produced racially differentiated subjects. It is clear that this aspect of 'racial time' is coterminous with the time of the emergence of governmentality as a dominant mode of regulation. Alongside this genealogical time, the concept of racial time also carries a notion of contingency in that 'racial meanings and social structures are always context driven' (Winant, 1994, p. 272).

At one extreme such meanings are located in and derive from coercive and repressive social orders such as Atlantic slavery or South African apartheid. However, democracies 'are forced to develop more hegemonic forms of racial rule. That is they must incorporate their racial oppositions, make concessions to their demands, and engage in ever-widening debate about the meaning of race in society' (p. 272).

Events in Britain since the Second World War would indicate the persistent relevance of the category 'race' and racial politics: a relevance which is continually re-articulated in specific conjunctures. It is, then, this aspect of racial formation theory in relation to sites of welfare on which I wish to focus. For, as Winant states:

> Indeed, we can speak of racial formation as a *process* precisely because the inherently capricious erratic nature of racial categories forces their constant rearticulation and reformulation – their social construction – in respect to the changing historical contexts in which they are invoked. (p. 271, emphasis in original)

The historical contexts in which racial categories are invoked in contemporary SSDs are in part comprised of developments in other areas of public policy and practice. Primary among these are immigration policy, policing and education, for each of these areas can be identified as making significant contributions to the discursive and social constitution of new black subjects, as migrants turned into settlers and their children began to stake out a claim to national belonging. The struggle over national belonging in part took the form of conflicts over racialized inclusions and exclusions within the welfare regime established by Beveridge and, decades later, its Thatcherite restructuring. Among these struggles the contest of black and Asian people for recognition and valorization of familial forms and relationships was prominent. This was posed particularly sharply in relation to fostering and adoption policy and practice, as I discuss in a subsequent chapter. Here, however, I briefly consider the ways in which developments in immigration, education and policing can be understood as constitutive sites of racial formation as racialized subjects of colour became inscribed into the national formation through processes of governmentality.

Immigration

A dominant discourse about the role of immigration policy in securing what is referred to as good race relations has been a feature of official and popular opinion for at least thirty years. There is a wealth of socio-logical and other literature which shows how this discourse has had the effect of structuring the normative and material relation of diverse groups of black (and other racialized) people to welfare services and benefits. In addition to this, the practical effects of immigration law, and the rules which govern their implementation, have progressively acted to circumscribe the access of first-generation migrants and their depen-dants to the facilities of the welfare state. Detailed discussion of the processes by which the claims of these groups to welfare have been dele-gitimated is beyond the scope of my concerns. What I am interested to point out is two things – one related to processes of juridical demarca-tion, the other to processes by which certain families are encompassed within the regime of welfare. Let me take each in turn.

In terms of a regime of governmentality, what successive immigration and nationality law has established is a redrawing of the boundaries which act to define which black (and other racialized) people and their families are legitimate residents and which are not (Lewis, 1998b). In changing the juridical status of vast numbers of those who were once British subjects, immigration and nationality policy has also acted to demarcate those populations who might still have a claim to British subjecthood – this time in the form of an 'ethnic minority'. Immigration policy has tended to be a practice and discourse of differentiation anchored to colour. This has certainly been the case between the Second World War and the ending of the cold war which accompanied the fall of many of the communist states of Eastern Europe. One point of contrast which illustrates this is that Irish people from the Republic, although heavily racialized, have never been subject to control under immigration legislation. The importance of immigration policy for my purposes is that, in progressively redrawing the lines of demarcation between ex-colonial subjects who could and could not make a claim to full citizenship/subjecthood, in the British constitutional sense, it estab-lished the juridical framework in which the move from 'immigrant' to 'ethnic minority' could be achieved. In that sense it is part of the process by which black and Asian people were to be encompassed within the field of governmentality as they underwent reconstitution as specific and new types of subject.

What kind of subject is the 'ethnic minority'? Kobena Mercer (1994) has suggested:

> The term 'ethnic minority' associated with social democracy in the 60s and 70s connotes the black subject as a minor, an abject, childlike figure nec-essary for the legitimation of paternalistic ideologies of assimilation and integration that underpinned the strategy of liberal multi-culturalism. A member of a 'minority' is literally a minor, a social subject who is *in-fans*,

without a voice, debarred from access to democratic rights to representation: a subject who does not have the right to speak and who is therefore spoken for by the state and its 'representatives'. (p. 295, emphasis in original)

Clearly, then, the 'ethnic minority' can be included within the nation but as a junior citizen/subject. In terms of my argument two things flow from this. One is that as infantilized people, those recialized populations who were now reconstituted as ethnic minorities could be included in the social relations of welfare as pathologized subjects. But since power is neither absolute nor uncontested, occupation of the subject position 'ethnic minority' was subject to contradictory processes. The counter-discourse of 'blackness' which aimed at articulating a 'people' across numerous ethnic divides always offered a site of refusal of the terms of 'ethnic minority' status. Simultaneously, however, resistance to dominant notions of what it was to be 'black' was also sometimes carried out by adopting notions of essential cultural characteristics which only insiders could know, understand and value. This of course resonates with the discourse of 'ethnic minority' and it is from this position that the second point emerges. For groups whose difference was demarcated around notions of essential cultural 'otherness', the time would come when representatives of these populations would be required to ensure the delivery of 'ethnically sensitive' welfare services. The tendencies towards pathologization on the one hand, and cultural specificity on the other, most keenly intersect on the terrain of the family, and in the two apparently discrete fields of education and policing this can be clearly seen.

Education

What education carries is both a version of the metamorphosis of the 'immigrant' into the 'ethnic minority' and the attempts to subject the occupants of this new category to a regime of governmentality. The problematic of 'race relations' was voiced by *The Economist* as early as 1958 when the 'immigrant' was the iconical figure of racial threat and difference:

The parents will probably still mostly be living in Harlemised districts in big towns and new arrivals will continue to import the *types of behaviour and attitudes* that disgust and annoy whites [whilst in the] not so distant future coloured teenagers' problems could then loom and it might be alarming. (27 November, p. 8, my emphasis)

Such expressions of alarm at the black presence in Britain were to become an increasing feature of both official and popular discourse and were to give rise to the cross-party consensus that the anticipated disruption which such black presence would cause could only be contained within a framework of 'strict but fair immigration control = good race relations'. This mantra was to attain such a status of 'truth' that it has structured black people's access to state services and benefits since the introduction of the 1962 Immigration Act. Within this 'race relations' paradigm, education was designated a special role – the task of producing new racialized subjects who would not display 'disgusting' behaviours and attitudes but rather exhibit the forms of behaviour appropriate to their newly acquired national status.

> A national system of education must aim at producing citizens who can take their place in society properly equipped to exercise their rights and perform duties which are the same as other citizens'. If their parents were brought up in another culture or another tradition, children should be encouraged to respect it, but a national system cannot be expected to perpetuate the different values of different immigrant groups.   (Department of Education and Science, 1964a)

In an analysis of the education of children of Caribbean origin or descent, Bonnick (1993)[3] has pointed out that the processes attached to the production of such citizens had to be depoliticized and that they concealed

> the underlying ideological process of reconstitution in which nuances of distinction and differentiation serve to particularise cultural and racial characteristics and construct them in such a way that they become major problems in themselves and a source of explanation of educational and social processes.   (p. 145)

In education the racialization which was necessary for the production of these new subjects was achieved through two convergent routes. On the one hand, there was the inscription of Caribbean-descent children into an historical discourse of slavery. Bonnick argues that this had the effect of denying such children any legacies in which they could take pride and establish a sense of communal and individual dignity. In this discourse, African-Caribbean children are said to be imbued with an ambivalent identity and to be embedded in familial and other socio-cultural networks which prohibit educational commitment and achievement. The term which carried this legacy was 'cultural deprivation', a label that enabled the second means of educational racialization. In the 1960s this was of course a term already saturated with educational meaning but in this case in relation to the education of white working-class children rather than their African-Caribbean counterparts. However, the process of racialization which was integral to the formation of new black subjects necessitated that the association between these two groups, which the use of the same term conveyed, be disconnected.

One way in which this disconnection was achieved was on the terrain of the family. 'The family' was accorded hegemonic status in official documents about the educability of the 'West Indian' child in British schools. For example, the DES report of 1971 identified the West Indian community as possessing the least cultural resources to deal positively with their new encounter. As Bonnick comments, there was

> a body of ideas about the Afro-Caribbean family contained in the early DES reports of the 1970s. These reports reproduced the view that the Caribbean family culture was weak and, as such, inadequate in generating the correct cultural predisposition for educational success.   (p. 179)

Having positioned African-Caribbean children as without a positive sense of their own histories and as outside of British class relations, they could now be interpellated as exclusively racial subjects who come from pathologized families and communities. By representing the 'black family' as an always potentially 'dysfunctional' institution, the discursive scene was set for the intervention of social workers in real live black families and the assimilation of social work to the production of 'ethnic minorities'.

Policing

From about the mid-1970s relations between the black communities and many of Britain's inner-city police forces became increasingly antagonistic. Moreover, these relations also became emblematic of the organic crisis of British capitalism, as a result of which their symbolic position extended far wider than the concrete relation between police and sections of the black communities. Analysis of this policy, practice and symbolic moment has been well rehearsed and has occupied much of the literature on 'race' in Britain in the mid-late 1970s and early 1980s (see, for example, Hall et al., 1978; Gutzmore, 1983; Gilroy, 1982; Sim, 1982). What each of these in their varying ways points to, is that developments in policing illustrated the ways in which 'race' was seen as being pivotal in the re-establishment of hegemonic social relations of which the crisis was both a manifestation and a partial resolution. What was missing from these analyses was the way in which the family, and therefore gender relations, was also emerging as a pivotal symbolic institution in both the identification of the causes and the solutions to the crisis. Elements within the police, however, understood this only too clearly and, as such, black family forms and putative relations were highlighted as central to the project of developing a 'new' policing style and practice.

It was in debates about community policing that discourses about black and Asian family forms were brought centre stage.[4] As one police spokesman put it:

> community policing requires the police to take the *initial* action within a community and become a pivotal institution within that society not only for matters which have been within the traditional area of police interests, but also in other areas which have hitherto been considered the exclusive province of other agencies. (Osborn, 1980, p. 34, his emphasis)

This reference to the police force becoming pivotal among a host of 'other agencies' all dedicated to the issue of crime, law and order, and all bound up in the project of regaining legitimacy and consent, was expressed in the development of multi-agency approaches. Formulations such as this embodied the utilization of a broader concept of 'police', more proximate to that older form sometimes referred to as 'social police'. For example, another major proponent of community policing suggested that

> There is a sense in which the concept of police can be used to mean a whole range of governmental departments . . . if to this battery of government resources one adds the idea that the common law explicitly commits the entire adult population to some policing responsibilities we are beginning to think in terms of policing by the body politic. . . . The implications for the police are profound. (John Alderson, when Chief Constable of Devon and Cornwall, quoted in Osborn, 1980, p. 35)

There is a close correspondence here to the idea of 'police' embodied in 'governmentality'. In this context 'police' suggests a cluster of apparatuses of security in which subjects have fostered among them co-operation, industriousness, loyalty, honesty, charity – all of which are central to the techniques of government (McNay, 1994, p. 119). In this regard the quotation from Alderson might be read as being concerned with the constitution of a nation of subjects who interiorize the responsibilities required of citizens. In this situation the 'dividing practices' through which the normal are marked off from the abnormal can flourish as part of an ensemble of institutions and practices through which legitimacy, consent and hegemony are achieved. Moreover, such strategies of normalization and legitimization are part of the social practices of 'repressive' and 'caring' agencies. Both types of agency may be involved in the production of citizens/subjects. But to say that a multiplicity of agencies is involved in this constitutive process is not the same as saying that there is a certainty of outcome, and it also suggests the instability of the subjects produced and the uncertain effectivity of the means of governmentality.

One way in which the instability of these subjects is managed is by the production of demarcations through which multiple series of 'us/them' are defined. Given this, the police demarcate boundaries between those with greater or lesser propensities to criminality; greater or lesser degrees of pathology; greater or lesser degrees of potential acceptance of an expanded or redefined remit for policing policy and practice. In this context a reminder of the position argued by Brown, which I quoted in the introduction, is timely. It will be remembered that he was concerned to establish the role of 'culture' in constituting groups who might be more easily assimilated to a reformulated project of policing. In so doing, discourses about family forms among racialized populations are introduced and subjected to differential racializations since 'Asian groups' were seen as exhibiting a greater capacity for inclusion in the project of 'crime control' than 'Caribbean groups'.

Moreover, it is within the interstices of processes of differential racialization that we can detect both contradictions and ambivalences carried within racial discourse. As Rattansi (1995) has pointed out, such ambivalence is particularly pronounced in relation to the British Asian family, which is simultaneously applauded for its apparently strong traditional and patriarchal structure and decried for its apparently backward – and oppressive – treatment of women within it.

Brown's approach can be characterized as a discursive strategy which explicitly mobilizes notions of family and culture, and implicitly notions of gender. These notions were subject to differential racialization but the overall frame acted to link putative ethnicized practices to the development of policing strategy. People of Caribbean origin and descent are constructed as culturally less susceptible to the techniques and aims of community policing, which is perhaps why 'it is the rough, difficult, potentially violent aspects of multi-ethnic areas that oblige police units having a more robust capacity' (Newman, 1983, p. 35) in these areas.

In contrast, people of Asian origin and descent are constructed as culturally more susceptible to community policing because of their assumed traditions of strong patriarchal control of family and community. All of this links to the construction of an essentialized cultural difference through which policing practice can be deployed and legitimated. This can be seen in relation to violence against women within Asian households. For example, in their work on domestic violence, Southall Black Sisters (SBS), a feminist organization formed in 1979, have found an appalling lack of interest on the part of Southall police in the application of the law concerned with domestic violence and thereby the protection of women facing such violence. A multi-agency Domestic Violence Panel operative in the 1980s assimilated the dominant discourse, which defines domestic violence as a 'family problem', to a 'race relations' logic. As such, they made it clear that their concern with domestic violence within Asian households was less about the provision of protection for women and more about the articulation of diverse agencies and populations to a policing agenda. This was achieved through the prism of 'cultural sensitivity', since

> Factors such as arranged marriages and different culture were cited as reasons for lack of intervention. . . . They also argued that older Asian women are supposed to have a higher tolerance level and therefore be in less need of help.   (SBS, 1989, p. 43)

So far I have argued that two interconnected elements were central to the incorporation of black and Asian populations into a regime of regulation known as 'governmentality'. These were the constitution of groups of people defined as 'ethnic minorities', and the differential incorporation of the families associated with these minorities into the social and cultural relations of welfare. I have attempted to give some indication of these twin processes in relation to immigration, education and policing policy. I have focused on these three areas for distinct but connected reasons: immigration, because it had a particularly significant role to play in the juridical reconstitution of 'immigrants' from the New Commonwealth and Pakistan into 'ethnic minorities'; education, because it was an early site in which the black family was marked out as pathological and unable to produce children fitted for the national culture (as such, education was charged with the task of producing new racial subjects); and policing, because it was in this field that black families were specifically highlighted as the struggle for a restoration of hegemonic relations took place.

Centring the black family (and the putative gender formations it contained) across these diverse but parallel sites opened the way for another set of agencies and professions to be brought into the project of assimilating reconstituted black subjects to a redefined political agenda. This was the profession of social work.

2

Now you see it, Now you don't: 'Race', Social Policy and the Blind Eye of Central Government

... in matters of race, silence and evasion have historically ruled literary discourse. Evasion has fostered another, substitute language in which the issues are encoded, foreclosing open debate. The situation is aggravated by the tremor that breaks into discourse on race. It is further complicated by the fact that the habit of ignoring race is understood to be a graceful, even generous, liberal gesture. To notice is to recognize an already discredited difference. To enforce its visibility through silence is to allow the black body a shadowless participation in the dominant cultural body. According to this logic, every well-bred instinct argues *against noticing* and forecloses adult discourse.

> *(Toni Morrison, 1992, pp. 9–10, emphasis in original)*

The Urban Programme was designed as a black programme in the aftermath of the 'rivers of blood' speech.

> *(Alex Lyon MP, 1977)*

I do not think we would all agree that the Urban Programme has in the past been a black programme. . . . My purpose is to deal, regardless of whether there are black or white populations, with aggregated problems of poverty and deprivation in our major urban centres.

> *(Peter Shore, Secretary of State for the Environment, 1977)*

Introduction

In the previous chapter I considered the connection between social welfare and the constitution of new racial subjects and argued that this be understood as a form of governmentality. By focusing on macro-level processes I was pointing to racial formation as part of a set of wider, somewhat abstract, processes involved in the constitution of nation and people. However, racial formation, like formations of gender or class, occurs in and across specific institutional settings and forms of social practice. These formations of 'race', gender, class or sexuality are also constituted more or less consciously as forms of iterative practice in the interstices of social, cultural, economic, political and psychic relations. In this chapter, then, I want to begin to link processes of racial formation to specific institutional contexts.

Specifically I focus on how 'race' is constituted and inscribed in particular measures at central government level. I consider the ways in which the central presence of 'race' and racism in the origin and implementation of certain policies is hidden from view by the use of a coded language in which certain terms come to stand for 'race'. By this I mean that the presence of 'race' only becomes apparent by reading the subtexts of parliamentary discussion; by considering the moment at which policy was legislated or adopted; and/or by considering the elisions which occur and the metonymic devices through which 'race' is commonly spoken in Britain. What I want to establish is that whenever an issue concerning the inner cities has emerged, policies, at central level, have been developed with regard to racialized populations of colour. However, the link between the policy and 'race' tends to move in and out of visibility, giving it a kind of 'now you see it, now you don't' quality. From this perspective it is possible to see that the deployment of discourses of 'race', and the related construction of racialized 'others', does not depend on an unambiguous visibility. To see this requires a view from the discursive shadows of the debate, focusing less on the detail and more on the language through which the detail is presented and explained. Thus, a grasp of the complexities of the processes of racial formation and its connection to social policy requires analysis both of the links between social policies and black and Asian people's access to centrally and locally provided welfare services, and of how and where 'race' as a discursive category influences the formulation of such policy.

The chapter is organized into three main parts. I begin with an overview of some of the national policy framework and introduce my argument that there is a general tendency to deny that 'race' is a deeply embedded feature of the British national formation. I then move on to suggest that this denial is, in part, achieved in the context of the construction of the social 'other' which is itself related to the psychic mechanism of turning a 'blind eye'. Categories derived from psychoanalysis enable this mechanism to be identified, thereby enriching social scientific analysis. Having outlined the contours of such an approach, I go on to apply this framework to a reading of those parliamentary debates outlined in the first part of the chapter. I highlight how 'race' is both seen and not seen and how a psychoanalytic understanding of the fluidity between visibility and invisibility deepens understanding of the relationship between 'race' and social policy.

The national policy framework

The first statute explicitly aimed at restricting the immigration of black and Asian people from the (ex)colonies was introduced in 1962. There was a clear link between the passage of this Act and growing concerns about Britain's relative economic decline as is evidenced by the attempts to control the categories of labourer entering the country (Sivanandan, 1982). However, the Act was also rushed in as a response to the growing concerns about the effects on the social and cultural character of certain locales that it was assumed would result from the presence of relatively large numbers of black and Asian people. As such, the Act was also the first statutory enunciation of the discourse which equated restricted black entry with the promotion of 'good race relations'. In this way it represented a defining point in the statutory representation of Britain's black and Asian populations. Since that time a dominant discourse has developed which has constructed this dualistic equation as a common sense. For example, Reginald Maudling, speaking in defence of the introduction of the 1971 Immigration Act, said:

> The main purpose of immigration policy . . . is a contribution to . . . peace and harmony. . . . If we are to get progress in community relations, we must give assurance to the people, who were already here before immigration, that this will be the end and that there will be no further large-scale immigration. Unless we can give that assurance we cannot effectively set about . . . improving community relations.   (quoted in MacDonald, 1983, pp. 16–17)

The message encoded here is that the 'good will' of 'the people' (who must, in this language, be white and 'British') will not be abused. Similarly, Maudling's language has another message embedded within it – the idea that prior to the post-Second-World-War migrations of black and Asian people there were no earlier periods of large-scale immigration to Britain. It also suggests that the people here 'before' were homogeneous, a seamless entity only now subject to the potential threat of an 'alien' and, if unrestricted, 'intolerable' presence.[1] This play of the myth of timeless roots and essential continuities is a common component in the construction of the nation (Anderson, 1983). Its danger lies in its 'othering' and exclusionary effects for black and Asian migrants and their descendants who, in this narrative, must always lie outside the line of descent and nationhood. Neither 'race' nor nation is explicitly named in this talk and yet they come together on common connotative terrain to 'people' those amongst whom harmony must be promoted under the rubric of 'community relations'.

As a subtext of this idea there are three distinct but overlapping, even if at times contradictory, ways in which black presence is associated with 'problems' in both official and popular discourse. One is that (what is considered) a significant black presence in an area is seen as a metaphor for social problems. The second is that black populations are concentrated in areas of high disadvantage so that colour and class become conflated. Material deprivation and disadvantage is assumed not to be determined by the colour of the residents in an area but rather by their class position. Articulation of the issues through this register allows an occlusion of racial disadvantage, a formulation that facilitates the denial of the nation as a racial formation but that stands in contradiction with the third way in which black presence and social problems are associated. This is as producers of problems. Here black people are represented as the cause of problems because of the cultural and social disorganization they are purported to induce as a result of their 'otherness'. The association of problems with black people is pervasive across many sections of the British population but the nature of the association varies. The slippages and moves between these will become clearer in the discussion of the parliamentary debates on section 11 and the Urban Programme.

The association made between a black presence and social problems has often been the rationale offered for the production of data on 'ethnic minorities' from the New Commonwealth and Pakistan (NCWP). However, despite the increasing incidence and call for such data and despite the idea that it is only on the basis of such data that appropriate policies and resources can be developed, most data are not used as direct indices for assessing the levels of financial and other resources to be allocated to help address these problems (Booth, 1988, p. 253). As a result, relatively few specific policies have been developed for this purpose, which is itself indicative of the tension between a need to recognize and deal with the issue of *racism* and an official resistance to just such a recognition. Here I outline those policies that do exist, all but the last being passed by Labour administrations although it is fair to say that in broad terms the dominant discourse embedded within them has been cross-party. The pieces of legislation are:

- Local Government Act 1966, section 11;
- Local Government Grants (Social Need) Act 1969;
- Inner Urban Areas Act 1978;
- Race Relations Act 1976;
- the Children Act 1989.

The second and third of these came to be known as the Urban Programme and this is how they are referred to here. These pieces of legislation are considered for two reasons. First, they provide the main statutory framework within which local policies aimed at combating racial discrimination and promoting equality of opportunity have been formulated. Second, the debates that accompanied their passage through Parliament in part mapped the discursive terrain on which the need for black and Asian social workers was enunciated and within which these workers, and indeed black and Asian client groups, were then inscribed.

The Local Government Act 1966

The key section of this Act in terms of 'race' and black and Asian populations is section 11. This is the oldest of the central government policies designed to increase financial resources available to local authorities that had 'substantial numbers' of black people settled in their catchment area. Such resources were to be used for the purposes of education and social welfare and some have characterized the section as a form of compensation from central to local government in recognition of the anticipated 'problems' associated with the presence of black people (Young and Connelly, 1981).

In its original form, section 11 allowed qualifying local authorities to apply for additional funds so as to employ staff so long as at least 50 per cent of the tasks associated with the post were devoted to work with residents in the borough who are defined as originating from the (New) Commonwealth and '. . . whose language and customs differ from those of the community . . .' (Local Government Act 1966, s. 11).

Local authorities qualified for such grants if more than 2 per cent of their school-age population had parents who were born in the NCWP *and* who had arrived in the United Kingdom within the previous ten years. As with much other financial support from central to local government the ratio for section 11 funded posts was 75 per cent : 25 per cent, central : local government respectively.

The 2-per-cent, ten-year rule was abolished in 1982 and replaced in 1983 with a more ambiguous criterion of what constituted 'substantial numbers', but the references to differing 'language and customs' alongside 'immigrant' made it very clear that it was immigrants from the New Commonwealth and Pakistan rather than the 'old commonwealth' who were being referred to. The change from the 2-per-cent, ten-year rule was a mixed blessing. On the one hand, it ensured that numerous local authorities escaped the disqualification that would have resulted from the impact of the immigration laws, since these had substantially reduced the numbers of people who had settled in Britain in the previous ten years. On the other hand, the vague and nebulous criterion of 'substantial numbers' opened the potential for arbitrary implementation of the Act (Bhat, Carr-Hill and Ohri, eds, 1988).

A second change to the rules governing the allocation of section 11 monies emphasized that such funds were for the employment of specialist staff. The change stipulated that all new section 11 post-holders be identified individually, and more detail furnished about the specific tasks associated with the posts. New bids were to indicate this information and there was a duty to regularly review all existing section 11 posts.

Section 11 was potentially relevant to social services departments because it could legitimately (i.e. within the letter and spirit of the law) be argued that these were departments having to provide 'work attributable to differences in language and customs'. Thus, in Circular 15/1967, issued by the Home Office, the list of staff explicitly mentioned included social workers alongside interpreters and liaison officers. The majority on this list, however, related to education – for example, head teachers, deputy heads, peripatetic teachers, teachers appointed to carry out language classes for NCWP-born children, etc. As one would expect from this, the majority of section 11 monies has gone to education – about 80 per cent in 1982/83 for example, with the remaining 20 per cent being distributed across other service areas. In 1993/94, 89 per cent of section 11 expenditure went to education projects. Nevertheless, local authority social services departments were able to make use of this clause and Johnson, Cox and Cross (1989) make the point that the vast majority of the remaining 20–25 per cent not going to education went to social services. Within social services the majority was used to fund social workers and staff in day nurseries and residential establishments (Johnson, Cox and Cross, p. 371). As we shall see, both of the social services departments considered here used section 11 in the attempt to develop 'ethnically sensitive and appropriate' services.

In 1993 it was announced that further changes would be made to section 11. Following the introduction of the Local Government (Amendment) Act, the original insistence on NCWP origin as a condition of grant was waived and broadened to include all 'ethnic minority' groups. Also, following the introduction of the single regeneration budget (SRB) in April 1994, those authorities previously accorded status as an urban priority area would have any section 11 monies incorporated into the SRB administered by the Department of the Environment. This was in keeping with the phasing out of the Urban Programme. Bids for section 11 monies from authorities in the remainder of the country would remain in the control of the Home Office. There is no published rationale for this split but it is in keeping with the general thrust of the Conservative governments of 1979–97. Thus the SRB brought together some twenty existing funding programmes from five central government departments under the control of the Government Offices for the Regions. The overall purpose of the creation of the SRB is to achieve greater focus and value for money in public expenditure on economic development and urban regeneration in England. The practices and principles of the SRB build on the experience of the City Challenge initiative which fundamentally changed the way in which resources for regeneration were allocated ... (letter to the author from Government Office for London, April 1995)

In this sense, then, the split reflects the attempt by the Conservative governments of this period to reduce the power of local authorities (see Lewis, 1998c). It also reflects the shift in the basis of central government intervention in area policy from a concern with social questions to one foregrounding economic issues. This change in emphasis was equally true in relation to funds specifically aimed at 'ethnic minorities'. Thus the Ethnic Minority Grant is 'a grant to support employment, training, and enterprise projects within voluntary organizations for black and ethnic minority adults with the objective of gaining access to mainstream opportunities'; the Ethnic Minority Business Initiative is 'a range of initiatives to encourage the development of ethnic minority run businesses'; whilst section 11 grants remain 'a range of grants to purchase additional services for ethnic minority adults and young people requiring additional assistance in order to gain access to mainstream opportunity' (all above quotes from NCVO, 1995, pp. 33–4).

The Urban Programme: the Local Government Grants (Social Needs) Act 1969 and the Inner Urban Areas Act 1978

Notwithstanding these very recent changes to section 11 and the Urban Programme, when it was first introduced section 11 explicitly made a link between 'race' and social policy in a way rather different from that usually found when introducing a legislative framework for provision of services to ethnic minorities. This explicit link was in contrast to the legislation ushering in the Urban Programme, sometimes described as a sister piece of legislation to section 11. Whilst section 11 is the

major vehicle of ... government support for local authority programmes designed to combat racial disadvantage, the Urban Programme is the major source of funding for voluntary sector schemes designed to combat racial discrimination. (HMSO, 1981, paras 52 and 67 HC 424–10)

Despite this explicit reference to racial discrimination, the terminology in the original Act (of 1969) is vague about the link to issues of 'race' and racism:

> An Act to authorize the payment to local authorities in Great Britain of grants towards expenditure incurred by reason of special social need in Urban Areas . . .
> 1 (1) The Secretary of State may out of monies provided by Parliament pay grants . . . to local authorities who in his opinion are required in the exercise of their functions to incur expenditure by reason of the existence in any urban area of special social need.

By the mid-1970s discussion was under way about changes to the original form of the Urban Programme that had been designed to be a flexible instrument with the aim of directing extra resources to inner-city areas. These debates culminated in the 1977 White Paper on the Inner Cities (HMSO, 1977) which proposed an expansion of the scheme and a reorganization into partnership and programme areas. The White Paper was to become the Inner Urban Areas Act 1978. The new scheme was administered under the Department of the Environment rather than the Home Office – a switch consistent with the shift in emphasis at this time from social projects to more economic ones. Ball (1988) argues that whilst the changed emphasis was to direct central government help to the inner cities which were by now beginning to visibly bear the effects of Britain's relative economic decline, it was generally intended that 'funding to ethnic minorities should take precedence' (p. 8). For example, the 1985 guidelines show a close correlation between areas defined as partnership or programme areas and those with the worst 10 per cent of unemployment and highest 'ethnic minority' populations (Ball, p. 9). Despite this reference in the Guidelines, and as with the earlier Act, direct reference to 'race' or race relations was omitted from the White Paper. Indeed there was explicit delegation of this arena of concern to the then newly established Commission for Racial Equality (CRE). Yet equally

> there [was] widespread belief that inner-city policy is race relations policy, and the Minister of the Environment has gone on record as suggesting that the White Paper is an important contribution to the fight against racism. (Rex, 1978, p. 9)

The effects of the reformulation of the Urban Programme heralded by the White Paper and instituted in the 1978 Inner Urban Areas Act were as follows. Seven 'partnership areas' were announced and fifteen 'programme authorities'. The difference between being a partnership area as opposed to a programme authority was that the former had the major share of the finance allocated to the scheme. There was also a special link to central government via the partnership committee and these areas had a number of additional powers delegated to them under the Act. Although already begun in the Shore announcements, the election of the first Thatcher government saw an increased emphasis on economic aims as opposed to social ones – such as that of redistribution. This switch was further evidenced by the introduction of 'enterprise zones', four of which were in, or became, new partnership areas. Programme authorities had only some of the powers allocated to partnership areas under the Inner Urban Areas Act and a much smaller share of the total budget. For example, Birmingham had £11.9 million allocated to it for partnership projects for the year 1979/80 compared to Bradford's £2.3 million for the same year allocated from programme funds. There was also a third category of authority – 'designated districts'; these had no advance (or ringfenced) allocation of funds under the Urban Programme, but such authorities did have the ability to bid for funds in the yearly round.

Despite the fact that 'race' and race relations are not explicitly spoken in the legislation governing the Urban Programme, from the beginning these issues were deeply embedded in it and indeed continued to be so right into the 1980s. Compare, for example, these two quotes on the Urban Programme – one from the Labour government of 1974–9, the other from the first Thatcher government of 1979–83.

> Where members of the ethnic minorities in inner areas suffer the kinds of disadvantage experienced by all who live there, they should benefit directly through the measures taken to improve conditions, for example, in housing, education and jobs. In addition, the government intend to ensure that their particular needs are fully taken into account in the planning and implementation of policies for the inner areas and in the allocation of resources under the enlarged Urban Programme. (Department of the Environment, *Policy for the Inner Cities* – White Paper 1977, Cmnd 6845)

> The Government's Urban Programme is of particular benefit to ethnic minorities, not only as a result of the projects designed to help them specifically, but also because nearly 40 per cent of the ethnic minorities live in partnership or programme areas. (Department of the Environment, 1981, *Ministerial Guidelines*)

'Race', then, is clearly embedded in this programme despite changes in its size and emphasis. Yet this has, at times, been denied, and it is noticeable that the language through which 'race' is spoken facilitates such denial. I return to both of these points later when I come to consider Parliamentary debates about the Urban Programme. Such denials are interesting because of the light they shed on the ambivalences buried deep in the British national psyche about its historical and contemporary implication in matters of 'race' and racism. Moreover, this feature crosses the political spectrum. As Hall (1978) puts it:

> It seems to me that the tendency to pull race out from the internal dynamic of British society, and to repress its history, is not, as might be supposed, confined to the political 'Right' of the spectrum. It is also . . . to be found on the liberal 'Left'. For the 'Right', immigration and race has become a problem of the control of an external flow, or as the popular press is fond of saying, 'a tidal wave': cut off the flow and racism will subside. The liberal 'Left', on the other hand, have long treated race and immigration as a problem in the exercise of 'good conscience'. Be kind to 'our friends from overseas': then racism will disappear. Neither side can nowadays bring themselves to refer to Britain's imperial and colonial past, even as a contributory factor to the present situation. The slate has been wiped clean. Racism is not endemic to the British social formation. It has nothing intrinsically to do with the dynamic of British politics. . . . It is not part of the English culture, which now has to be indeed protected against pollution – it does not belong to the 'English ideology'. It's an external virus somehow injected into the body politic and it's a matter of *policy* whether we can deal with it or not – it's not a matter of *politics*.   (p. 24, emphasis in original)

If there was a wide-ranging tendency to depoliticize the issue of 'race', even in the policy arena, there is a clear discomfort in explicitly talking of 'race'. As Morrison (1992) reminds us, noticing 'race' is taken as a display of ill-breeding and so it is interesting to think about the times and ways in which 'race' and racism are acknowledged. What the foregoing discussion shows is that in the British policy context such niceties demand that at best 'race' can only be explicitly mentioned in relation to two points: first, when policies with the stated aim of facilitating integration are being developed and implemented; second, when the point being established is that no disadvantage will accrue to 'ethnic minorities' as a result of the adoption and implementation of specific policies. Processes of racial exclusion and 'othering' cannot be explicitly recognized, and therefore confronted, because, as Hall points out, to do so would entail a recasting of the English (or British) culture on different representational terms. This in its turn would demand a very different national self-image and historiography, and may necessitate a shift in policy emphasis and content.

Race Relations Act 1976

After long and intense discussion with the TUC and the CBI, and following the 1971 Immigration Act which came into effect in January 1973, the third Race Relations Act was passed in 1976. This Act sought to rectify some of the omissions of the 1968 Act, particularly in the field of employment, and is therefore the Act with the widest applicability. The general ethos guiding the Act can be gleaned from the White Paper which preceded it. Apart from outlawing discrimination (the definition of which closely followed that contained in the Sex Discrimination Act passed one year earlier), the Act only *enabled* employers to adopt positive action policies and programmes and did not require them to do so. A second feature was a commitment to flexibility in the interpretation of the meaning of discrimination. It was thought that too literal an interpretation might preclude the elimination of discrimination in fields such as training (CRE, 1980). Closely linked to this is the third feature: that in the ideal scenario the Act was envisaged as a *temporary* measure, which would only be on the statute books for as long as it took to eliminate the effects of past discrimination and to educate away any prejudice found in the population at large. This is another indication of the refusal to see racism as endemic to the British social formation. From this perspective, time will ensure the erosion of any discrimination facing black populations as their numbers are restricted to levels 'acceptable' to the 'host community' and the 'immigrants' and their descendants become 'acculturated' into the 'British way of life'. In this sense the Act is another example of the inscription of dominant discourses about 'race' and race relations discernible across the whole ensemble of social policy (and indeed the whole social and cultural spectrum).

The Act sought to establish a legal framework to outlaw discrimination and provide for the possibility of action aimed at overcoming the effects of accumulated prior discrimination. To this end the White Paper promised:

> provisions allowing [but not requiring] employers and training organizations to provide special training facilities to members of such groups and to encourage them to take advantage of opportunities for doing particular work. There will be similar exemptions allowing . . . the provision of facilities and services to meet the special needs of particular ethnic or national groups [for example in relation to education, instruction, training and health and social services].   (quoted in CRE, 1980)

These aims became encoded in sections 5 (2) (d), 35, 37 and 38 of the Act and they enabled employers, including local authorities, to provide special or targeted training or service provisions for ethnic minority populations.

These provisions have all been used by local authorities in pursuit of the promotion of equal opportunities and 'good race relations'. Arguably, however, another section of the Act has had greater implication for local authority employment and service delivery policies – that is section 71 (see Nanton and Fitzgerald, 1990, p. 159). This section establishes a general statutory duty on local authorities to promote equality of opportunity and good race relations and to ensure that their employment, and service delivery and administrative arrangements, pay 'due regard to the need to eliminate unlawful discrimination' (Ousley, 1990, p. 134). The section reads as follows:

> S. 71 Without prejudice to their obligation to comply with any other provision of this Act, it shall be the duty of every local authority to make appropriate arrangements with a view to securing that their various functions are carried out with due regard to the need –
>
> (a) to eliminate unlawful racial discrimination; and
> (b) to promote equality of opportunity, and good race relations, between persons of different racial groups.

Importantly, it was the enduring relevance of this clause that resulted in an amendment to the 1988 Local Government Act on the politically loaded issue of contract compliance clauses in contracts between local authority departments and their suppliers. As a result, the clause in this Act prohibiting influence of 'non-commercial' matters on the contracting process in local authorities was amended so that the duties imposed under section 71 of the Race Relations Act (RRA) remained intact (Solomos and Ball, 1990, p. 217).

Taken together, the clauses in the RRA have been important in providing a legal framework which some local authorities have used in an attempt to address racial inequality. Broadly, three interrelated types of initiative have been developed:

1 training – in terms of both awareness and skills development;
2 contractual – attempts to extend the pursuit of equal opportunity by imposing conditions on supplier organizations to the local authority;
3 positive action generally – the overhaul of arrangements across and within departments of the local authority to remove barriers to equal opportunities.

These clauses form a backdrop for many of the strategies adopted by local authority departments, including the social services departments discussed in the next chapter.

The Children Act 1989

This was a major piece of legislation codifying existing laws governing the care and control of children; parental rights and duties; the rights and duties of local authorities in relation to children; and the relations between parents, children and local authorities. In relation to 'race' it has been greeted as a step forward because of the oft-quoted clause relating to religious, racial, cultural and linguistic background. The clause comes in Part III of the Act concerned with the duties and responsibilities of local authorities' support for children and families. Among the duties imposed on local authorities in relation to children looked after by them, section 22 requires local authorities to ascertain the wishes and feelings of the child, parents and significant others and to have (among other things) due consideration '. . . *to the child's religious persuasion, racial origin and cultural and linguistic background*' (s. 22 (5) (c), my emphasis).

There are a number of interesting points about this clause. One is its relative weakness. It only imposes a general duty to have 'due consideration' where 'reasonably practical'. Second, where it is situated within the Act raises interesting questions. It occurs within that part of the Act dealing with the imposition of general statutory duties on local authorities. Prior to this, notions of 'race', on ethnic or national origins, do not figure. This is so even in those sections dealing with the rights accorded to parents and children, to the assignment of guardians *ad litem* or indeed to any other part dealing with the rights (and duties) of individual families or children. This is suggestive of a blindness to issues of 'race' where benefits and/or legal protections are enshrined. Moreover, it is reminiscent of the ways in which, in other pieces of legislation, it is only at times when racialized populations of colour are problematized (and pathologized) that explicit reference is made to them. In this sense 'looked-after' children are automatically problematized because they are most often seen as the effect of inadequate family structures and/or parenting skills. This in turn links to both the attempts by central government to increase its control on local government and, more contradictorily, the wish by the centre to push matters of 'race' to the local level.

Before going on to discuss how and when 'race' enters parliamentary debates on the social policy legislation outlined above, I want to suggest a framework for reading these debates. I emphasized the visible/invisible character that 'race' assumes in national social policy. At times explicit connection is made between 'race' and the reasons for, and the anticipated outcomes of, the policies. At other times such visible connections to 'race' are elided by referring instead to conditions of social malaise and deprivation. In other words, sometimes 'race' will be seen to stand as a biological metaphor for a system of social, historical and political significations, while at other times structural factors, understood as class or spatial inequalities, are invoked as the metaphor for 'race' and race relations. In a context where issues of 'race' and racism are cast as epiphenomenal, or at most the property of a few 'bad apples' and not endemic in British society, recourse to class or spatial structure is a means of avoiding the embeddedness of 'race' and racism in the British social formation. At one level it is possible to understand this as emerging from the lack of commitment on the part of successive central governments to do anything other than restrict immigration and pass the appropriate legislative framework to ban discrimination and promote 'good race relations' and equality of opportunity. Indeed, this dualism delineates dominant discourse and practice in the field of 'race relations'. Only at moments when it seems politically unavoidable is more than this done and even then never without an awareness of the potential political minefield that may open up when dealing with 'race' and racialized popu-lations of colour, particularly if a redistribution of resources in favour of greater equality is involved. Some interesting and important analyses of the links between 'race' and social policy at the level of local politics have been made and these have gone a long way in helping understanding of the dynamics and contradictions of this interrelation (see, for example, Saggar, 1993; Ben-Tovim et al., 1986; Solomos and Back, 1995). Here, however, I want to suggest an additional reading or interpretation of the forms of articulation between 'race' and social policy by drawing on psy-choanalytic understandings of the formation of 'the other' and processes of denial, forgetting and turning a blind eye.

Reading through the psychoanalytic

Constructing the social 'other'

Although a term with Hegelian roots, 'the other' has come into preva-lent usage in recent social and cultural theory because of the conver-gence of post-structuralism, feminism and postcolonial criticism. In both the Lacanian and object relations schools of psychoanalysis, and in femi-nist analyses seeking to theorize the links between the psychic and social formation of sexual difference, the idea of 'the other' has occupied a central place. The ubiquity of the notion of 'the other' across these diverse but overlapping theoretical approaches has meant that the term has a kind of ambiguity referencing an interiorized psychic 'other', sexual difference, or a more generalized alterity. Such a wide range of refer-ences can potentially lead to conceptual ambiguities and/or conflations. Despite this, the concept of 'the other' acts as the point of articulation between psychoanalytic and post-structuralist approaches and in this capacity it has provided a powerful analytic tool in the deconstruction and theoretical destabilization of fields of power constructed around axes of difference.

There are three interrelated points emerging from conceptualizations of 'the other' that I wish to focus on. First is the idea that the 'self' is constructed relationally (that is in terms of the distinction between 'self' and 'other'). This process of constitution of 'self' is, however, an unstable process precisely because the self contains within it sameness *and* difference. This leads to the second point, that maintenance of the fiction of a unitary self comprised of internal sameness in opposition to external difference is achieved through an active process of expulsion, denial, rejection or even ingestion. In terms of the social relations of 'race', this process of ingestion equates to a process of appropriation or assimilation of difference into sameness, so that which was different – 'the other' – is no longer so. Finally, the psychic process of the constitution of a self through the expulsion and denial of 'the other' has its wider social and cultural supports and expressions. Indeed, it is precisely the mutual imbrication of these psychic and socio-cultural processes that has been the subject of much psychoanalytically inspired feminist theory (see, for example, Alexander, 1994; Benjamin, 1995; Brennan, 1989; Hollway, 1989). In these cases it is sexual difference that has been at the centre of their concerns. However, some psychoanalytically inspired feminism and much postcolonial theory has centred on racial difference and the formation of a racial 'other' (see, for example, Kovel, 1995; Lane, 1998; Mama, 1995; Rose, 1996; Bhaba, 1994; Rattansi, 1995). These have drawn directly on the work of Freud (especially *Civilization and its Discontents*) and the ways in which concepts and methods developed by Freud have been extended and appropriated by Fanon, Memmi and other more recent postcolonial critics.

Drawing on a theoretical framework concerned with the process of formation of the 'self' and its psychic 'other' to elucidate the processes of formation of a social subject and its social 'other' may be seen to sit uneasily in a discussion of social policy. Yet the analytic utility of the psychoanalytic approach lies in the way in which the structure of the relation between 'self' and 'other' has been theorized. Thus, formation of 'the self' has been conceptualized as dependent on 'the other', and involving an *active* process of recognition, loss, separation, expulsion (abjection) or ingestion. When this theoretical insight is allied to the understandings of the constitutions of difference rooted in various forms of post-structuralist analysis (as relational, always in process, and never quite closed or achieved as in Derrida's *différance*, with its double inscription of difference and deferral), then we have a powerful analytic tool through which to comprehend and narrate the constitution of a (series of) social 'others' in social policy. It is this that I wish to appropriate and deploy in my analysis of the parliamentary debates of central policy initiatives on 'race', particularly in relation to the dual processes of expulsion and ingestion – or not seeing and seeing.

*Turning a blind eye*²

In an interesting application of a reading by Vellacott (1971) of the Oedipus myth, Steiner (1985) has attempted to think about the ways in which people often construct a set of meanings or interpretations about a situation which go against all the fully available facts before them. They 'turn a blind eye'. Steiner argues that the idea of the blind eye is a complex one conveying the ambiguity between whether the knowledge being denied is conscious or unconscious. What I am interested in appropriating for the analysis of how and where 'race' is spoken or unspoken in social policy debates and texts is precisely the ambiguity and ambivalence revealed by the twofold reading that can be made of the process of turning a blind eye. Steiner tells us that Vellacott offers two readings of the Oedipus myth.

First, is the traditional interpretation in which the central characters are as being caught up in the play of fate or forces outside of their control. For social policy analysis, 'structural forces' understood as class and/or spatial inequalities can be substituted for 'fate' such that when thinking about 'ethnic minorities' words such as 'inner cities', 'disadvantage' (with its connotation of class) and 'deprivation' (which is associated either with class or cultural pathology) can be substituted for discrimination and/or racism. In this view the conditions in which many members of 'ethnic minority' populations live their lives in Britain are a product of one or two factors. It can be an effect of urban deprivation and decay, factors they share with their white working-class cohabitants. Matters of 'race' or colour do not enter the equation. On the other hand, the conditions of life of racialized populations of colour can be explained as the product of their internal cultural and social attitudes and habits – the result of cultural pathologies. Either way 'race', as an axis of differentiation and power and as a principle internal to social relations in Britain, is elided.

A second interpretation of the Oedipus myth is that it shows that in many complicated and difficult situations social actors have some awareness of the relation between factors and their effects, but for a complex set of individual, and possibly overlapping, reasons they deny or displace this knowledge. In the play, the chorus, which constantly speaks of the catastrophe to come, represents the simultaneously known and denied. It is my argument that such a process of denial and displacement in terms of the relation between 'race', racism and particular policies is evident in the parliamentary debates I discuss in the next section.

I want to consider the ways in which these interpretations of a Greek myth may be applied to readings of British social policy in the mid- to late twentieth century. Let me begin by unpacking the substitution of 'structure' for fate because the issue of structure is itself a complex one. In the dominant reading of the Oedipus play, the central characters – Oedipus, Laius, Jocasta, Creon, etc. – were locked into a tragic set of relationships and actions because the play of fate was outside their control. Fate would have it that Oedipus is cast out to die by his parents because Apollo's oracle foretold that he would kill his father and marry his mother. Fate would have it that the shepherd saves Oedipus' life by giving him to a shepherd from another city; that Oedipus would then be adopted by Polybus and Merop and that it would be these that he later flees from to avoid carrying out the abominable prediction. Fate would have it that he would be on the road at the time that his real, but unknown, father is passing in the carriage, that he would kill him, arrive in Thebes, be crowned the king because of solving the riddle of the Sphynx and end up marrying his mother. As a result of these fateful occurrences, a plague would befall the city because of the inner corruption at the very centre of the city. All of this was, as it were, 'written' by fate and all of it was beyond human control, even though a result of human actions. The characters were the objects of fate, their actions determined by an invisible hand. Whilst this is the moral of the tale, there is within it another tale and that is the seemingly contradictory one of the power, indeed imperative, of human action on the basis of fully available knowledge (see, for example, the introduction by Knox to the 1984 Penguin Classics edition of the play). Thus Oedipus, the very embodiment of the inner corruption, is also compelled to act to reveal the truth of the relationships and the cause of the city's troubles, and the chorus, positioned as onlookers who bespeak the tragedy and its causes, represents the knowledge that is available.

In the functionalist school of sociology, 'structure' is afforded the same kind of determining quality as fate in the Oedipus myth but without the additional imperative to act. Human actions are conceived as constrained within a set (or sets) of invisible presences which are external to these actions and themselves ineluctable. The long-accepted consequence of this formulation of social structures as sets of immovable girders is that the social divisions characterizing a society are seen as natural and immutable and the social processes produced by, and productive of, action are made invisible. The problems with this conceptualization of structure reside both in what gets defined as a structure (i.e. the closures it leads to) and in the way that certain actions are cast as inevitable whilst others are cast as impossible.

'Structure' conceptualized in this way has a double effect. It leads to a privileging of class as the key element in the social structure, such that at the level of the social formation as a whole, structural relations are seen as encapsulated by class relations. Within certain social science and political traditions, this has had the additional effect of constructing these relations as both natural and normative.

I should make it clear that I do not wish to propose an abandonment of the concept of structure. Thought of in Giddensian terms as a framework produced by the repetitions of social processes and actions, which then in turn help to fashion or pattern future actions and processes, the concept of structure allied to agency is invaluable in social theory. However, affording structure a methodological and causal privilege leads to analytical closures (methodological, ontological and epistemological) that are unacceptable and unhelpful. In this vein, I want to consider what it is possible to elide in the invocation of dominant conceptions of structure and, in turn, how these elisions are related to psychic as well as social and political processes.

In this sense my interest in the Oedipus myth and Steiner's use of it lies in the latter's notion that turning a blind eye involves a vague awareness that certain facts are being avoided whilst simultaneously not being conscious of what it is that is avoided. In this sense Steiner's appropriation of the Vellacott reading is useful because of the links made in the myth between what is seen or denied and how these in turn are related to what it is deemed possible to do; or to put it another way the link between, on the one hand, 'knowing' and 'not knowing' and, on the other, the issue of constraint or opportunity to act. The two link together because 'not knowing' is often couched within the idea of externally imposed constraints which are then used to dismiss that which is being avoided without having to explicitly name it. In terms of a 'self', this can equate to an expulsion or denial of the 'other' within. In the fields of 'race' and politics, such 'constraints' are mediated through the electoral process and systems of legitimation, which in turn are articulated on a discursive terrain that continuously severs the link between contemporary black settlement in Britain and the country's imperial past. The effect of this is both the erratic acknowledgement of Britain's imperial history and the denial of 'race' and racism as enduring *internal* factors in the social formation. It is this which accounts for the 'now you see it, now you don't' quality of 'race' in social policy and the abjection of 'ethnic minority' populations.

How are we to understand the pervasive social amnesia in relation to 'race' that is manifest in British policy and politics, given that all of the pieces of legislation outlined here have been enacted in the heat of, or subsequent to, moral panics about 'race' and the black presence which Powellism, understood as the incorporation of racist discourse and policy into mainstream politics (Hall, 1978), articulated? Cultural theorists have noted that periodically societies fall prey

> to periods of moral panic. A condition, episode, person or group of persons emerges to become defined as a threat to societal values and interests . . . [after a flurry of policy and rhetorical activity] . . . ways of coping are

evolved, or more often resorted to; the condition then disappears or sub-merges or deteriorates and becomes more visible. Sometimes the object of the panic is quite novel and at other times it is something which has been in existence long enough, but suddenly appears in the limelight. Sometimes the panic passes over and is forgotten, except in folklore and collective memory; at other times it has more serious and long-lasting repercussions and might produce such changes as those in legal and social policy or even in the way the society conceives itself. (Cohen, 1972, p. 9)

This suggests that the search for an analytical understanding of the simultaneous 'forgetting' and panic about 'race' needs to incorporate notions of social neurosis and phobia into more predominant ways of understanding the genesis of social policies. The insights provided by psy-choanalysis show that panics, irrational fears and other forms of neurotic behaviour are related to processes by which repression of that which is too horrible to bear in consciousness occurs. However, that which is repressed has a habit of revealing itself in a whole array of symptoms – from slips of the tongue, through dreams, to neurotic and psychotic behaviours.

Application of psychoanalytic methods to the analysis of cultural forms requires a heuristic mechanism by which a move from the level of the individual to that of the collective can be achieved. Obeyesekere (1990), in developing a psychoanalytic anthropology, suggests that just such a mechanism is provided in the notion of 'symbolic remove' (p. 57). He means by this the levels of distancing between deep motivations and the representational forms which both express and reconfigure these motivations. Thus, he suggests that by holding the notion of symbolic remove it is possible to develop a means for interpreting systems of rep-resentation and meaning as they are expressed in diverse cultural forms. These cultural forms may carry an array of condensed psychic concerns but in their progressive distancing from their motivational roots they can also link to collective anxieties and social neuroses whose sources are social and historical as much as psychic. Analysis of the unconscious motives contained but repressed in cultural symbols is what 'the work of culture', as Obeyesekere calls it, is about and its value lies in the disso-lution of the conventional divide between the material and psychic, or the structural and representational.

Such a dissolution facilitates powerful and innovative analyses of specific social situations, as Krikler (1995) has shown. He attempted to uncover the set of circumstances which 'nourished a particular moment of acute anxiety amongst whites in a region of South Africa' (p. 491) in the early part of the twentieth century. In developing his analysis he drew on the Freudian notion of social neurosis to understand the collective anxieties that arose as a result of a failure on the part of the white people concerned to consciously confront their implication in the history of South Africa's racially ordered society. Through a detailed analysis of one phobic moment, Krikler shows 'how seemingly irrational fears – about black revolt – arose from a process of repressing from conscious memory historical experience' (p. 492). Such repression of historical experience and implication resulted in social neurosis, understood as 'a psychological malady arising from the repression of uncomfortable facts by an entire social grouping' (p. 507).

Just as at the level of the individual, the social repressed can be glimpsed in a variety of ways. Turning a blind eye, social amnesia and moral panics can then be understood as some of the forms in which the socially repressed returns to haunt the society attempting to 'forget'.

Part of the process of turning a blind eye to the embeddedness of 'race' in the British social formation is that structural forces are foregrounded and become the language through which 'race' is spoken and yet discrimination or racism is denied. However, *racism* is also a major structuring force within British society. Turning a blind eye then also involves the denial of a central 'structure', such that structure can only be equated to class relations and not to other axes of power which organize social relations in contemporary Britain. I think there are a number of ways in which the reformulation of structure outlined above is helpful.

First, functionalism's 'structure' gives political legitimacy to the failure to 'see' and act on racism because it suggests that nothing could be done anyway. The play of fate, as it were, dictates the possibilities. In the field of social policies, this is to reduce racism to disadvantage, which is to privilege class (in both its Weberian sense as socio-economic position and status, and its Marxist sense as social relations of production) as the determinant of all. By adopting a conceptualization that neither equates structure to class, nor sees structure as all determinant, a wider field of action is potentially opened up.

Second, if this reconceptualization makes it conceivable that action is possible, then the next step is to delineate the structural and discursive factors involved in producing the conditions of life of black people. It is here that the issue of 'knowing' and 'not knowing' enters. Steiner makes it clear that for the process of 'turning a blind eye' to be understood the insights afforded by both readings of the Oedipus myth have to be taken simultaneously.

> We are meant to accept the idea that *both* can be simultaneously true, that he knew and at the same time did not know. It is this which I mean to convey when I suggest that he turned a blind eye to the facts.   (1985, p. 165, his emphasis)

If turning a blind eye involves two simultaneous processes what is even more important for my purposes is the consequences it has. To elicit these in the arena of social policy I want first to quote Steiner at some length in relation to the psychic effects because I think these can be reworked to shed some light on the situation in the field with which I am concerned.

> If the Oedipal crime is not acknowledged to have taken place, but is misrepresented, distorted or covered up, then there is nothing to mourn, and the reparative processes . . . cannot operate. There is nothing to fear because no crime is acknowledged, except, of course, the fear that the cover-up will be exposed. The result is that the external couple is not attacked as it would be if psychic reality was acknowledged but instead the attack is mounted against an internal representation of a good intercourse, namely one in which truth is respected. The external status quo is apparently preserved but there is an inner corruption which is represented by the plague in the play and specifically confirmed by the oracle. The personality is then felt to be based on an insecure foundation and the need to cover up leads to further evasions and distortions. (p. 168)[3]

I want to suggest that we can use this insight in looking at the blind eye of 'race' and social policy. No full-scale and systematic 'reparative' process is necessary if the internally generated or organic racism of British society and institutions is denied or 'not seen', and the problem is displaced on to those constituted as racialized outsiders. Once so constituted these outsiders can be represented as the 'inner corruption' threatening the 'personality' or character of the body politic/nation. This threat or insecurity results either if too much attention is paid to the outsiders, or if they are not limited in numbers nor subjected to processes of social regulation. The 'good intercourse', which could just possibly arise if processes of racialization were acknowledged and then undermined, is prevented because the 'truth' of 'race' and racism is denied or turned a blind eye to. The fear that the 'cover-up' will be outed is always present because of those moments of political, social or cultural 'plague' – such as sporadic urban rebellions, when racism is riotously resisted, or moral panics when racializations are made explicit. These and other factors must be constantly misrepresented and evaded and I would argue this ideological and psychic imperative is revealed by the constant slippage to 'deprivation/disadvantage' alongside, or simultaneous with, the evocation of 'race' and/or ethnicity at certain moments in the evolution in social policy.

This approach can elucidate the points at which, and the ways in which, particular policies can be explicitly presented as aimed at black and Asian populations *and* those where such acknowledgement is not possible. What will become clear is that 'recognition' of the 'race' aspect of a policy is most likely to be explicit when the discourses inscribed in the policy problematize racialized populations of colour. In this sense Ann Phoenix's (1987) formulation that there is a 'normalized absence, pathologized presence' in relation to black people is particularly sharp. The effects of turning a blind eye to 'race' and racism are profound. As Ousley (1984) has pointed out in relation to the effects of the legislation detailed earlier:

> Over the past two decades pathetic attempts have been made by central government and local government to deal with the perceived threat posed by the black presence in Britain. There have been discriminatory immigration legislation to stop black people's entry, race relations legislation with restrained enforcement provisions and the exemption of the Crown from all charges of racism, 'Section 11' funding for local authority posts intended to deal with 'new commonwealth immigrants' in their areas; the Urban Programme; Educational Priority Areas; MSC schemes; and the Inner City Partnership. Because none has addressed the central issue of racism, these programmes have all had marginal benefits for black people and in many ways have been discriminatory.   (p. 98)

The effect of this approach is to appear to do something whilst simultaneously constituting and reconstituting black and Asian people as 'outsiders' and 'other'. Similarly, this has the effect of constituting the British, and 'their' culture, as internally 'good'. There are no internal complexities or contradictions to be acknowledged, no 'seeing' of processes which produce racist social relations.

I now want to go on to illustrate these points with reference to the parliamentary debates that preceded the introduction of some of the policies outlined above. In particular, I concentrate on debates about section 11 and the Urban Programme.

Analysing the unseen in parliamentary debates

Section 11

At first sight it could be thought that because section 11 was explicitly introduced as a policy linked to the presence of black communities in urban centres up and down the country, there is little to be said about it within the framework of the 'blind eye'. Contrary to this I would suggest that an exploration of debates as recorded in *Hansard* about the section from its second reading (1966) until the time of writing (1995) shows many of the elements of the blind eye at play.

In June 1966 the Bill which became the Local Government Act 1966 had its second reading, marking the occasion of its first full parliamentary debate. Roy Hattersley, then MP for Sparkbrook, Birmingham, opened the debate by situating clause 11 in the context of the then Labour government's immigration policy, stating that 'those of us who believed it essential to do something *to make integration and absorption possible* supported Part III of the White Paper then and support it now' (*Hansard*, vol. 729, column 1333, my emphasis). In so doing he immediately establishes the link between control of entry and 'good race relations', one of the dualisms providing the discursive parameters for debate on these issues.

Soon he also makes the second common link – that of black presence and deprivation – by saying

> I call Clause 11 the second part of the implementation of those policies [i.e. on immigration and integration] because the first example of special help being offered to *areas* with a high concentration of immigrants was the additional assistance announced . . . for housing authorities with particularly pressing slum clearance problems. By and large, they are immigrant areas, and by and large they will benefit. Moreover, they are the *areas* which will have the most benefit and assistance from Clause 11 of this Bill. (vol. 729, columns 1333–5, my emphases)

I have stressed his use of the word 'areas' because it exemplifies the point that the beneficiaries of the monies proposed in this clause were not black and Asian people but local areas which had to be compensated for their presence. This in turn is related to the issue of 'reparation' which the notion of the blind eye raises, for once again reparation – in the form of attempting to undo processes of racialization and racism – is not seen as the issue. Rather the matter at hand is deemed to be 'compensation' to those who have to 'suffer' the presence of black and Asian people. In so constructing the problem, British complicity in the historical and contemporary reproduction of racist social relations is avoided. Despite this avoidance, 'race' is simultaneously reinscribed as a key axis of social relations because it remains a marker of differentiation, pathologization and 'trouble', albeit spoken through the metaphor of urban deprivation or the 'inner city'.

Hattersley, however, has more on his agenda than to argue for monetary compensation to be paid to specific local areas. In the continuation of his speech he manages to raise the 'distinctiveness' of the 'problems' associated with immigration from the (New) Commonwealth; to pathologize black and Asian family forms; and, thereby, to argue that such families be subjected to instruction in 'British ways'. Moreover, he manages to do this all in a tone that establishes both his concern for 'his' immigrants and his foresightedness in matters of community relations – for which read 'race'. He warns that he will touch upon contentious issues but that he will establish the specificity of 'problems' arising from Commonwealth immigration.

> It is vital that money could be provided under the Clause for some services which the unenlightened would regard as essentially peripheral both in education and health. . . . I know very well that to enumerate the problems of constituencies like mine, with 30 per cent of its inhabitants immigrants from the Commonwealth, is to court the accusation that one is emphasizing the problems for most unworthy reasons. . . .
>
> [Nevertheless] there are in my constituency schools in which 30 per cent of the children speak no English at all. There are schools in which 50 per cent of the children speak English in a quite minimal way. Also – *this is probably more important*, and it is the central issue which I put before the House and the Government – there are schools in which 70 or 80 per cent of the children have *really no experience of English customs and English mores.*
>
> I hope that, when the money under Clause 11 is distributed, the Secretary of State will bear in mind that, as well as providing smaller classes in which English can be adequately taught, as well as providing extra visitors *to remind parents of their new obligations in Great Britain, it is essential to make provision to teach these children basic British customs, basic British habits and, if one likes, basic British prejudices* – all those things which they need to know if they are to live happily and successfully in an integrated way in this community.
>
> I hope very much that the special grants under Clause 11 will be available for teaching in that sense as well as teaching in the more formal sense. The immigrant areas are usually areas where schools are too old and the classes too crowded. But as well as the great problem of providing formal education, there is the need for formal instruction of both the children themselves *and their parents.* There is here a great work of education and encouragement to be carried out. I know from my own experience in Birmingham that those who carry on this work with immigrants, who are there to give informal advice and assistance, and to *persuade* as well as to teach are often regarded by the unenlightened as unnecessary and unimportant . . .
>
> I welcome the grant, because this is the first occasion when money has specifically been set aside for authorities which *suffer* this problem.
>
> (vol. 729, columns 1335–7, my emphases)

There are a number of moves discernible here. First, we can see recourse to, and slippage among, the discursive pairings that have structured social policy formulations (and the lack of them) concerned, directly or indirectly, with 'race' in post-Second-World-War Britain. Thus, for example, we see 'race' as a metaphor for problems in the notion of 'immigrant areas'. The idea that a 'substantial' black presence in an

area is productive of problems is also embedded in Hattersley's plea
for education to be defined widely in the name of integration. But then
just as he gets dangerously close to doing what he states he will not do
– i.e. blame black people themselves for the problems they and the
areas they live in face – he veers off into issues of spatial structure.
'Immigrant areas' are those 'where schools are too old and the classes
too crowded'. Recourse to structure, here where class and geography
overlay one another, provides the route by which not to 'see' where he
is going discursively. Simultaneously it provides the detour via which he
can return to the racialization of problems yet still avoid the issue of
racism.

What is also striking about Hattersley's speech is how he simultaneously manages to problematize black and Asian *families*. He does this by
proceeding as if it is axiomatic that 'their' values, customs and traditions
are 'alien' to those of the 'British way'. Here we have the introduction
of a theme that is replayed on numerous occasions in official, academic,
media and professional discussions about, and representations of, the
black and Asian presence in Britain.

Indeed if we look at parliamentary debates of section 11 in recent
years, at least as they are recorded in *Hansard*, this last point is clear. For
example, in a House of Commons debate held on 5 July 1994, Max
Madden, speaking on behalf of Walker, the MP for Keighley, near Bradford, read a statement about section 11 (now subsumed under the SRB)
which included:

> Having visited schools in my constituency where up to 95 per cent of the
> roll are of ethnic minority origin, I know how important this issue is [i.e.
> discussing the changes to section 11]. . . .
>
> An understanding of English and an ability to use language are vital
> prerequisites to the learning process. Any child who lacks those basic skills
> is bound to be at a serious disadvantage and to start losing time which can
> never be made up. . . .
>
> To that end more section 11 money should perhaps be devoted to the
> pre-school sector and to *working with parents* who, in most cases, are very
> anxious to give their children a good start in life but who *may be poorly
> equipped to do so*. (*Hansard*, vol. 246, column 291, my emphases)

So here again there is a slippage from the issue of educational need
to that of the adequacy of the 'ethnic minority' family and, implicitly, the
gender formations they are assumed to contain. The retention of this discursive register is all the more striking given the very changed economic
fortunes of Britain in the mid-1990s compared to those in the mid-1960s,
and especially compared to the dominant approach to state supported
and promoted welfare which now centres on notions of self-reliance and
independence from the 'nanny state'.[4]

Once again the recourse to the notion of invisible but determinant structures provides the means by which to return us to the 'problem' of black and Asian presence and, at the same time, to elide the issue of racism. Thus Walker (the Keighley MP) continues with this in his written statement:

> All too evidently, the problems are here and now. Money spent today, if wisely used, will certainly be repaid in the future by cutting the cost of *tomorrow's unemployment* and *tomorrow's social disadvantage.*
>
> I hope that Bradford will combine with Government to put together a bid within the context of the Single Regeneration Budget which, among other things, *clearly addresses the problems which section 11 was intended to resolve,* and which also provides good value for taxpayers' and Council Tax payers' money.   (vol. 246, column 291, my emphases)

Exactly which problems section 11 was aimed at resolving – language provision for those who needed it, a means of gaining extra financial resources to a particular area, compensation to local areas for carrying a national burden of New Commonwealth settlement, a means of promoting integration – is not made at all clear. Moreover, it sits alongside the new language of 'good financial management' and is part of a co-ordinated plea to get extra monies into Bradford.

What is plain is that whatever the prime motivation behind this contribution to the debate the whole issue is played out on the well-established terrain of numbers and problems. This despite the fact that primary New Commonwealth migration into Britain had been reduced to a trickle. Max Madden, for example, foregrounds the issue of numbers when he takes up the debate in his own right: 'By the year 2000 one in every two pupils in schools in Bradford will be of ethnic minority origin. At present, nearly 82,000 are on roll, 27 per cent of ethnic minority origin' (column 291). Really his 'origin' refers to descent, a distinction of which he is aware since he uses this to make recourse to the ubiquitous 'problem' of black families, for he goes on to say:

> Although most of our children are *second generation few have parents who were educated in Britain.* There is still a propensity for a spouse in an arranged marriage to come from overseas, often speaking little or no English. It is not surprising that *those* parents cannot teach their children at home. Because of the number of parents who cannot speak English, there is a significant need for more adult literacy provision.   (vol. 246, column 292, my emphasis)

So the language needs of 'ethnic minority' children slip to the problems of '*a* spouse' from overseas which slips to the inadequacies of 'those parents'. The needs of individual children suddenly get constructed as familial lack and inadequacy. And here, at the level of the psychoanalytic in its Lacanian variant, one is reminded that the process of 'othering' and 'self' (and thereby the constitution of the subject) always involves an ascription of 'lack'.

What is also presented here is that limited language proficiency (real or presumed) is presented as if it were the sole reason for the under-achievement of many black, Pakistani- and Bangladeshi-descent pupils in schools. Madden cites the figures and, though he has no recourse to a language of structural disadvantage, racism, as a contradictory but powerful structuring factor in underachievement, is once again unrecognized.

> Continuous monitoring of 20,000 ethnic minority pupils in Bradford suggests that on leaving first schools aged nine, 27 per cent of those pupils have still not achieved national curriculum level two. That has an impact on subsequent achievement because assessment records show that 59 per cent of ethnic minority pupils entering upper schools, aged 13, have not yet achieved national curriculum level four. The proportion of Bradford students who do not achieve GCSE grade C or above is the highest in the country.
>
> Bradford still has a number of pupils and students who arrive at school with no English. Of the September 1993 intake, there were 177 such children in first schools, 114 in our middle schools and 48 in our upper schools. (columns 291–2)

Of course the importance of substantial proficiency in received English for educational achievement cannot be denied. As such I would argue that all those pupils who need specialist classes in English language (however small or large that number may be) should have access to them. However, here my concern is not with the issue of rights to, and distribution of, educational resources. Rather it is to analyse the moves by which the issue of racism is 'not seen'; the ways in which, and moments at which, discourses of 'race' are foregrounded in the parliamentary debates; and the moments when racial discourses are supplanted by, or overlaid with, those of class or – more accurately – disadvantage.

Earlier I commented that section 11 had been analysed as a means of compensation from central government to those local areas which were seen as having to bear the 'burden' of black settlement. As such it is a policy at the heart of centre–local relations. This remained so in the 1990s when these relations underwent radical restructuring in the wake of the reforms of Conservative governments and their retention in broadly similar form by Tony Blair's first New Labour government. The debate on section 11 quoted above took place in this changed context and the contributions of the Bradford MPs were in many senses appeals to central government to recognize the special circumstances of the city and therefore the need for continued access to section 11 monies. This is because of the 1993 incorporation of section 11 monies into the single regeneration budget. As a result of these changes Bradford would no longer receive section 11 funding. Black 'problems' and black 'needs' were therefore used as the basis of an appeal for the maintenance of financial resources to the city, arguing that without it the pursuit of equal opportunity would be seriously undermined.

The issue of equality of opportunity is already present in some of the debate previously quoted. For example, the need to support English language teaching as a prerequisite to educational attainment. In the contribution from Gerry Sutcliffe (Bradford South), the issue is stated directly and related to other sources of area-based financial support, i.e. City Challenge and the Urban Programme: 'Initiatives such as city challenge and the urban programme were the result of problems in inner-city areas. We do not want to return to the days of a lack of funding to provide equality of opportunity' (column 294). Whose equality of opportunity is not specified at this stage but his use of one of the key code words by which 'race' is spoken – i.e. 'inner-city' – gives a very strong hint. And anyway the term 'equality of opportunity' has moved from its post-Plowden (1960s) association with (white) working-class school-children to its post-1970s association with women, 'ethnic minorities' and, to a lesser extent, disabled people. So one is not surprised that Sutcliffe continues with reference to the need to recognize that: 'In areas such as Bradford and most other Metropolitan Authorities, there must be greater concentration on section 11-type schemes to support people in dramatic need' (column 294).

So 'race' again works as an implied shadow, or what Althusser referred to as 'an absent presence'. It has something to do with the production of need but how and of what order is elusive. For here we have a statement about 'dramatic need' without any specification as to how this either arises or is quantified. The earlier contributions had given some idea. Out of a total of nearly 82,000 pupils in Bradford schools we had been told that in one year's intake a total of 339 with no English had entered schools. Is this what is meant by 'dramatic need'? Or is it the issue of overall disadvantage and lack of resources found in Bradford's educational facilities? If it is this latter issue, then section 11 monies should not be available to help alleviate such need. The details of the issue then are not spelled out. What is clear is that the discursive terrain on which the debate took place was that of only 'seeing' 'race' when black or Asian people were constituted as a metaphor for wider social and economic problems; as being located in 'problem areas'; or when they were seen as producing problems because of their 'otherness'.

This last point is most clearly put in the contribution from Terry Rooney (Bradford North).

One problem is that Bradford has *never had a race riot*. If it had been otherwise, large sums of money might have followed, as happened with Bristol, Toxteth and Brixton. Fortunately, we have never had such happenings, and part of the reason for that is the extensive and profitable use of section 11 funds in the Youth Service and in further education. (column 294, my emphasis)

There is a wealth of discursive moves discernible here. First, there is the clear identification of black people – especially 'black youth' – as productive of major social disruption in the extreme form of riotous behaviour. Second, there is the paradoxical suggestion that such behaviour brings with it local reward in the form of injections of finance from the centre. Third, there is the idea that the social control of problems caused by black youth is achievable by the use of section 11 monies.

What is quite remarkable about this discursive journey is the act of 'forgetting', or social amnesia, on which it is premised. For no mention is made of the 1981 case when twelve local youths of Asian descent were charged with conspiracy. They became known as 'the Bradford Twelve'. The event occurred after police were reportedly informed that preparation was being made for a major riot in the city and that a huge quantity of petrol bombs was being stored in a disused site in the city. The twelve charged were said to be the 'ringleaders' of the said conspiracy. This was one of the key 'law and order' trials of the decade and figured quite significantly in the recasting of second- and third-generation young men of Asian descent as (at least potentially) a new source of trouble and concern for inner-city police forces. Moreover, it served to locate Bradford firmly on the map of areas of tension between black and Asian young people and the police in the wake of the riotous rebellions which began in Bristol in 1980 and were to sweep up and down the country for the next ten years.

The Urban Programme

It has already been shown that the link between the Urban Programme and 'race' was not explicit in the language of the statutes introducing and extending the Programme, but the fact that it was first introduced in the immediate aftermath of Powell's infamous 'rivers of blood' speech of April 1968 meant that to officials, politicians, 'race relations' personnel and the black communities the link was crystal clear. It was also clear in the debates that accompanied the announcement of changes to the Programme in 1977. This juxtapositioning makes it possible to discern the blind eye mechanism at work – a process of avoidance being played out on the terrain of moral panic.

To reiterate: the main changes introduced at this time were all aimed at trying to regenerate the life of inner cities, which the inner-area studies had shown as rapidly collapsing. The six main proposals were:

1   to give a new priority in the main policies and programmes of government to help improve inner-city life;
2   to develop a more unified approach to such policies and programmes, part of which would be accomplished by the transfer of the Urban Programme from the Home Office to the Department of the Environment;
3   to strengthen the economies of inner-city areas;
4   to review and change policies aimed at directing and encouraging population movement within and across regions;
5   to recast the Urban Programme so that it covered economic and environmental projects as well as social ones;
6   to establish special Partnership areas, with additional Programme areas.

(Hansard, vol. 929, 6 April 1977)

In introducing these proposals, Peter Shore, then Secretary of State for the Environment, made explicit reference to black and Asian populations using the old formulation of 'substantial numbers' and in such a way as to constitute them as problems: 'Over the past decade inner cities have suffered a massive and disproportionate loss of jobs and exodus of population. *Substantial ethnic minorities* in some cities have added an extra dimension of *difficulty*' (vol. 929, columns 1226–7, my emphasis). Yet still Cabinet ministers were maintaining a distinction between policies that were explicitly deemed to be about managing the purported problems of a black and Asian presence and those that were supposed to be only tangentially cast in the shadow of 'race'. This distinction also reflected departmental rivalries between the Home Office and the Department of the Environment; the division of labour between them also giving some hint at how matters of 'race' were perceived. Thus, in a written answer from the Prime Minister to a question about the effects of the transfer of the Urban Programme to the Department of the Environment, we find this:

The Urban Programme has proved its worth as a valuable source of support for projects benefiting those living in urban areas of special social need. So long as the programme was innovatory, responsibility appropriately rested with the Home Office. It is now to be greatly expanded and there will be room for measures going beyond specifically social projects.

I have, therefore, decided to transfer responsibility for the Urban Programme ... to my right honourable friend the Secretary of State for the Environment. ...

The Home Secretary will retain the central responsibility for the Government's race relations policies and for Section 11 of the Local Government Act 1966 . . . the Voluntary Services Unit will also remain in the Home Office. The interests of the ethnic minorities and the voluntary sector will be fully taken into account in the allocation of resources under the enlarged Urban Programme.   (vol. 929, p. 510w)

Here again the factors at work are the two simultaneous processes by which a blind eye is turned. On the one hand, the 'knowledge' that 'race' has something to do with the Urban Programme is evident because both Shore and Callaghan (then Prime Minister) link the need to do something about inner-city regeneration to the presence of 'large' black or Asian populations. Structure, in the form of economic decline and urban decay, is there, and so the government must intervene in the forces producing these in an attempt to halt and alter their course. Structure in the form of racism is, however, known and not known. 'Ethnic minorities . . . add an extra dimension of difficulty' and will have their 'interests' 'taken into account', but the policies for dealing with 'race relations' are outside of the orbit of the Urban Programme and the Department of the Environment. Black and Asian people are designated as part of the problem but racism is not recognized as part of the structural dynamics which result in the need for the policy in the first place. 'Race' is a factor in the 'inner corruption' which needs to be addressed, but there is no resulting reparatory process for the racism structuring the lives of inner-city residents. For the simple reason that this is denied, it is seen and not seen, known and not known.

Further reference to the 1977 debate as recorded in *Hansard* illustrates this still more clearly and also shows that some politicians were less reticent in openly speaking the link between the Urban Programme and the presence of black populations. Alex Lyon, MP for Bradford Central, said,

> I congratulate my right honourable friend on what may turn out to be the most important decision that the government have made. However, it is not with unalloyed joy that I look on the transfer of the Urban Programme to a *completely non-black programme. The Urban Programme was designed as a black programme in the aftermath of the 'rivers of blood' speech, and has never been fully used for that purpose.* If my right honourable friend is taking over the Urban Programme, why is he not taking over Section 11? In the choice of cities to be helped by the planned improvements, why is Bradford omitted when it is third in the list of census deprivation indicators and third in the number of New Commonwealth immigrants who live there?

To which Peter Shore replied,

> The Section 11 programme under the 1966 Act remains unaffected by what I have said and will continue to be used by the Home Office, which has its particular responsibilities in this field, linked with its responsibility for

immigration policy. *I do not think that we would all agree that the Urban Programme has in the past been a black programme. If it has been, it has been extremely ill-directed, because an extremely small part has gone to areas where black communities are strongly established.*

My purpose is to deal, *regardless of whether there are black or white populations*, with aggregated problems of poverty and deprivation in our major urban centres. That is my purpose and policy. In some of the inner cities black communities are very small and in others they are very large. I believe that is the best way to proceed.   (vol. 929, columns 1235–6, my emphases)

What factors is it possible to see at play in this sequence of talk? Again there is the explicit denial of any knowledge of 'race' in Shore's rejoinder to Lyon's declaration that the Urban Programme was a 'black programme'. Formation of the policy in terms of disadvantage and deprivation enables Shore, as spokesman for the Government, to deny that any 'reparation' has been or indeed should be paid to black and Asian communities for racism which they may face. Such a denial has been a consistent necessity in British politics since the 1950s when black settlement was viewed with increasing alarm and there were an ever-growing number of calls to ensure that no special favours were accorded to 'them' at the expense of the 'indigenous' population. Moreover, this debate took place in the same year that various tabloid papers had headlines which screamed about 'Malawi Asians' staying in £600-a-week hotels at the expense of the Department of Social Security. So an expanded Urban Programme – from just under £30 million a year to £125 million – could not be presented as a black programme. Such sensitivity might have been heightened in the context of the 1976 IMF-imposed retrenchment and a general election looming in the following eighteen months to two years. A recourse to 'colour blindness' was, then, a third expedient that can be read in this debate. The Urban Programme both does not make any 'reparation' for the particular conditions black and Asian people may face, it is also 'racially' neutral, aimed at achieving the tasks of economic and environmental regeneration regardless of whether the populations are 'black or white'. In so declaring its colour blindness, British parliamentary practice and government aims are devoid of racial bias and once again knowledge of the racial structuring of disadvantage is denied.

However, knowledge of 'race' *can* be spoken when to do so reproduces the discursive constitution of black people as the problem. Shore achieves this by reiterating the purpose of section 11 funding and more importantly its position alongside immigration policy. The subtext is that such special funding, which is after all *compensatory* spending to local authorities for having to put up with the presence of 'immigrants', is only ever possible within the context of control of the entry of black people to Britain. Moreover, the same discursive terrain is occupied by Lyon, who defines the Urban Programme as a black programme, within a speech designed to make a claim for Bradford as worthy of partnership status. It is the links between the high numbers of black and Asian people in Bradford and the incidence of deprivation indicators that, in his view, make Bradford a suitable case for treatment.

In this section I have analysed some of the main parliamentary debates on section 11 and the Urban Programme between the years 1966 and 1995 for it is here that the links between 'race' and social policy are discernible. With the exception of the 1976 Race Relations Act, there was no elaborated discussion of 'race' or racism in the debates accompanying the passage through Parliament of the other pieces of legislation referred to in the first section of this chapter. Even the debates accompanying the second and third readings of the Children Act 1989, with its clause relating to the ethnic, racial, religious and cultural origins of looked-after children, contained no detailed discussion of these links. Such omissions are further evidence of the ways in which 'race' is both seen and not seen in British social policy. Even where 'race' is evident it is often present in an elusive or implicit way.

More generally, this chapter has moved through three stages. It began by outlining the legislation that both had a 'racial' aim and yet was simultaneously denied as having such an objective. Next I outlined an analytic framework capable of understanding this contradiction. I then applied this framework to a reading of a number of parliamentary debates on inner-city legislation. Throughout I suggested that an examination of the discourses through which racialization occurs reveals the points at which a blind eye to 'race' and, more importantly, racism is evident. What this showed was that the denial of 'race' as a structuring principle is a psychic as well as a political process. If the notion of governmentality points to the processes of formation of racial subjects and their subsequent incorporation into forms of regulation, the psychoanalytic notion of 'the blind eye' points to the attempt to deny these processes and the amnesias, slippages and anxieties such denial produces. The knowing and not knowing of 'race' is part of the ebb and flow through which British national implication in the production and reproduction of racism is denied. It is also part of the process through which central and local politics are negotiated. In this context Britain at the level of the national is not constructed as a racialized space in contrast to those special (and often pathologized) areas deemed 'inner city'. Thus, responsibility for dealing with the effects of racialized space is delegated to the level of the local. As a result, questions of 'race', racism and racial formation are not denied or turned a blind eye to at the local level. Racial discourse still constructs particularized, essentialized and pathologized subjects but it does so explicitly rather than through processes of denial, slippage and amnesia. I turn now to a consideration of some of these matters at the local level.

3

Sites of Condensation: Social Services and Racial Formation at the Local Level

Introduction

In the previous chapter I showed how 'race' was discursively produced in central policy debates and how it was mapped onto the terrain of inner-city policy. I suggested that in parliamentary debates on key pieces of legislation Britain's status as a racial formation at national level was denied. This denial was effected by a process of turning a blind eye which allowed 'race' to be both seen and not seen.

I want now to consider the ways in which the process of racial formation was played out at the local level. In particular I want to show how, in the 1980s, two local authorities used central policy initiatives to make social services more 'culturally appropriate' or 'ethnically sensitive'; how these policies were linked to wider local events in which 'race' and racism were key factors; and how, as the discursive and organizational context of social services changed, policy aimed at promoting racial equality became reformulated. This reformulation had an especially marked effect on employment policy for black social workers. In the 1980s recruitment of black and Asian social workers into the SSDs of these two local authorities was given high priority as racial tensions became especially sharp in many inner-city areas.

Of especial importance were the training schemes introduced by the two SSDs, since these provided black women with an opportunity to gain professional social work qualifications and many of the women whose voices we hear in this and later chapters gained their professional qualification through this route.[1] Throughout this chapter I analyse numerous social services committee reports to gain a picture of policy development and change with respect to 'ethnic minority' employees and service users in the two authorities I selected for my enquiry. I was concerned to analyse how black and Asian recruitment to qualified social work positions was achieved; what issues such recruitment was seen to address; and what subject positions were being textually constituted by these policies.

Secondment policies are analysed as key mechanisms facilitating access to professional training. They are also illustrative of the complexities of equal opportunities policies. Therefore, analysis of such policies needs to be situated within the wider complexities, contradictions and contestations to forms of inequality operating within and outside of the organizational context. As such, much of this chapter centres on a delineation of some of the wider elements, including political, organizational and financial changes which resulted in shifts in emphasis in policies dealing with 'race'. This is linked to my concern to analyse social services *employment* policy, as opposed to service delivery. The predominant emphasis in the literature on 'race', racism and social policy has been on issues of service delivery. This has meant that not only has the employment of racialized groups in the welfare sector been generally neglected, but that also there is a paucity of analyses of the specific circumstances which led to the entry of qualified black and Asian social workers into some local authority SSDs. Having already considered the way in which the general terrain facilitating this move was configured in terms of the concept of 'governmentality' and the denial of Britain as a racial formation nationally, here I consider specific recruitment policies at the local level and the continuities and discontinuities with central government policy and discourse.

The chapter is organized into two sections. The first focuses on the London Borough of 'Coolville', and the second on 'Inland City' Council. In each section I outline the development of policy aimed at recruiting black and Asian social workers. On occasion I also include some of the women's accounts about employment policies. I deal with the authorities in the order in which they introduced specific recruitment and training policies aimed at enabling black and Asian women (and men) to gain professional social work qualifications.

The London Borough of 'Coolville'

As an instrument of central government policy concerning 'race', section 11 can be said to embody all of the pitfalls and ambiguities of other, albeit sparse, government policies on 'race'. This is particularly so in terms of the reinforcement of negative perceptions of racialized populations of colour, and in terms of their permissive and ambiguous characters (Ben-Tovim et al., 1986, p. 112). Despite these limitations, local authorities have been able to use central initiatives in their attempts to develop what are often termed 'strategic race relations policies'.

During the mid-1980s the social services department in the London Borough of Coolville did just this. This was the result of a combination of simultaneous factors which centred on the senior personnel recruited to the department and the pressures imposed by local black groups and others similarly defined as 'ethnic minority'. These came together within a wider context of sporadic street rebellions, or 'riots' in the dominant discourse; widespread pressure within the social work profession for a radical change in the practices of adoption and fostering; and the intense struggle between radical Labour controlled boroughs and the Conservative governments of the time.

During 1983 and 1984 the authority recruited a new director of social services and three new assistant directors. Some, if not all of these had already gained a reputation as key figures in raising the issues of, and campaigning for, a radical review of social services practices in relation to multi-ethnic populations. That the senior staff of the department should all be newly recruited in such close proximity to each other suggests some major changes in the overall political direction of the borough in relation to equal opportunities.

It is evident from the work of Solomos and Singh (1990) that major challenges to local authority approaches to 'race' and racism – in both service delivery and employment – were generally occurring at this time. Although the focus of these authors' work is on housing in one or two particular boroughs, it is clear that the combination of formal policy statements, an investigation by the CRE into the housing department (and the subsequent issuing of a non-discrimination notice) and local political pressure from black and anti-racist activists led to a dynamic process of change in relation to the approach to race equality across all departments in the authorities they consider. As they state:

> The final stage of policy formulation which has culminated in the present policies resulted from critiques of existing policies, the linking of these critiques with wider notions of race equality and iterative modifications arising from implementation. By formally committing themselves to race equality soon after the Race Relations Act (1976) and taking limited measures to effect it, both Hackney and Haringey created a policy gap. The discrepancy between formal commitments and reality, between radical rhetoric and the space between the words, was seized upon by . . . policy entrepreneurs and by political activists of the urban left, and voluntary groups with an interest in housing in their attempts to define and redefine policies. (p. 106)

This description of the combination of forces which effected change at departmental level can be said to characterize the process of change in other departments and numerous authorities. Indeed a key social services committee document from the London Borough of Coolville directly referred to the CRE investigation into Hackney as indicative of the need for all service departments to review and alter their policies and practices (London Borough of Coolville, *Towards the Development of a Transracial/Cultural Model of Service Provision*, 20 September 1984). Certainly the SSD in this borough had been subjected to sustained critique about its service delivery from local black organizations. For example, as early as March 1982, the social services committee received a report from Coolville Black People's Association which identified what it saw as the major gap between Council-wide and departmental rhetoric on the one hand, and practice on the other.

> [the] Borough Council is committed to the idea of a race-relations policy and to the enforcement of an equal opportunities policy, yet it is our experience that what are entrenched, traditional Council services and provision can have a deleterious effect on, and are sometimes inimical to the interests of the black community. Consequently we find ourselves forced to question, to what extent have the ubiquitous ideals of race-relations policies and equal opportunities managed to survive endless rounds of Council theorizing and exist as concrete practice. (*Report to Social Services Committee*, 15 March 1982, item G)

Some months later social services and other relevant committees (such as the community development committee) received several reports concerned with future working relations between the SSD and two grant-aided local organizations which were offering services to people of Caribbean origin and descent. Both of these organizations had been subjected to a major review. Whilst it was recommended that the two organizations implement changes to their administrative and recording systems, it was agreed that the working links between the department and these organizations should continue in the interests of 'race' equality and equal opportunity in service delivery. One of the reports received was from an independent consultant who was later to become one of the three new assistant directors. These examples – Coolville Black People's Association's critique of current practice and the review of the two organizations – suggest that a process similar to that identified for Hackney housing department by Solomos and Singh was proving a successful way to apply pressure to service departments in the interests of 'race' equality. These events were precursors to the recruitment of senior personnel to the SSD, and in its turn this recruitment was indicative of the development of a political atmosphere in which 'race' equality measures were foregrounded.

An examination of social services committee papers for the 1980s gives some insight into the impact that this had on the policies guiding service delivery and links with black community organizations. In early

June 1984 the social services committee received a joint paper from the Director of Social Services and the Principal Race Relations Adviser entitled *Bid for Section 11 LGA 66 Resources Progress Report: A Strategy for Race Relations in Social Services*, which makes it clear that they were going to utilize revised central government policy in an attempt to develop more appropriate services for black and other 'ethnic minority' communities. The report outlined the problems of the existing practice in relation to section 11, arguing that it had 'very serious implications . . . for the Black community and good race relations generally . . . [and that it would] reinforce class division, perpetuate racial disadvantage and lay the foundation for conflict'.

Furthermore, the authors of the report argued that existing practice and interpretation of section 11 by the Council, with its tendency to centralization, conflicted with the Council's stated commitment to decentralization. The implication of this pattern for black communities was that they tended to be seen only as *consumers* of services and not as *providers* (para. 3.1, my emphasis).

The report also noted the abolition of the ten-year rule, and suggested that the impact of this made claiming resources from central government under section 11 worthwhile. The need to act was clear, not only in order to realize a potential source of central government money but also to ensure that the established contradictions within the system were not intensified and institutional racism reinforced. Section 11 money had a clear potential in promoting positive action so long as its use was linked to a broadening of the structures of accountability to include the black community (para. 4.2).

The Committee then resolved to adopt a number of recommendations which included an assurance that funds intended to benefit black communities be used for that purpose; that new financial and administrative arrangements be established for the management of section 11 monies; that a special section 11 vote be established within the Committee to ensure that successful bids to central government not be forfeited because of a failure to secure the 25 per cent required from the local authority; that proposals which accorded with the Council's decentralization strategy be prioritized, especially if they also established and/or strengthened links with black community organizations; and that a detailed package of proposals consistent with a race relations strategy be developed and brought to the Committee as a matter of urgency.

This report was soon followed by another (*Towards the Development of a Transracial/Cultural Model of Service Provision*, September 1994) emphasizing the need for development and implementation of a transracial/transcultural model for service delivery. This laid out what it saw as the problems in existing patterns and procedures of service delivery; established the philosophy underlying a new model of service provision; set out a long-term programme for achieving change; and detailed a shorter-term programme to be accomplished in the year ahead.

This programme for immediate action had six main features, including the refocused use of section 11; the development and implementation of a record-keeping system, including one relating to employment; and a goal of achieving 35 per cent black and ethnic minority staff. This report can be read as very clearly setting the tone for future developments in social services policy on 'race'.

There are two aspects I want to focus on. One is its perspective on the link between 'race' and class as axes of differentiation and domination affecting user experience of social services. The other is the philosophical approach to anti-racism underlying the proposal for change. This focus enables a contrast to be drawn between the local approach to questions of 'race' and racism and that discernible in the debates about central policy discussed in chapter 2.

In identifying the need for change it is clear that the authors of the report begin from what might loosely be called a 'political economy of the welfare state' perspective. The wider economic and social context in which council departments operate is conceptualized as one of 'class struggle and class domination'; whilst the 'knowledge' base of social services provision is seen as located in middle-class norms and values. Together, these mean that as a service provider the department (and its personnel) is ill equipped to deliver appropriate services to the diverse population it serves (section 4 of the committee paper, 'the need for change').

> Social Services provision has evolved a structure and a body of knowledge which is dominated by and sustains the middle classes. Its norms, values and practices are shaped and carried out by the middle class. . . . a second major feature of Social Services provision today [is] . . . its racist nature. The perceptions and insights and the way that officers go about their business are largely dominated by racist tendencies.   (paras 4.2 and 4.3)

Class and 'race' as axes of differentiation sit alongside one another as the twin pillars guiding the delivery of social services. Gender, despite women being the vast majority of recipients and deliverers of social services, is absent from this analytical frame. This is an interesting reformulation of the slippages and elisions between class and 'race' which could be seen in approaches at the centre. More radical in orientation, this local level formulation wants to hold onto the two axes as separate but running parallel to each other, suggesting that both aspects need to be tackled if service delivery is to become more appropriate to the needs of the populace. In national policy debates class is the universal, often in ways that obscure 'race' as an axis of inequality, except when 'race' is to delineate the particular.

However, as the report goes on to delineate the philosophy underlying its approach to change, it is clear that a reverse form of conflation occurs – that class gets collapsed into 'race', rather than the other way round.

> In offering assistance to people of a different race and social class, it is essential to understand their care patterns and viewpoints, especially their culture, their values and goals about family/child care.
>
> Most Social Services personnel are not knowledgeable about differences in class and cultural values, beliefs and practices of black and ethnic minority people.   (paras 4.7 and 4.8)

Inappropriateness and conflict arise from the interface between the white middle-class social worker and the black/ethnic minority, working-class client. To understand the issue in this way allows 'culture', understood as determined by both class and ethnicity, to become the privileged modality in policy development aimed at change. Moreover, this approach occupies the same discursive formation as positions articulated at the centre, for it constructs social worlds, values and cultures as mutually exclusive elements of the binary 'white, middle-class'/'black, working-class'. Despite this, the approach is presented with a tone of moral certitude when it asserts: 'This section of the report sets out *the* basic philosophy of *race relations in Social Services*' (para. 5.1, my emphasis). It rejects all notions of integration and proposes what it calls a multi-cultural and multi-racial approach to service provision. This is

> one which actively addresses, promotes and caters for the aspirations and needs of a multi-racial and multi-cultural community. It would therefore be working towards change rather than acting as a reservoir for the casualties of social injustices. The primary focus revolves around those functions provided under the heading of Care and Community services. Care and Community services by their very nature involve a high level of interpersonal contact between the Directorate's personnel and individuals and families in the community. It is the interpersonal contact which is informed exclusively from a European care perspective that has to be transcended and supplanted.   (para. 5.1)

This means that social services have to meet different needs in different ways, or meet similar needs in different ways according to cultural group. Moreover, 'cultural differences are most striking in family life – the very basis of the services offered' (paras 5.2 and 5.4).

This is interesting for in addition to 'class' becoming conflated to 'race', 'race' itself now becomes synonymous with 'culture' and the point of conflict is reformulated as that between an homogeneous European culture and various minority cultures, which presumably are also internally homogeneous. This slip between registers is achieved by retaining the terrain on which social work makes its claim to professionalism – i.e. the family. To this the authors are then able to add the second key component of social work's claim to professional status – psychology. The application of psychological frames of reference *appropriate to black people* is an essential feature of transracial/transcultural care (para. 5.12).[2]

Following the moves amongst the various registers inscribed within this report, it is possible to delineate more clearly the shifts in what is being identified as in need of change. At first one would think that the very nature of social work itself would be the focus of change because it is deeply implicated in the maintenance of a social formation based on the inequities of class and 'race'. The move to 'culture' as the key modality elides this and in fact social work, although in need of reform, is identified as a field of professionalism requiring only minor change. The necessary reforms will be achieved by a rethinking of patterns of service delivery through the frame of what is now called 'transculturalism' and 'black psychology [which] enables accurate analysis and comprehensive explanations of black life' (para. 5.12).

In this way social services will be radically changed and social work made more appropriate to multi-racial/multi-cultural Britain.

> Transracial/cultural care is a necessary new development in the field of social work, which [in turn] owes its theoretical origins to the advances made in the disciplines of medicine, medical anthropology, psychology and psychiatry.
> Transracial/cultural care offers new insights for relationships, and advances the ability of social workers to care for others who are of a different race and culture. (paras 5.13 and 5.14)

We can see, then, the evolution of a discursive framework that guides the delivery of services to a multi-racial/multi-ethnic population. However, implementation of this new approach required a mechanism to ensure the staff mix of the department was adequate to the task. In this vein the numerous projects proposed as part of the strategy designed to implement the new approach would increase the staff complement by 121 posts. This was in addition to an earlier commitment to an equal opportunities recruitment programme, and a special black secondees scheme for social workers.

Recruitment

The black social workers' secondment scheme was supplementary to a general secondment scheme, and was an early demonstration of

Coolville's attempt to increase the numbers of social workers from 'black and ethnic minority groups'. Proposed late in 1982, the black scheme was initially aimed at recruiting ten secondment places to a two-year CQSW course. Upon completion of the course, candidates would be obliged to return to work for the department. At first recruitment was skewed towards internal staff. However, external applicants were not excluded. There was fierce competition in the first round with more than 100 internal staff indicating an interest in the scheme and its degree of popularity is evidenced by it being continuously oversubscribed throughout its lifespan (until 1987).

Development of the scheme, and other more general comments about the Council's role as a local employer, indicate the concern to promote equal opportunities in employment. Moreover, this scheme demonstrated the desire to promote equality of access to professional grades and not just those occupations which were traditional sources of employment for women from racialized groups, for example home helps, unqualified residential workers, cooks and cleaners.

> Although the Directorate has a well-established secondment programme it is felt that a *special recognition of the needs of black staff for training opportunities should now be made*. It is important that the proportion of the population from black and ethnic minority groups should be reflected by the staff serving the whole community. In the first instance an increase in those *directly serving the public by social work* is sought. (*Report by the Director of Social Servies, Training Opportunities for Black Staff*, 7 September 1982, para. 3.1, my emphases)

Because the proposal was to offer black staff substantial support for professional training, it was recognized that it would need to be handled sensitively (para. 7.1) as a certain amount of disquiet might be expressed by white staff. As it was to turn out, this note of caution was to prove rather prescient.

The departmental concern to develop professional training opportunities for black staff in and for itself was an important moment in facilitating entry of black and Asian women (and men) into qualified positions. Three of those interviewed in this London borough had used this route, one having support only for the second year of her CQSW course. She was one of the external recruits, prompted to apply as a result of an advertisement about the scheme. Another had gained her professional qualification (CQSW) via the general secondment scheme. It was factors such as this that led to the authority gaining a reputation among black and Asian social workers as a progressive or radical borough.

However, this reputation often became quickly tarnished once actually employed by the borough. One factor contributing to this scepticism is that the period when full support for professional training was offered was relatively short lived although the reasons for its cessation are not well documented or open to public scrutiny. No doubt the reasons are multiple and complex but what is interesting is that popular understandings among some black staff in the SSD are framed through a discourse of racial and gender antagonism. For example, it was suggested to me that the demise of the black scheme followed from a legal challenge by a white man, not employed by the Council (interview, 1995). In this narrative the argument against the scheme was that it was unlawful for the department to offer such schemes to black candidates only.

Whatever the 'truth' about the legal challenge to the scheme it was clear that between 1982 and 1987 the climate in the department was a very different one. This change in culture was brought about by a mix of factors which were played out over a number of years. These included the major antagonisms between central government and certain Labour controlled authorities, this borough among them; rate-capping and the abolition of the Greater London Council and other Metropolitan Counties; the introduction of the poll tax (community charge) and the challenges to it; and finally the shift in the social relations of welfare that accompanied the changed arrangements for financing local government services and the successful ideological onslaught on 'loony left' councils and their commitment to equal opportunities.

However, if the withdrawal of support for such training was commensurate with the new climate, the cessation of the secondment scheme had a demoralizing effect on the part of many black women in the department. One woman put it this way:

> because people were brought into the organization with the understanding that if they weren't qualified there would be opportunities to qualify and they would be seconded, and shortly after I was seconded . . . they stopped all secondments, without any discussion or anything. So people that had just come in without being qualified and who were waiting because people had to apply and they only took a certain number every year . . . When they closed a lot of residential establishments . . . they had this idea that they would be qualified, because generally interviews, when you are asked questions about, you know, what would you like from the organization . . . further training, etc. They always say there is support there, . . . so I think that has hit hard really. (interview, 1994)

This woman's account conveys some sense of the long-lasting effects of cuts in support for professional training. Her account also raises other issues. One significant issue is that of raised expectations. She suggests that the previous existence of secondment schemes resulted in an enduring expectancy regarding such support. But it also seems to suggest that management in the department failed to make it clear that such support had ceased and this ambiguity was further compounded by the experience at interview panels.

Second, the account raises issues about the general effect on career mobility. It is difficult to gauge whether these effects were greater for black women, although the demise of the *black* secondment scheme must at least have had some disadvantaging effect. In addition there is the specific mention of the residential sector which has been known as a sector in which black and Asian women have been concentrated as unqualified workers. It was the desire of at least some black and Asian women to escape this occupational ghettoization that made the black secondment scheme so attractive. Yet with the closure of more and more residential institutions in the wake of the introduction of community care, cessation of secondment schemes was likely to be felt even more intensely.

The black secondment programme came out of a short-lived and specific moment when the perspective on equal opportunities was such that its commitment to promoting access to *employment* was seen as important in its own right. The original initiative pre-dated the major strategy papers of 1984 indicating that employment was early on the agenda. It was successful in getting black and Asian women (and some men) into qualified positions in the department, and this did not go without notice. '[The] . . . political climate [here] changed and they were actually trying to get more black workers employed in [Coolville]' was how one woman saw it, whilst another said, 'about that time [December 1983] there was just like an influx, if I can use that term, you know of black workers, and all of a sudden there were all these black workers'.

'This bridge called my back': the distillation of racialized bodies

As we have seen, this recruitment process had its roots in two developments. On the one hand, the adoption by the SSD of a 'transcultural' perspective, and on the other, a concern to promote the authority as an equal opportunities employer. However, while employment had formed part of the strategy for promoting racial equality and good race relations, service delivery had always been a major concern and this was soon to become the privileged concern with consequences for black professional training.

Indeed the emphasis on quality of service delivery in a multi-racial, multi-ethnic, multi-faith community is already evident in the policy papers summarizing the 'transcultural' approach. As one report put it:

> All the proposals . . . are concerned primarily with the development of
> a wider range of services to meet the needs of a multi-racial community

[particularly to promote an] increase in resources to alleviate social stress and their use specifically to assist members of the black and ethnic minorities community. (*Report from the Director of Social Services, Summary of Section 11 Proposals 1984/85*, 20 September 1986, paras 1.2 and 2.3)

Clearly, from an equalities perspective, patterns and processes of service delivery are important matters to be addressed. However, it is also my argument that where service delivery is the privileged area of concern, questions of how to promote equality of opportunity in employment and training potentially become obscured.

Where service provision occupies the primary focus of changes in SSD policy and practice, the form and quality of policy aimed at promoting equal opportunity in employment is greatly altered. In the context of SSDs with a concentration of black and Asian women staff at the lower and unqualified ends of the employment spectrum, commitment to equal opportunity in *employment* carries with it a need to address such occupational concentration. Thus, where the focus is entry into professional jobs, training and career progression strategies tend to be foregrounded. However, once the predominant emphasis is on delivering 'ethnically sensitive' services such concerns can be sidestepped. Of course it could be argued that so long as statutory duties under the 1976 Race Relations Act are met the issue of the creation of new or wider employment opportunities for those groups previously excluded is beyond the legitimate purview of local authority departments. From this perspective the quality and equality of service provision is the only responsibility local authorities have towards local taxpayers. However, it seems to me that there was more than this at play in these particular examples.

I would maintain that this is related to the tendency to constitute black and Asian workers as racialized bodies whose qualification to deliver 'ethnically sensitive' services resides in what is seen as their *natural* ability to act as cultural translators for the department. The notion of the 'racialized body' refers to the ways in which phenotypic or somatic traits are used to divest certain categories of people of individuality and to accord them only a group belonging understood in terms of 'race'. Bodies become the sites of condensation of the plethora of signs through which 'race' or 'culture' are delineated, most obviously skin colour but also factors such as hair texture, nose shape or accent. Thus, the racialized bodies of, for example, liaison workers or development workers are simultaneously at one with, and differentiated from, the racialized populations they represent. They are at one with these populations because of the phenotypic or linguistic traits which they are said to have in common with those they represent. They are differentiated from them because they stand in the position of a social services department worker who has the power which comes with statutory duties. But for the actual social worker – i.e. the qualified worker with the potential to use the coercive powers assigned them by the state – this differentiation is starker still and though their bodies can still mediate the welfare relation between the SSD and populations defined as ethnic minority, there is a greater distance because of their position in the welfare agency. From this perspective the post of development worker constitutes an intensification of processes of racialization because it focuses almost exclusively on embodiment. In this racial discourse the need for professional qualification in social work is much less necessary because the 'qualification resides in the skin'.

One area where this was clearly evident was in those jobs entitled 'liaison worker'. A number of such posts – ten – were identified in the London authority's composite report on section 11 bids already referred to. That such workers are viewed as physically embodying the skills of racial or cultural translation is apparent from the ways in which the tasks of the post are defined.

> The postholder will concentrate on the dual function of helping members of the black and ethnic minority community in understanding and using existing statutory health and personal social services and in assisting statutory agencies in being more responsive to the needs of a multi-racial community. (*Section 11 Proposal – Community Social Workers, Report to Social Services Committee*, 20 September 1984, para. 4.6)

Attached to area teams, their skills of 'translation' would be fed into the department at this level. What level of experience of social services or professional qualification those appointed were expected to demonstrate is not clear. This confirms the point, because in taking the proposal forward for agreement by elected members, what is highlighted is 'ethnic' or 'community' belongingness. In other words, the proposal is presented through a highly racialized or ethnicized discourse, for although aimed at communities whose 'mother tongue is not English', it is not presented as a *language* translation scheme. This conflation of language and 'culture' is particularly interesting because in practice the 'liaison workers were used as interpreters and community ambassadors' (interview, July 1995), suggesting that at least in the first instance the language needs of the department were the focus. However, the delineation of the duties attached to posts as outlined in the committee paper provided for a greater flexibility in the jobs and we can see evidence of the de-emphasis on the need for qualified social workers in the fact that 'at least two of them became unqualified social workers' (interview, July 1995).

To say this is not to ignore the complexity of the issue nor to deny the need to increase equality of access and provision to marginalized and under-represented sections of the population. Moreover, it is clear that at this time the views, needs and levels of voluntary provision within populations defined as 'ethnic minority' were an unknown quantity. As a result, alongside the liaison worker posts, there were also to be community social workers. The proposal for such workers was justified on the grounds of its consistency with the move to a patchwork structure and the departmental commitment to undermining racism in its approach and inequality in its provision.

However, the central rationale and associated tasks were to ascertain the views towards, and knowledge about, social services; the extent and location of informal networks of support within the 'community'; and the development of an ethnically sensitive and responsive approach from the department and its representatives (*Section 11 Proposal – Community Social Workers*, 20 September, 1984, para. 3.1). To the extent that this investigative work involved a process of enumeration of sections of local inhabitants about which little was felt to be known, we can detect a strategy of 'population'.

It is notable that no reference is made to the required or desirable ethnicity or 'race' of the would-be community social workers. One must remember that this proposal was advanced within the overarching philosophy on racial/cultural difference and equality laid out in the earlier 'transcultural' paper. Thus, it is from these that one gains an insight into the discursive and ideological terrain on which this proposal is written. In these, physical embodiment was the guarantor of an ability to discern community needs and responses. Therefore, one would be justified in anticipating that the community social workers would ethnically 'match' those 'populations' identified as in need of development work. Moreover, the construction of those populations as homogeneous and univocal is evident in the use of the singular 'community' in the preamble to the delineation of tasks.

Black workers were constituted as racialized bodies because the much needed work to amend SSD practice was often understood and developed within a discursive framework which 'fixed' black or Asian social workers and 'populations' in rigid and essentialized racial and cultural categories. Instead of examining ways in which such frameworks and categories could themselves be undermined in the process of changing the SSD, the reports suggest that anti-racism consisted of applying additional perspectives, values and methods to existing social services practice and 'knowledge'. As such they simply reproduced the binary categories of racialized discourse and reinscribed the minority status of the populations whose interests they wanted to protect.

Such an approach has become the dominant one within welfare institutions concerned to tackle racial disadvantage and discrimination. For example, an advertisement placed in the *Guardian* in 1995 for an African/Caribbean social worker read:

For the African/Caribbean social worker a knowledge of the culture of children/young people from the African and African/Caribbean communities and how their social care needs can be met. (2 August)

Yet it is unclear what similarities exist between the cultural and social care needs of young people who share the same skin colour but who inhabit widely differing social, geographical and cultural worlds. For example, how similar are the care needs of the recently arrived refugee child/young person from, say, Somalia and the second- or third-generation British-born child/young person of Montserratan or Jamaican descent? To suggest an essential similarity between these two categories of black person is to confuse an enunciation of *political* 'sameness' with cultural 'sameness'. Moreover, it is difficult to imagine how one social worker is expected to be able to 'demonstrate' such 'knowledge'. However, by constructing them solely through the essentialized and homogenizing categories embedded in discourses of racialization and community these points are occluded.

The 1990s

Reference has already been made to the change in approach and organizational culture that occurred from the late 1980s. One of the key features of these changes in terms of the employment and career development of women social workers from racialized groups was the privileging of service delivery in the department's equalities agenda and the simultaneous de-prioritization accorded equality of access to employment at *all* levels in the department.

Of course the de-emphasis of employment was not stated as a formal policy but a reading of the committee reports from that time onwards indicates primacy of service delivery. With this in mind, I want to explore the trends of the early to mid-1990s around three main themes: the disappearance of the language of transculturalism and equal opportunity in training and employment from general committee reports; the switch to the language of 'equalities' rather than specifically named areas of inequality, such as 'race', gender, etc.; and the overall emphasis on 'service'.

The case of the disappeared: 'race' and the general departmental direction

In anticipation of the introduction of new legislation aimed at radically reorganizing local authority social services departments, Coolville SSD underwent two major restructurings – one in 1990/91 and a second in

1992. The final details of these reorganizations are not important for the issues being discussed here but a reading of the reports outlining the proposals for change are revealing in their absence of 'race' (and indeed any mention of other axes of inequality) except in the most general of terms.

Take, for example, a Joint Report of the Directors of Social Services and Corporate and Information Services – *Social Services Restructure 2nd Phase* – which went to Committee in July 1990. The general tenor is evident in the last page of this report where equalities considerations are dealt with. In the 1980s it had become customary in many local authorities for all committee reports to give consideration to their implications for those sections of the population who suffered some form of discrimination and disadvantage. Often the content of these paragraphs became no more than an endless repetition of a form of words templated on the computer. Nevertheless, at their best, they made it incumbent on officers to give some thought to these issues, and moreover each area of discrimination was considered separately. By the 1990s, this convention had (at least partially) stopped in Coolville. Thus, paragraph 12.2 of the report referred to above reads:

> *Implications for Black People and People from Ethnic Minorities, People with Disabilities, Gays and Lesbians, and Woman [sic].*
>
> The Directorate of Social Services aims to provide the above groups with an improved level of service by restructuring the second and third tiers of management in order to make managers more accountable and responsive to these community groups.

Any specificity of service needs which might exist among these disparate groups is completely occluded in this amalgamation which, in its homogenizing effects, reinscribes their marginalization as those who are at once 'different' yet non-specific. Given this, how the restructuring of management organization will result in more accountability is unclear, but it does not have to be made clear. Non-specific needs do not demand specific remedies. Moreover, any employment needs which might emerge in connection with these groups, whose 'group' status is the product of the intersections between identities and social positions, is completely ignored. Yet one would expect that the restructuring of a whole directorate would have at least some implications for employment levels and prospects, and therefore for the possibility of pursuing equal opportunity in employment. Indeed the report itself recommends the abolition of at least thirty-three posts and the establishment of the same number of redefined posts in their place.

It is not that the issue of equal opportunity is entirely absent from elsewhere in the report but rather that it is couched within descriptions of the management arrangements and lines of command. This reflects the shift in emphasis to modes of presentation and the lines of connection within and between departmental sections. Even here the relative marginalization of equal opportunities issues is expressed in the lack of precision about the complexities of the issues. Thus, we see that the deputy director will be responsible for equal opportunities, but no more detail about the accompanying terms of reference is given anywhere, unlike the situation for compulsory competitive tendering, transport, meals on wheels, etc. This point is covered in the following way:

> The Deputy Director is to be responsible for Resources, Training, and Strategic Services within the Directorate . . . and also Equal Opportunities and Liaison Officers. It is proposed that a manager will be responsible for each of the following:
>
> 1 Resources
> 2 Training
> 3 Strategic Services
> 4 Liaison Officers
>
> (para. 6.1)

Equal opportunities is mentioned within the overall responsibilities of a senior officer but any more detailed discussion is reserved for the other points. The areas that are given more detailed attention is illustrative in itself. For it is precisely those areas that, as a result of central government legislative and policy change, had become subject to new forms of organizational arrangement where the language of markets and business prevailed. In this context equal opportunities matters which cannot be dealt with in the discourses and practices of 'managerialism' are unspecified and marginalized.

The final reference to equal opportunities is as follows:

> After consultation with relevant officers however it was agreed to create a manager responsible for Planning, Grants, Research of Freedom of Information, Quality of Service and *Black and Ethnic Minority* issues, as well as New Technology and Stats. This sub-division will provide a cross Directorate resource for the above functions to all service providers and managers in Social Services.   (para. 6.9, my emphasis)

Here, the previously undifferentiated field of equal opportunities has become reformulated as, and reduced to, 'Black and Ethnic Minority issues', again suggestive of the homogenization, marginalization and narrowing of equalities issues.

We find yet another example of this as the report goes on to outline the structure of the main departmental divisions. Here we find that within Adult Services, there will be a manager responsible for:

Disability Residential Unit
HIV/AIDS
Sickle Cell
Visual and Hearing Impairment   (para. 7.4.i)

which seems to take care of 'people with disabilities', who are ungendered but include those of Caribbean, African and south-east Mediterranean origin or descent who might suffer from sickle cell anaemia and related blood conditions.

This report provides ample illustration of the ways in which new organizational discourses provide opportunities for the marginalization of equalities issues. To approach equal opportunities issues within such a framework suggests two distinct but perhaps overlapping effects: either the adoption of a technicist approach which assumes that achievement of the 'right' organizational arrangements will ensure the emergence of effective processes for dealing with inequality; or, perhaps more perniciously, adoption of an approach that avoids any serious consideration of processes, practices and structures that produce inequality can be read as a conscious attempt to marginalize equalities issues in times of 'realism'.

Yet another report – *Service Contract 1990/91 – Towards 3-Year Objectives* – illustrates this process still further (11 July 1990). This was the first service contract statement issued by the authority and its aim was to outline the activity programme, resource availability and constraints, and detail achievable targets within the directorates' 'overall twin objectives of *customer or user care* and *sharing power*' (para. 8, emphasis in original).

The detail of the report is beyond the scope of my concerns except in so far as it illustrates the closures resulting from the adoption of what was understood to be a discourse and practice of managerialism.[3] Five areas of major change are identified as providing the context in which the service contract was drawn up. These included legislative change; restructuring; the establishment of an adequate information strategy; and 'the *Training*, *re-Training* and *creating* of an effective and efficient professional, managerial, administrative, technical and basic care *staff mix* so that both flexible and accountable employment patterns ensue' (para. 2.5, emphasis in original).

No mention at all is made of any equalities issues which may arise in relation to these *employment* issues. This is a further illustration of the shift from the situation in the early 1980s. Another section identifies 'other significant changes' and refers to the imminent introduction of a form of internal market and suggests that inter-directorate service level agreements will have to be established. It is in this context that some reference to equalities issues is made.

A more adequate and widespread transcultural approach to all services has to be implemented, with fully fledged ethnic monitoring of services as part of Quality Service Review. Anti-discrimination and anti-poverty measures will be adopted wherever they can within activity programmes. (para. 3)

But these issues are themselves to be tackled within a situation where:

Service Budgets and staffing resources have been disaggregated substantially and key activity monitoring is being put in place. Budget scrutinies, quality monitoring and service contract reporting will be progressively brought together. Non-priority activities will be increasingly defined, and given the need to maintain a budget without deficit, critical choices on service level changes and reductions where resources do not match expectations will have to be put before Members.   (para. 4, emphasis in original)

Given this scenario, and given the relative marginalization of 'race', gender and other equalities issues which we have detected in other reports from this time, it is not surprising that no high-profile and detailed discussion of these issues is present here. 'Race', gender and other categories of social inequality can disappear from the policy focus because the discursive frame of efficiency, value for money and balanced budgets act to subsume a highly differentiated population under the rubrics of 'customers' and 'service users'. The 'market' is the equalizing force embedded in this discourse and the form of organizational links and efficient management of that market is the way to ensure its equalizing effects are realized. Ironically, the then Director[4] seems to be aware of the subsuming and closure effects resulting from the imperatives of the new orientations. For as the minute to the meeting records:

Members expressed concern that there did not appear to be an equal opportunities emphasis running through the report . . .
   The Director of Social Services responded that he had deviated from using transcultural and equal opportunities statements in the report and had *looked instead at resources, targets and measures* as well as equality and quality.   (*Minute of Social Services Committee held on 11 July 1990, no. 28*, my emphasis)

Clearly these are not commensurate terms and the 'deviation' represents a discursive and *political* shift in which economic forms and indicators replace others concerned with questions about the distribution of power within welfare relations. However, it is precisely these changes in welfare relations that become hidden under the language of markets, resources and targets. For whilst these latter terms are devoid of 'people' they nevertheless partially act to define the relationship between constituencies of clients and sets of resources held and allocated by the SSD.

The language of 'equalities'

As part of the restructuring exercise, functions concerned with the promotion of equal opportunities were decentralized to the relevant directorates. First proposed in late 1991 by the Assistant Chief Executive (Equal Opportunities and Community Affairs), the idea was that social services (among other directorates) would have four equalities officers with each post assuming lead responsibility for one or two of the Council's four priority equal opportunities categories. Their functions were centred on service delivery (*Equal Opportunities and Community Affairs Corporate Review*, 9 October 1991, para. 2).

One of these posts was established as a senior equalities officer, who would have line management responsibilities for the other three. The senior post would hold a generic equalities brief, with the three lower-level posts assuming responsibility for the areas not especially covered by the senior office holder (*Equalities Officers – Social Services*, 14 April 1992). At one level this structure was devised as the pragmatic solution to the overload of control functions that would accrue to the strategic services manager if the posts were established as originally conceived. It was also partly the result of '. . . the Council's response to the loss of substantial amounts of Section 11 funding previously used to employ Race advisors' (para. 3.1).

Changes in the organization of financial relations between central and local government, departmental restructuring, and an atmosphere in which equalities specialisms were seen as increasingly unrealistic, led to a merger of functions and blurring of conceptual distinction and complexity. The overall result was the conceptual simplification and policy marginalization of the diverse and complex world of (in)equalities. This was especially in relation to the promotion of employment opportunities in the higher-grade posts within the department, and a decline in the resources, including personnel, committed specifically for such work. That this was the directional pull prevalent from the 1990s is evidenced by a 1995 report on equalities issues (*Developing Equalities Work Within Social Services*, 5 July). This shows that in the intervening years: 'Budget cuts and restructuring have decreased the number of posts to one Equality Development Officer, managed directly by the Strategic Services Manager. This post [i.e. EDO] is presently vacant' (para. 3.1).

It is self-evident that major reductions in resources led to the need to find 'efficiencies'. In this context, experience tells us that such efficiencies are frequently made in employment via a whole panoply of measures – from redundancies and severances, early retirements, non-filling of vacancies, etc. Other ways include a redefinition of tasks and job descriptions and a general restructuring of work organization and labour process. In terms of equal opportunities issues, this often means an incorporation of equalities tasks into a wider range of posts. In keeping with this the 1995 paper states:

> All members of staff will continue to hold responsibility for equalities issues and therefore the range of other (i.e. apart from women's since there is a seconded women's development officer) equalities functions across the Directorate will be maintained. These include:
>
> (a) All staff continuing to be responsible for assessing the needs of individuals in relation to their personal requirements including ethnic and cultural background, religion, gender, disabilities and sexual orientation.
> (b) All service managers continuing to hold responsibility for developing equalities policy initiatives within their areas. Equalities Developments will be detailed as key objectives within Local Service Plans.
> (c) All service managers continuing to be responsible for user/public consultation mechanisms, which take into consideration equalities issues, within their service.
>
> (para. 6.5)

Such devolution of responsibility across the range of departmental staff is an important part of establishing 'a sense of ownership [empowerment] of equalities initiatives' (para. 5.1). However, in such an organizational culture, the issue is how to valorize equal opportunities commitments alongside all the other 'objectives' that managers and staff are supposed to 'own', otherwise it is just a nominal commitment. Such devolution and the existence of specialist personnel with responsibility across the range of axes of inequality are not mutually exclusive, although this view did not seem to be held by senior management in the London SSD. Therefore, they were to redesignate the equality development officer post to that of equalities inspector who would assess the equalities work across the department. Moreover, it is apparent that the focus of attention for equalities was in terms of service delivery and that this was spoken of in the language of 'customers'. Policy development and implementation for employment was less firmed up. For example, in terms of training it was stated that the possibility of 'prioritizing applicants from minority groups when allocating places on the new employment based Diploma in Social Worker courses' (para. 6.6) was under consideration.

There is some echo here of the situation in 1982 where support for professional training was provided to enable people from 'ethnic minority' populations to become basic-grade social workers. Given the lack of representation of some such populations who form a sizeable proportion of this London borough (for example Turkish) this remained important. But in the 1995 formulation the possibility of such training is not at all guaranteed, nor does it necessarily address the career progression needs of ethnic minority women social workers already employed by the department. It is as if the department was unable to recognize the changes that had occurred in the staff profile and to respond accordingly. One area where such action was needed was in relation to what became known as the 'area manager barrier'. This referred to the fact that by the 1990s no ethnic minority person held a post higher than that of area manager. In this context even those actions implemented since the restructurings in the early 1990s were of limited use for assisting ethnic minority staff to reach the upper levels of the management structure.

There were some developments, including the creation of a new senior practitioner level post between that of social worker and team manager; the provision of training and work experience opportunities for staff displaced by the restructuring of the department; and the introduction of NVQs in Social Care for residential and day-care manual staff.

These failed to address the problem because they did nothing to break the clustering of black and other 'ethnic minority' women at the lower end of the professional scale. Similarly a measure designed to support 'women middle managers on high level managerial courses', bypassed many black and Asian women because only two of them were at this level. This illustrates the problems that can result when structural and discursive inequalities arising from multiple and intersecting axes are conceptualized as both distinct and internally homogeneous.

This returns me to my argument that the way in which particular posts and areas of work are conceived influences the ease with which they are cut, redefined or assimilated. To redefine the separate but intersecting axes of domination into one field, to homogenize, lays the foundation upon which the need for distinct and specific measures can be denied. Superimpose this notion upon that of 'customers', 'value for money', 'resource constraint' and 'missions' – in other words the significations of the new organization of welfare relations – and departmental requirements can easily become redefined as the ability to respond to diversity (not inequality) by getting the organizational arrangements right. Add to this the idea that all that is required to demonstrate growing equality is representation among the staff of populations defined as 'ethnic minority' and the need for resources to respond to a constantly evolving situation is denied. This is in contrast to a conceptualization of hegemonic discourses as productive of institutional practices which reproduce the logics and effects of inequality organized around 'race', 'sex', 'sexuality' or 'disability'.

The imperative of 'service'

The discourse of 'service' mediates the relation between black social workers and black 'consumers' or 'customers' because they are both positioned as racialized or ethnicized subjects. The presence of the former within the department is necessary if the 'service provision' to the latter is to be 'appropriate'. This formulation raises many concerns, among them being the elision of the need for a rolling programme of substantial departmental support for initial qualification and career development. If quality of service delivery to racialized 'customers' only depends upon the *presence* of their counterparts as employees, then issues of recruitment and/or training of black people into qualified positions is subordinated to the imperative of service. This formulation of the issues was apparent in the London authority in the early to mid-1990s.

The inability to maintain the distinction between issues of service delivery and those of employment stems from two overlapping processes. One is the conceptualization of black employment issues as always and only about policies designed to facilitate entry into areas of employment where women (and men) from racialized groups have traditionally been absent or under-represented. Equal opportunities in employment policies were designed to address this problem and the black secondee programme offered a particularly focused example of what can be achieved given resources and political and organizational will. However, if the focus of equalities strategies is *employment*, initial entry into non-traditional sectors is only the starting point. For a more systematic approach aimed at widening the employment profiles of excluded or under-represented groups an additional emphasis on career progression, further training and transformations in the organizational culture is needed. In the absence of such developments, entry into the occupations may well be secured but at the lower grades. In short, change and the promotion of equality in employment must be understood as an ongoing and dynamic process.

A second, equally important issue is the conceptual conflation of analytically distinct, but intersecting, axes of social inequality into one homogeneous mass captured under the rubric 'equalities'. In the absence of a conceptual mapping capable of capturing the complexities and points of similarity and difference among areas of inequality it will be impossible to delineate the organizational processes preventing particular groups from advancing further within the occupational field.

These two points suggest that it is necessary to avoid a situation where employment equality becomes subsumed under other organizational imperatives that emerge from the process of welfare reorganization and a discourse of 'service' and the 'customer'. I would argue that just such a process of subsumption occurred in both the departments considered here and this carried implications for black women's employment within the two SSDs. Moreover, I would suggest that this process is related to the idea that a mere presence of black or other racialized staff on social work teams is enough since the main objective is to deliver 'ethnically sensitive' services.

The issue of attracting a more ethnically diverse staff mix, and ensuring this was reflected at higher professional levels, was placed high on the agenda by a unit with a specialist focus on race relations in a report that went to Committee in October 1991 (*Progress Report of the 1990/91 Race Relations Work Programme within Social Services Directorate*, 9 October 1991). Yet it is clear that the issue of employment was embedded in a wider frame where service delivery was by far the main focus. Thus, in the original work programme to which this report of the Principal Race Relations Advisor was responding, there was only one reference to employment issues and even this single reference was in relation to the functions of the race relations team where 'employment' was identified as one of five areas to which they were to have regard. No special mechanisms for facilitating access to departmental professional occupations was mentioned and all the other points concerning the team's terms of reference were about service delivery.

This emphasis on service was further exemplified in the departmental Race Relations Work Programme for 1991/92 but in this the 'imperative of service' is even starker. In referring to the imperative of service I am suggesting more than just a focus on getting services out to the 'service user'. Instead I am suggesting that 'service' now carries the idea of 'business' and thus the 'business of serving customers' implies a different rationale behind the organizational arrangements and priorities. In part this is reflected in the concern for 'operational objectives', 'targets' and 'performance indicators', all of which suggest an evaluation on the basis of accounting techniques rather than socially produced needs being met. For example, the report outlining the social services service contract (1990/91) had as one of its targets for children and young people 'To facilitate transcultural provision'. This was to be achieved by the following measures: '1. Ensure precise ethnic/cultural monitoring; 2. End of year report in liaison with Race Relations' (p. 8).

Moreover, the whole of the Race Relations Work Programme for 1991/92 was written in these terms as is reflected in the view that 'areas targeted by the Race Relations (sub-committee) correspond with the key areas chosen by the SSD in accord with the Corporate Specifications for Service Contract for 1991/92 as set out by the Policy and Resources Committee in its Report Service Planning 1991/92'. The rest of the report is then all set out under headings dealing with operational objectives and performance indicators.

A shift to the language of business reflects a shift in the understanding of the relationship between sections of the local populace and state organized welfare delivery. It also reflects a shift in the role accorded to state agencies for the delivery of welfare and as agencies offering a wide range of employment opportunities. In this move to a new welfare regime, inequalities are either unacknowledged or conceptualized as outside of the direct concerns of the local authority. Diversity is a part of the new welfare regime but it is a diversity divorced from socially produced power inequalities and instead harnessed to a notion of consumer choice. Thus, a diverse range of 'customer' needs become articulated through, and satisfied by, the equalizing force of the market. This refocuses attention on reorganizing institutional structures and arrangements as if state welfare agencies were businesses and the tackling of inequality (recoded as diversity) was simply a matter of organizational techniques and accounting.

It is in this context that a high-profiled employment strategy was lost. The language and imperative of service created the potential for the demise of the pursuit of equality of opportunity in employment, especially at higher levels in the occupational hierarchy. This tendency was mapped onto a formulation that saw the mere presence of racialized staff in social work teams as sufficient to facilitate a 'transcultural' service. Any further developments therefore focused on getting the mechanisms for service delivery right rather than providing opportunities for access to occupations defined as professional and ensuring opportunities for career development within that. These intersecting processes were reproduced in 'Inland City' and I will now turn my attention there.

'Inland City' Council

In 1980 the then Director of Social Services of this city council visited India and Pakistan 'with the aim of gaining a deeper understanding of Asian culture and the needs of Asian people in [the local area]' (Inland City Council, *Strategy for Ethnic Minorities – Report to Social Services Committee*, 6 June 1984). The visit had been funded by the Commission for Racial Equality as part of its programme of providing such trips for public officials whose remit included work with sections of Britain's black populations. These visits were premised on the idea that they would provide relatively quick and easy access to the cultural characteristics, values and social patterns of the predominant 'ethnic minority' populations found in British cities. Knowledge and understanding of these cultures was deemed necessary if equality of service delivery was to be achieved and 'good race relations' promoted. Having become so acculturated, the Director 'as part of his continuing awareness of the special

needs of minority communities . . . encouraged a variety of initiatives'
for the delivery of culturally appropriate services (ibid.).

The centrality given to this visit in the early development of services
for the Inland City authority black and ethnic minority populaces raises
many points about the overall approach to black presence adopted at
this time. All the more so since the visit itself, and the ensuing initiatives,
had been prompted by the publication of *Multi-Racial Britain: The Social
Services Response* in 1978 by the Association of Directors of Social Services and the Commission for Racial Equality. This report had identified
'newness', 'cultural differences' and 'racial prejudice and discrimination'
as the reasons why SSDs needed to give special thought to the appro-
priateness of their provision. 'Culture' and 'difference' had been placed
centrally on the agenda.

The immediate response to the 1980 visit focused on awareness training for elected representatives and departmental officers, and on developing consultation with the Community Relations Council (CRC) and
those identified as local community leaders. For example, training was
organized to give both members of the social services committee and
departmental staff greater (cultural) awareness of Asian and African-
Caribbean communities and their needs. Some staff attended racism
awareness (as opposed to cultural awareness) courses, and there was
also the possibility to attend courses more specifically service-focused
such as services for 'ethnic minority elderly' (June 1984, Appendix 1,
paras 3.1–3.4). Similarly, quarterly meetings were established between a
subgroup of the Committee and the CRC. In addition, representatives
from at least one department met regularly with leaders at the local
mosque.

It appears that between 1980 and 1984 this was the extent of developments aimed at improving services for black residents in the local
authority area. Notably there were no initiatives at all aimed at recruiting black and Asian social workers, one of the central recommendations
of the ADSS/CRE publication, although the 1984 report puts this down
to an embargo on recruitment that was in operation at the time.

That year, 1984, marked a shift in this impasse. This was the result of
an instruction from the race relations and equal opportunities committee that all departments produce details of a race relations policy. The
committee had itself only been established in that same year as part of
the changes introduced by the incoming Labour administration. Prior to
this the Council had formally adopted an authority-wide equal opportunities in employment statement in July 1983 – a statement introduced
by the preceding Conservative administration.

Although the 1984 strategy paper aimed to pick up where the 1980
initiatives had ended, what is different about this later document is
that it introduced the first departmental *policy* statement, providing the

guiding framework for all work in the directorate. The paper also introduced a *strategy*, the main elements of which centred on training, recruitment, monitoring and review (of both clients and staff) and liaison. The
limits to the liaison and consultation process were soon to become apparent, as I show later. Meanwhile, and in contrast to Coolville, the London
authority, there was no detailed analysis of the class and 'race' basis of
current social services philosophy and social work practice. As with the
London case, however, gender was entirely absent as a clearly identified
category of social signification and power. The policy statement attempts
to follow what had become accepted as the first step in equal opportunities 'good practice', but rather than displaying elements of a 'political
economy of welfare' approach it was heavily grounded in a cultural pluralist perspective. This perspective expands the idea of cultural diversity
and draws on obvious or assumed cultural differences between groups;
there is also a commitment to positive valuation of these differences
and to the preservation of group culture and tradition. The thread which
binds these diverse cultural groups is that of the overarching and secular
political authority. However, as Mullard (1982) has pointed out this is an
idealistic formulation and completely ignores the inequalities of power
between groups differentiated around axes of 'culture' or 'race'.

The key elements in the social services policy statement were

(i)   recognition and valorization of the multi-racial/multi-cultural com-
        position of the City;
(ii)   opposition to all forms of racism and commitment to the promotion
        of racial equality and justice, including its obligations under the 1976
        Race Relations Act;
(iii)   a responsibility to provide culturally appropriate and sensitive ser-
        vices to all residents who need them, 'within available resources';
(iv)   a responsibility to implement the Council's equal opportunities in
        employment policy.

(1984, Policy Statement, paras 2.1–2.6)

The paper's cultural pluralist hallmark focuses attention on the
concern for 'ethnic sensitivity' in the delivery of services and deflects
from the statement of opposition 'to all forms of racism'. Indeed the
tension between, on the one hand, espousal of opposition to racism and,
on the other, commitment to ethnic sensitivity was reflected in the discussion of the report by the elected members. The minute of the Committee meeting which approved the report recorded that an amendment
was proposed that the statement of opposition to 'all forms of racism' be
altered to remove the word racism and focused instead on the promotion of 'racial equality and justice'. The vote was lost – seven to twelve
– but it is interesting that any members were opposed to direct reference
to racism (minute of Committee meeting).

If the policy statement contrasts with the approach contained in the (September) 1984 policy report in the London Borough of Coolville, *Towards the Development of a Transracial/Cultural Model of Service Provision*, the proposed strategy compares more closely. Thus, in a similar way to that in the London authority, this SSD makes reference to two of the key elements of the 'transcultural' approach noted earlier. For example, first there is an espousal of a belief that 'western concepts' are 'alien' to the City's ethnic minorities and, second, there is reference to the requisite mix of professionalism and 'cross cultural' communication skills. Cultural diversity, then, implies hard, immutable boundaries and the binary opposition between 'the West and the rest' (Hall, 1992b) is steadfastly reinscribed, as is evident from the following:

> 3.1 For a sizeable proportion of . . . residents, *Western* concepts of social services are likely to be *alien*. With a variety of patterns of family and other relationships, different religious beliefs and customs and a large number of people who are not able to communicate easily in English, there is a clear obligation to determine the most practical, efficient and effective way of providing services. Provision of good services for all client groups depends on the *attitudes* and ability to *communicate* as well as on the professional skills of workers. In the development of services there will be a recognition that patterns of family and other relationships, the *boundaries of what is normal* behaviour, and criteria for assessing both *situation* and *need* are *culturally determined*. (Inland City Council, *Strategy for Ethnic Minorities*, June 1984, my emphases)

Issues of culture, language or diversity in familial forms and relations are important and should form part of developing a strategy for service delivery. Critically, however, this recognition of diversity takes place on a terrain in which 'culture' is the privileged site of differentiation and 'culture' as the determining axis in social relations is only 'seen' in connection with the City's (and Britain's) black and Asian populations. The result is the reinscription of these groups as 'other'. Moreover, cultural traits and boundaries are conceived as immutable across the generations.

This conceptualization of the issues facilitates the mutual exclusion of 'English/Western' and 'Asian'. Thus, the appendices to the report can show both that the SSD is supporting 'a play group for Asian children, an unemployed Asian men's group and a girls' group which assists *with problems that Asian girls have in Western society*' (Appendix 1, para. 5.7, my emphasis)[5] *and* that the 1981 Census showed that 43 per cent of what were deemed New Commonwealth or Pakistan heads of household were *born* in Britain and that most of the 'non-white' children were *born* in the City (Appendix 2). Figures such as these beg the question as to what it is that determines 'racial', ethnic or national group belonging; what, exactly, it is that 'Asian' girls born and raised in Britain are having problems with, and if they are, why.

In the model utilized by this social services department the answer to these questions can only be found in terms of cultural alienation and cultural conflict. The task for social services, then, is to develop forms of support and communication able to cope with this. Moreover, this becomes translated as the same thing as anti-racism which is conceptualized as equality of provision and cultural sensitivity. Anti-racism as practices and discourses which attempt to undo the bases and fabric of racial categorization, subordination and 'othering' is occluded in this approach. An attempt to elicit the processes which may act to constitute as 'Asian' girls born in Britain to parents whose own places of birth are in south Asia (or the Caribbean, etc.) is similarly prevented. Social services practice can then only be to treat such girls as 'not British' – even if the adjective 'second-generation' is added. Ethnic descent and ethnicity become conflated with 'race' and either way are envisaged as a fixed characteristic inherited across the generations.

Given this, the development of forms of support and communication depended in large part on the recruitment of black social workers to the department's offices and divisions. It is notable that the emphasis on recruitment at this time (1984) was still focused on training and monitoring of new recruits and internal transferees. Three new 'ethnic minority posts' had been established – one inspector charged with evaluating current services in order to propose change; and two training officers 'who will be improving the knowledge and skills of the Department particularly of Afro-Caribbean and Asian communities' (para. 2.3). The big push for a significant increase in the number of qualified black social workers employed in the department's field, domiciliary and residential services was to wait another eighteen months.

This notwithstanding, there were attempts to use section 11 monies to fill posts with a specific 'ethnic minority brief'. The June 1984 report refers to 133 such posts being bid for, though it is not clear how many of these were for social services directly, nor how successful that bid was overall. Similarly, the department was attempting to recruit interpreters for one specific district by use of inner-city partnership (ICP) monies gained under the Urban Programme. Central government initiatives were being used in a way that permitted local government to privilege (and reify) 'culture', while central government remained 'blind' to 'race'.

If the 1984 policy statement and strategy provided the conceptual framework guiding social services department practice, further development and the process of implementation were slow in coming. Events in one area of the City in 1985 were to change all this. These events were subsequently named in such a way as to mark and racialize[6] the events and they ushered in a flurry of activity across the Council's departments, and even led to a specific Riots Action Plan in 1986. Prior to this and immediately after the 'riots', the social services committee received a report on 9 October 1985 which outlined a strategy for the extension and implementation of the services for 'ethnic minorities' first begun in 1984.

The report stressed the urgency of the situation.

> There are a wide range of issues on which action needs to be taken immediately . . .
>
> Discussions have been proceeding within the Department . . . to produce an action programme to advance the strategy . . .
>
> The discussions to produce the action programme and involvement with various ethnic minority groups, have shown that there is a considerable amount of work which needs to be done to improve the level, type and quality of services available to ethnic minorities and appropriate to their needs. (*Strategy for Services to Ethnic Minorities, Report to Social Services Committee*, 9 October 1985, introduction and paras 2.1 and 2.2)

In terms of the recruitment of black and Asian social workers to the department, the key aspect of the report was the proposal to establish a Positive Action Unit. The Unit's main functions were to revise the existing strategy and progress its implementation; to review and monitor service provision; to encourage positive action policies; and to co-ordinate consultation processes (para. 3.1).

However, at least

> for the first two or three years the prime function of the Unit would be in the area of equal opportunity and personnel practice, with the aim of increasing the proportion of ethnic minority employees at all levels and in all parts of the Department.   (para. 3.2)

There was also some sense in which the urgency of the situation dictated that a greater commitment for mainstream funding of initiatives aimed at the 'ethnic minority' populations be forthcoming. Thus, although the 1985 report recommended a review of existing section 11 provision, the Positive Action Unit was to be funded from mainstream budgets and not via a re-allocation of reviewed section 11 funds. Certainly the director of social services sought to secure commitment for the 25 per cent local authority share of such posts, but anything else was envisaged as additional to that which already existed. There was therefore an identifiable shift towards more mainstream funding of posts and projects aimed at ethnic minorities. This was significant because of the widespread understanding that the paucity of such mainstreaming was indicative of a national lack of commitment to black and Asian communities. However, one should not be tempted to over-read the shift. For example, at a committee meeting in July 1986, one councillor expressed concern at the continued preponderance of black projects being funded by section 11 (*Minute 4818-8 to 9 July Social Services Committee*).

Nevertheless, it is evident from committee activity that finances from mainstream funds were being sought in a more consistent way, suggesting that the 'riots' so sharpened the issues that they acted to redirect resources somewhat, if only temporarily. For example, at the July 1986 committee meeting, which considered progress of the Riots Action Plan, extra funds of £212,000 per annum (and pro rata equivalent for that year) were sought for five projects aimed at delivering services to sections of the local black and Asian populations (*Riots Action Plan – Progress, Report by the Director of Social Services*). This was supplementary to those projects already identified in the *Action Plan – First Report* of April 1986. The document was an interdepartmental report laying out what each directorate was doing in response to the riotous events. In the part detailing the social services response, seventeen projects were identified as being wholly or partially aimed at the ethnic minority communities, eight of which were to be mainstream funded. The remainder are identified as being funded under the ICP (Urban Programme). However, in terms of the argument about an increase in mainstream funding, it is noticeable that only one of the main programme funded projects had not yet secured its money, compared with five of the Department of the Environment projects. Moreover, a further four of the latter were still awaiting Department of the Environment approval for the project itself.

Recruitment and the work of the Positive Action Unit

Against the background of the riotous events and the political pressure that the race relations and equal opportunities committee represented, the work of the Positive Action Unit was to prove pivotal for the further development of employment and service provision initiatives. Consistent with received equal opportunity wisdom of the time, awareness training (racism and cultural) was given greater emphasis (*Riots Action Plan – First Report*, p. 22). Frontline workers were to have an expanded programme and staff involved in recruitment were compelled to attend racism awareness and equal opportunities selection courses. Similarly, the 1984 emphasis on culturally appropriate dietary provision in meals on wheels, day centres, etc. was reiterated, as was the commitment to recruiting prospective foster and adoptive parents from the City's 'racial' and cultural minorities. Emphasis was also placed on the need to recruit black and Asian social workers to the department and the creation of specialist posts for some aspects of the work was agreed.

The scheme which was to prove pivotal in providing entry routes for black and Asian social workers to the department was the social worker trainee scheme for black and ethnic minority people developed by staff in the Positive Action Unit. Agreed early in 1986, 'the scheme was intended to be part of a 5-year programme which, allowing for turnover, had as its target at least 15% of qualified social workers being of black or minority ethnic origin' (*Social Worker Trainee Scheme, Committee Paper*, 12 November 1986).

By July 1986 the Council had agreed an across-the-board target of 20 per cent of employees drawn from the 'ethnic minority' population; a figure roughly in proportion to the percentage of the total population of the City. For social services, reaching this target figure required concerted effort as in 1983 the figure was only 8.2 per cent (Solomos and Back, 1995, p. 181) and there was no evidence to suggest that there had been any significant increase in the three intervening years. In order to bring the trainee recruitment target up to the 20 per cent figure, it was agreed that the scheme be expanded by an extra ten posts. This raised the total level to thirty. The scheme attracted an enormous amount of interest and a total of 900 applications were received, belying the previously held view that black people were not interested in social work as an occupation (report of Director of Social Services, 12 November 1986, and interview material). There is no doubt that this scheme was tremendously important in opening up professional social work to black and Asian women (and men).

In many ways the trainee scheme was a secondment programme but it had more of a developmental aspect to it than its counterpart in the London authority (Coolville). Two or three of the appointed trainees went directly to the local Polytechnic to begin the two-year CQSW course. The majority spent their first year working in the SSD. These were the people who did not have the necessary qualifications or experience for direct entry to the CQSW course. They rotated between sections of the department, staying in each for about ten to twelve weeks. In this way they gained the required experience for entry to the social work course. Interestingly, given the gender balance of social work as a profession, amongst the trainees there was only a slight skew towards women.[7] On completion of the social work course, trainees were under contract to return to the department for a minimum of two years. The initial agreement was that they would return at level one but the cohort was a tight knit, politically vocal group, and they renegotiated this and returned as level two social workers.

The scheme lasted until 1989 and really had only one cohort; after this a second, smaller and differently focused scheme was introduced. The changes came about as a result of cuts in departmental budgets for training, but dissatisfactions were also being voiced by some other members of staff.

> There were a number of grumblings from people who worked internally and had been here for a long time and obviously saw these people as having privileges they weren't getting. They had served their time and they had been waiting for their opportunity to go on secondment internally. So having done that big external push, the department was more inclined, in my opinion I have to say, to look internally for people to go on training courses.   (interview with ex-member of the PAU, 1995)

Against this background, the trainee scheme was redesigned into a smaller development worker programme. Those recruited were direct employees and placed in the children's and elderly teams. They received support from a training officer in the PAU and from a sectional supervisor who was on hand for the more day-to-day issues. After one or two years the development workers could seek secondment to a recognized social work course through the general secondment programme, but although still within the framework of the positive action initiative, there was no guarantee of success.

Along with a change in the structure and size of the scheme the general brief was altered so that it resembled the London authority's liaison worker project. The development workers' remit was to initiate direct development work with groups in the local population who were seen as under-represented in terms of the take-up of departmental services. It was envisaged that the workers would act as a two-way conduit between the department and the targeted 'communities' themselves. On the one hand, they were to introduce the SSD to the communities by informing them of the range of services, eligibility criteria, frontline organizational structure, etc. On the other hand, the development workers were to feed back information to the department on services that had been developed voluntarily. The department would then consider how it could support such voluntary-sector provision or begin to meet the needs directly. In this way it was thought both that there would be an increase in the use of departmental services amongst sections of the City's 'ethnic minority' populations and that the provision would be more 'culturally appropriate'.

Clearly this department was working through a cultural pluralist approach. As in the London liaison workers scheme, the development workers were constructed as representative of 'their' communities and as 'translators' who could decode the internal logic of both the under-represented groups and the department. The ability to perform this precedes any professional qualification in social work because they physically embody the skills required by the department. As with the London case, the departmental concern to address equality of opportunity in employment in its own right is undermined.

Furthermore, as inhabitants of racialized bodies these workers were located in a different form of work organization. In the earlier secondment programme, a formal training scheme was envisaged with routes to professional qualification, personal development and work experience. In the latter scheme all that was guaranteed was a full-time job with the opportunity to apply for secondment in the general scheme that was undergoing constant cuts. 'Race' or 'culture', then, were the axes around which a different organization of work was instituted for the development of services to populations defined as 'ethnic minority'. This provided the context within which these racialized bodies were to labour.

In the absence of any further departmental schemes aimed specifically at black and Asian recruitment into qualified positions, these workers' dependence on the general secondment scheme was total. However, this scheme was itself cut in size between the late 1980s and 1995 when it was estimated that it offered opportunities for 'no more than ten if that' (interview with ex-PAU worker). In the view of this ex-PAU staff member, the result of this change in the link between 'race'/ethnicity and employment and training opportunity, was

> that black people were back where they started. Well not back where they started because they got more support. [But they were] dependent on filling in their application form. Dependent on managers supporting their application. Dependent on an interviewing panel being made up of a variety of people so that you stood a chance of getting through the process of getting secondment, which was becoming more difficult.

This formulation highlights the bureaucratic nature of the general secondment process and there is a clear inference of the racial disadvantage it carries. Similarly, the tone implies that racial disadvantage can enter at any of several stages in the process. It implies a deep scepticism about the procedures for guaranteeing equality of opportunity in selection and recruitment. To the extent that this characterization is accurate there is a clear suggestion that formal policy and procedure is regarded as a poor substitute for hard, targeted schemes offering the possibility for black people to gain entry to professional employment in the SSD. From this perspective the days of 'back to where they started' are multilayered in that they refer not just to the time when entry to the department was virtually non-existent, but to times when access to professional training routes was closed off.

The anticipation (or fear) of a return to the pre-1986 situation resulted in individuals adopting creative ways of gaining access to routes to qualification. The above participant illustrated the creative response on the part of black women in the following way:

> In my experience, more and more black women were using the career break scheme to go to the Polytechnic . . . so they would actually take time out of work . . . be unpaid. [The] career break scheme is an unpaid leave scheme that was used initially for women on maternity leave. You could have up to five years unpaid leave and return to work with the post held open. So a number of black *people* who did not get secondment used that route to get training. But of course they would have to apply for a grant. The department didn't pay anything. (ibid., my emphasis)

Three interesting points are embedded in this statement. First, in worker/management terms it is illustrative of the ways in which employees attempt to subvert employer policies and practices for their own advantage. Second, it is interesting for what it reveals about the ways in which policies aimed at promoting gender equality are utilized by black women in the name of 'race' equality. As might be expected, the career break scheme was formally available to all women regardless of 'race' and/or ethnicity. In the context of a situation where 'race' equality measures are perceived as being eroded or downplayed, it is possible to discern 'race' being spoken through gender. It is a form of subversion of one field of (in)equality in an ideological and discursive context which divides these axes into separate spheres.[8] The third point relates to the ways in which these fields are spoken. Thus, despite the example being about the ways that black *women* use a scheme that attempts to take into account the impact of motherhood on women's career opportunities, there is a slippage to 'black *people*'. In this part of the account, then, there is an inversion – i.e. gender disappears as an explicit term, and by extension any suggestion about gender inequalities and differentiation within black populations is hidden from view. Simultaneously the account suggests that attempts to gain access to training opportunities are created on the terrain of gender while being articulated in the metalanguage of 'race' (Brooks-Higginbottom, 1992). The dual process of speaking 'race' through gender whilst making the latter invisible in terms of the internal relations of black populations is something that, as we see in subsequent chapters, is often repeated in the accounts of other women.

The 1990s

As with Coolville, by the late 1980s/early 1990s the situation in Inland City was much changed. The number of black and Asian women and men in the SSD had risen to just over 28 per cent, but this general figure may well mask clustering at the lower end of the scale. For example, in mid-1994, the highest level attained by any black or Asian social workers was that of area office manager, exactly the same as in the London authority. There were two of these, both women: one of Caribbean origin, the other of south Asian origin. There were no other black or Asian people (women or men) at levels above this, of which black staff were acutely aware. Moreover, a few months later, departmental rumour had it that a further reorganization of the department would mean that even these women might well have to reapply for their jobs. This was generally greeted with despondency and cynicism by black and Asian women since, as they saw it, all previous reorganizations had left them in a worse position within the organizational hierarchy.

The woman who had been centrally involved in the PAU characterized the situation in this way:

> I don't see any specific initiatives or advantages, or any huge drives to improving the position of black people through training in the department. I don't necessarily think that is the only thing they have to look at either. Because I know of a lot of people who were already able but who didn't get those positions. So we're in the glass ceiling thing. So you get qualified but you're not becoming an AD [assistant director] or you're not becoming an area manager, so that's the battle really. What I would like to see and what a number of people would like to see, is people having gained their qualifications, gaining rapid access to management in the same way that their white counterparts do. Because they don't have to wait ten years to become a senior manager, so why should black staff now that they are qualified. So what we realize is that the goalposts are kind of changing. (op. cit.)

A number of points arise from this. At the level of policy, we see again that 'race' equality in employment is understood as being only about initial entry into professional grades and that once this is achieved career progression is not a major departmental concern. At the more abstract level, this account is revealing because of what it tells us about what is 'seen'. We are given an account in which 'race' is the privileged site of what is seen, whilst gender at best is accorded a kind of subtextual quality, at worst made completely invisible. Thus, which white people are progressing (women or men) is left unspoken, whilst we are left to guess whether it is black men as well as black women who are caught in the 'glass ceiling'. However, the use of this last term is notable for its association with gender inequality – a factor of which the informant would have been well aware given her current position in the organization (within corporate training and development). Yet it is clear that both 'race' and gender intersect to construct the terrain on which struggles to maintain access to professional training and career progression are waged. For example, in 1989 a group of black women got together as black women to form the Black Women's Training and Development Group. This was a self-organized group with the aims of redirecting the focus of SSD training away from an emphasis on assertiveness and awareness training and towards a more specific focus on career development and progression. After gaining support from the then director of social services and a budget from the training manager, they began to develop supervisory and management courses. There are two key points about this. First, the development of a proactive strategy such as this began to establish the kind of training that black women themselves thought necessary to meet their individual and collective needs. The result was, and this is the second point, training that foregrounded career progression. It started from the assumption that many black women were now qualified, with the implication that training that began from a premise of some kind of deficit was unable to speak to the needs of a new situation. As a result, this kind of self-organized, self-defined training programme attempted to increase the labour market power of black women by undermining some of the factors and assumptions that facilitate the emergence of 'glass ceilings', for example lack of relevant qualification or experience. Black women realize that the obstacles they face are multifaceted and constantly shifting, making the need for self-organization more pressing.

> Now that we've got equal opportunities policy and we've introduced a black perspective into most of the policies of the department and people realize that the culture has got to change, what happens is that they actually make it difficult for you to get to those levels [senior management, etc.] so that you can initiate changes. (op. cit.)

There is, however, some evidence to suggest that the department felt it necessary to provide some form of career development training for black staff. For example, in 1992 a training programme was established for black managers in conjunction with the local university. The aim of the programme was fairly straightforward, seeking to encourage black managers, from home care organizers and team managers upwards, to apply for senior posts across the directorate, and to provide a management development programme. It was a modular course leading to a certificate in Social Services Management. There were three main modules – managing self, managing people, and managing resources and finance. However, the course only ran for approximately eighteen months, in part because participants were not very satisfied with the course content or with the extra workload it generated. There was no time off to study and a lot of motivation and time was needed to get through the course requirements. This too, then, was a different kind of career development support in comparison with either the original CQSW secondment scheme or the Black Women's Training and Development programme.

This is in keeping with the shift in emphasis since 1985 towards service provision and away from 'race' equality in employment and is clearly discernible in an early 1995 committee report, *Race Equality in Service Delivery* (11 January). As with the London authority reports of the same period, one notes the shifting understanding of the objectives of equal opportunity in employment once service provision is privileged. Similarly, in both the Inland and London authorities, the language and imperative of 'service' (and a kind of managerialism) is pre-eminent. Indeed in reading both these papers one is reminded of the point made in an early Coolville committee report which referred to the tendency not to see black people as service *providers* and only as service users (London Borough of Coolville, *Bid for Section 11 LGA 66 Resources Progress Report*, 1984).

Thus, in the entire ten-page main part (there are several appendices) of the Inland City report (1995) there are only two explicit references to the issue of 'race' equality in employment. The first is in reference to the recruitment of staff to a non-professional/non-qualified occupation – i.e. home care workers. Moreover, this is raised in connection with the increasing ability to provide 'equality of access' by the City's multi-ethnic population to the department's home care service.

> The Department provides Home Care Users with greater choice. Since April of this year [1994], 196 additional home carers have been recruited to the service. Particularly encouraging is the breakdown of their ethnic origin: 60% white European, 22% African-Caribbean, 14% Asian and 5% Other. (*Race Equality Service Delivery Strategy*, report to social services committee, 11 January 1995, para. 3.1.4)[9]

Some pages later there is a more general or rhetorical statement regarding Local Race Action Plans. These were annual plans outlining 'race' equality targets and the means by which they were to be achieved and monitored. They were produced by all area, divisional, team and unit managers and co-ordinated centrally by the department's race and equalities section. The plans began to be produced in 1993–4 and included statements about, but little substantive detail on, 'race' equality. For example, 'the continual development of [local race action] plans on an annual basis, will ensure that they reflect those initiatives which are current to the achievement of race equality in service delivery and *employment* practice' (para. 5.1.3, my emphasis), or 'issues of race feature significantly in this and reaffirm the Department's commitment to ensuring equality for its black and minority ethnic *employees* and users' (para. 4.4.1, my emphasis).

Other, more tangential, references are made elsewhere. For example, reference is made to the Black Workers' Support Group, but in their capacity as members of the Policy and Services Monitoring Group, which concentrates on service delivery. Similarly, awareness training for staff '. . . to ensure that its employees are aware of the need to deliver services within a framework of equality' (para. 4.4.3). Even the reference in the report to section 11 is in terms of funding services, rather than the type of job it supports as part of the provision (para. 4.5.2).

It could be argued that since this is a strategy report on service delivery, there are no grounds for raising issues about its lack of reference to 'race' equality in employment. However, there was no parallel report on employment. Moreover, as early as the 1978 ADSS/CRE report on the social services response to Britain's multi-ethnicity, increasing equality in service provision has been seen as premised on the employment of black staff in SSDs up and down the country. We can conclude, therefore, that such received wisdom, which had been temporarily scorched into departmental policy in the wake of the riotous events of the mid-1980s, was now eroded. With this in mind, the question that arises is not why issues of employment should be included in such a report, but rather, what factors are at play that result in their exclusion.

Perhaps the emphasis on employment, which began with the adoption of the equal opportunity employment policy statement in 1983, and had its apex in the work of the PAU, was de-emphasized once the department exceeded the 20 per cent across-the-board target pushed through in 1986. However, even this needs to be understood in the context of the overall discourse of 'race' and racial equality. Consistently over the years black and Asian people had been recruited to the SSD as racialized subjects who were perceived as embodying (quite literally) the skills and knowledges deemed necessary for the department. This was the first and fundamental characteristic facilitating their entry at a time when local political and 'community' relations forced the issue of racism onto the municipal agenda. Since racial and cultural 'translation' was the SSD's primary requirement, recruitment and training of appropriate 'representatives' was a key focus. At one particular moment, opportunities for professional training were superimposed on what was seen as the more pressing issue of developing culturally sensitive services and being seen by 'ethnic minority' communities to be doing something. Once the numbers were reached (the critical mass being 20 per cent across the board) such schemes were no longer necessary. This was particularly so in the very altered financial and organizational contexts of the 1990s, in which customer-centredness relied on getting managerial and organizational arrangements 'right' as a precursor to the delivery of equality. In this sense it is also possible to discern the shift to an imperative of service, with its language of targets, performance and consumers, in these later committee papers.

Take, for example, the substantial report on race equality that was presented to the Committee in January 1995. Its very title 'Race Equality Service Delivery Strategy' is itself revealing. So, too, is its 'current strategic approach', which reads:

> 3.1 The broad strategic approach taken by the Department has been as follows.
>> 3.1.1 The Department has re-established the Race and Equalities section, which is now fully staffed. The section provides strategic direction on service delivery to people from Black and Minority Ethnic communities and also deals with equality issues around race and gender to ensure services are delivered within a framework of equality and equity. The unit has become closely integrated into the Department's Planning and Management processes. The benefits of a sharper definition of role are becoming clear in a number of areas.

Subsequent sections of the report emphasize targets and achievements in developing 'ethnically sensitive' services; monitoring and data collection; and review of future service delivery systems for specific communities, in, for example, day-care facilities for African-Caribbean and Asian elderly, foster care for children from these communities, and home care services (paras 3.1.2–3.1.4).

The remainder of the report goes on to outline the 'Corporate Requirements' by which 'race' equality in service delivery is to be achieved. This provides a new context from which to view even the reference to the employment of the home care workers, since it is clear that they are recruited to meet service delivery targets and not because the department, as a major employer in the area, sees itself as having a responsibility for the development of policies aimed at achieving equality in employment in its own right.

In this chapter I have considered the process of racial formation at the local level by exploring policy development and change in relation to black and Asian women's entry to professional social work. I have argued that changes in access to professional training in two social services departments resulted from the combination of conceptualizations about the link between 'race', 'culture' and employment and the reorganization of public welfare around notions of the market, the customer and the homogenization of 'equalities issues'. Where relevant I considered the slippages and elisions that occurred between 'race' and 'culture', and these and other axes of social differentiation. As with the situation at central government level, moves between these registers were deeply embedded in local policy documents. In broad terms there was considerable similarity in the approaches adopted by the two authorities. Both had a 'high' moment of commitment to facilitating entry of women from racialized populations of colour to professional social work and developed schemes specially designed to achieve this. Both were pushed in this direction by a confluence of events in the local area and used a combination of central and local finances to support their policies. Moreover, both authorities operated within discursive frameworks that essentialized 'racial' difference. However, there was some distinction between the two authorities in relation to the key signifier of this essentialized difference. Thus, in Coolville 'race' as a biological category tended to be predominant, whilst in Inland City it was 'culture' that was the privileged signifier of difference. Of course in both authorities these terms were substituted and elided, but that there was some tendency to foreground one rather than the other is interesting. In part this may be related to the predominant 'ethnic minority' in the local area, but more than this cannot be said. When one compares the two authorities with the situation at central government level there are more discernible differences. Thus it was not so much that at local level 'race' slipped in and out of visibility, but more that the ways in which it was 'seen' was a product of local social/political conditions, and the organization of relations between central and local government. As we saw in chapter 2, recognition of Britain as a racial formation nationally is denied at central government level, whilst specific localities are seen in racialized terms. Indeed, in central policy debates, one feature marking the specificity of inner-city space was precisely its changing racial character. Management of these specific places was devolved to local government within the existing framework of central/local organization. In this context the 'blind eye' of 'race' does not operate at the local level yet the tyranny of racial discourse is such that at local level the specificity of place is occluded, hence the broad similarity between the policies considered here.

Thus, discourses of 'race' circulated at both central and local level which positioned black and Asian women social workers in ways that racialized them and 'fixed' them into specific organizational and occupational locations. How such women occupy and resist these positionings forms the subject matter of subsequent chapters.

4

'The Call of the Wild': Contestatory Professional Discourses on 'Race' and Ethnicity

Introduction

The preceding two chapters have identified the policy formations at national and local level in which racialized welfare subjects were constituted and which shaped the employment of social workers from these populations. These, however, are not the only formations that were at play in these processes. As an arena of employment for racialized populations, social work is a distinctive occupation given its claim to (quasi-)professional status. Between the late 1970s and early 1990s, issues of 'race' and ethnicity became increasingly significant within the professional discourses of social work. In examining the specific organizational settings of social services departments, we need also to consider how the professional discourse has articulated these issues as part of social work theory and practice. This chapter, then, explores another level of encounter between 'race', gender and social work. Specifically, it considers the ways in which 'racial' and ethnic identities were conceived and addressed within the professional discourse of social work in the 1980s and early 1990s.

The aim of the chapter is threefold. First, it is intended as a critique of some of the dominant conceptions of 'race' and ethnicity in much social work literature. I argue that accompanying a recognition by SSDs, and others involved in social work, that issues of racism and ethnicity needed to be addressed, was a discourse of 'ethnic absolutism' (Gilroy, 1987) with regard to racialized or ethnicized groups. I use the terms 'racialized' and 'ethnicized' to refer to the idea that all of an individual's or group's needs, patterns of behaviour and value systems can be reduced to, or derived from, their 'race' or ethnicity. I use the term 'ethnic absolutist' to refer to the practices in social work which are premised on these ideas and which also have the effect of reproducing processes of racialization and ethnicization. Such ideas are very pervasive and more or less explicit traces of this form of thinking can be found across a wide spectrum of political and social policy thought. We can see it in social work texts, in social services department policy and practice, and, perhaps paradoxically, in critiques of these. An example of this latter form is provided in the highly vocal, and indeed contentious, critique which the Association of Black Social Workers and Allied Professionals (ABSWAP) mounted against traditional social work practice with black clients, especially in the field of adoption and fostering. As Gilroy (1987) has noted, there is a high degree of correspondence between New Right conceptions of 'race' and those used by ABSWAP. Within the profession of social work and the discourses which circulate within it, the encounter between 'race' and social work occurs as an encounter between opposing sides of a shared discursive formation.

Following from this, my second concern will be to show a link between conceptualizations of 'race' and ethnicity and the practical effects of such conceptualizations. In order to explore this relationship I focus briefly on the transracial adoption and fostering debate in a way which conveys some of the complexity of the issues. Thus, I attempt to make a distinction between, on the one hand, the *political agenda* of those black professionals and activists who sought to intervene in and disrupt dominant social work policy and practice, and, on the other hand, the discourses of 'race', ethnicity and identity which they utilized. I argue that these discourses, although ostensibly posed as an alternative to the dominant ones circulating the profession, are equally problematic in that they act to reposition black people (professionals and clients) in racialized social relations. It should become clear that both the ways in which 'race'/ ethnicity are thought about and the policies which emerge from this thinking are terrains on which struggle has taken place.

Finally, utilizing work by Brah (1992), I will offer a reconceptualization of 'race' and ethnicity which more adequately grasps the complexity of lived social relations as they are structured through and by 'race', ethnicity and gender. I argue that 'race'/ethnicity needs to be understood and analysed as a major, but only one, axis of differentiation organizing a set of contingent social relations, the exact configuration of which will alter with varying moments and contexts.

What do we mean by 'difference'?

As we have seen, an implicit notion of difference has underwritten much of the literature and debate on local government employment and service provision. In social work this has largely been concerned with how to ensure that the needs of 'ethnic minority' clients are met, the emphasis being placed on service provision. Because the assumption has been that the 'black/white' divide equals the 'client/social worker' one, the key issue was initially seen to be how to ensure that in areas of high 'ethnic minority' populations social work staff would become equipped to deal with clients who had 'racially' or ethnically defined needs and were therefore 'different' by definition from the 'normal' social services client. Already in this situation we enter the terrain in which certain sections of the population have become racialized or ethnicized. 'Racial' or ethnic belongingness is not seen as something applicable to all people – including those implicitly defined as the (de-ethnicized) *majority*. It is not a field of ethnic differences that is conceptualized, but a difference from the otherwise universal structuring of need.

Two key strategies evolved as the way to resolve this problem: first, to train white social workers to be 'ethnically sensitive'; second, to go out and recruit people from these 'ethnic' communities to social work courses and social services departments.

The two strategies were not mutually exclusive, for, as Basil Manning wrote as early as 1979:

> the role of the black social worker would then be important in providing an ongoing in-service training for white workers helping them to understand more fully the cultural background of their black clients, their lifestyles, their norms and values, their use of words, the 'do's and don'ts' of relating to other cultures.   (in Cheetham et al., 1981, p. 32)

The remedy for white bias in social work was racially mixed staff teams and training courses for white staff organized by their departments. Here too we can see traces of absolutism. In this perspective ethnicity can only be 'decoded' by 'insiders' (i.e. black or 'ethnic minority' social workers) who will then 'translate' them for 'outsiders' (i.e. white social workers).

What was not spelt out so clearly was the notion of 'difference', as applied to ethnicity, which underlay these strategies. Each strategy was to have major policy/practice implications, but the idea of difference (or how ethnicity was defined) and the meanings that accrued to it were taken for granted – treated almost as self-evident, unquestionable and certainly uncontested. This was especially so in the context of cultural misunderstanding which was assumed to be a major problem facing SSDs and their staff. For example, as late as 1987 Ely and Denney wrote:

> Most of the original 'immigrants' arrived here through the process of 'chain' migration whereby they took up employment and housing

opportunities found for them by relatives already here. It was *natural* and *beneficial* for them to locate themselves in the midst of members of their own group, where a shared language, shared memories and cultural heritage provided a bridge between their past and present worlds. (p. 13, my emphasis)

Embedded within this statement is the idea that cultural barriers are generated only by the 'immigrants' and that they will prevent any easy assimilation or integration with the 'host' society. Such cultural barriers are assumed to be 'natural'. Moreover, 'natural' used here also suggests 'healthy' and perhaps it is from within this premise that we get the straightforward inversion of the more common complaint about the pre-sumed proclivity of 'immigrants' to 'mass together', with its implication that this obstructs the development of good race relations.

Upon closer examination it is possible to detect more at work here than a benign notion of 'ethnic solidarity' and adaptation. Both the 'ethnic sensitivity' model and the 'black social workers' model are premised on a Manichean notion that white and black are fundamen-tally and eternally different from one another. The root of this differ-ence, it is suggested, resides in cultural 'otherness'. This is a core in each model, but there are distinctions between them. Before going on to consider these two models in more detail I want to explore some of the discursive terrain on which 'race' and ethnicity were conceptualized, as there was increasing recognition that social work policy and practice needed to adapt to the changing demands imposed on it by having to work with multi-ethnic client populaces.

Freezing the frame: discursive hegemony and ethnic absolutism

Whilst much social work literature has embedded within it (more or less explicitly) a dominant notion of 'race'/ethnicity, this should not be taken to mean that there has been no struggle over the conceptualiza-tions of, and meanings attached to, 'race' and ethnicity. Recognition of this area of struggle is important because much of the debate about social work with multi-ethnic clientele proceeds as if it has been totally untouched by the important contributions made by post-structuralist, feminist, black and anti-racist movements to the understanding of 'race', ethnicity and identity. Moreover, since policy itself is developed upon, and has embedded within it, historically specific, albeit sometimes con-tradictory and conflicting, notions of 'race', ethnicity, identity and nation, it is important to try and elicit what these might be in any given his-torical moment.

The struggle over meaning results in one coming to occupy the position of 'truth' and dominating the terrain. Alternative conceptions are assigned to the margins but do not disappear. In this situation it may be the case that oppositional discourses traverse the same terrain as dominant/hegemonic ones. The point of distinction between them may reside in the political outcomes envisaged or struggled over. Despite differences in political project it is often possible to trace a discursive convergence rooted in the play or deployment of binary oppositions.

In this context the concept of 'discursive formation' is useful. Foucault defines a discursive formation arising 'whenever one can describe, between a number of statements a system of dispersion, whenever, between objects, types of statements, concepts, or thematic choices, one can define a regularity (an order, correlations, positions and functionings, transformations)' (1972, p. 38). The statements which comprise the discursive formation are such as to imply a relation between any one and all the other statements. In a sense, and paradoxically, the statements in a discursive formation constitute a structure since 'They refer to the same object, share the same style, and support a strategy . . . a common institutional or political drift or pattern' (Cousins and Hussain, 1984, pp. 84–5).

Two points flow from this. First, a discursive formation does not have to have a series of statements which are all the same; rather, 'the relationships and differences between them must be regular and systematic' (Hall, 1993, p. 292). Second, despite the fact that different speakers may articulate the statements in a discursive formation, once so spoken they become positioned within the discursive formation. Thus, statements that attempt to contest the underlying structure of relationships which are articulated by the discursive formation are deprived of their oppositional content and power. This is because the structure of meanings which they produce act to subordinate these oppositions.

This means that there is no guaranteed trajectory which can be plotted from a specific starting point. At the beginning of this chapter I referred to a number of authors (ABSWAP, Cheetham, Ely and Denney) who had argued that anti-racist social work strategies could only develop from a specific understanding of racism and the dynamic of 'race relations'. Clients' needs were to be seen as emerging from their location in social structures, as indeed were the potential benefits of employing black social workers. However, I want to argue that such benefits cannot be guaranteed, and I want to begin to illustrate this by an examination of some of the work of David Denney.

In an article plotting perspectives on 'race' and ethnicity in social work literature, Denney outlines four major approaches and offers a consideration of each (Denney, 1983). Adopting a version of the typology developed by writers such as Sivanandan (1982) and Mullard (1982) of the phases through which 'race relations' was apprehended in political circles and public policy through the 1960s, 1970s and 1980s, Denney examines the potential strengths and weaknesses of each model as it is presented in the social work literature. These models he calls the anthropological, the liberal pluralist, the cultural pluralist and the structuralist approaches. In this piece he offers a rather thorough critique of the liberal pluralist model in which a focus is placed on the '. . . principal ethnic/cultural factors which should be borne in mind when considering the possibility of "adapting" social work methods to the multi-ethnic context' (1983, p. 159). Similarly, this perspective calls upon social workers to develop an appropriate interpretative framework from which to 'translate the "rules" of interaction' (p. 157). As Denney argues, rightly in my view, 'one wonders exactly how the social worker goes about this complex interpretative procedure . . . whose reality finally dominate[s] the situation', and what happens to 'the vital question relating to the distribution of power . . . even at the micro level, i.e. in the social work interview' (p. 157).

Interestingly, and unfortunately, he goes on to conclude that a variant of this view, that of cultural pluralism, as exemplified by Ballard, does have a role to play (alongside the positive aspects in the other three) in the generation of a reformed, ethnically sensitive social work. This is because 'knowledge of specific cultures and the development of ethnically sensitive services are essential and important goals' (p. 171). Certainly Denney argues this must include a recognition of the structural determinants which position 'immigrants' or black populations in British society and the racism which can permeate social workers' interactions with black clients. But such structural determinants are envisioned as running parallel to ethnic cultural systems. The consequence of this is that the structuralist approach with which he began becomes subordinate in the reformulation where 'immigrant' culture is understood as static and predetermined. This is rather different from a framework which sees 'culture' as 'the play of signifying practices' (Brah, 1996) and understands that these signifying practices will be produced within, across and (sometimes) in opposition to the structural determinants of, and constraints on, black people's location in British society. These forces and processes will intersect with and undermine the diverse and internally heterogeneous cultures so that the meanings attached to culture and ethnicity become reformulated in new and different circumstances.

This more complex and fluid understanding of 'culture' has far more potential as a basis for developing policy and practice that will be flexible enough to meet the differential needs which a highly diverse society will produce. Moreover, 'culture' in this sense becomes a contingent force operating with or against processes which act to produce a highly differentiated population. Unlike the approach adopted by Denney, to think in this latter way pre-empts the emergence of forms of ethnic absolutism. However, given Denney's conceptual frame it is not surprising to find that, in a later co-authored work, he seems to have subscribed to a form of ethnic absolutism. We can see this in the context of a discussion of the 'ethnic sensitivity' model.

The ethnic sensitivity model

Central to this approach is the idea that 'difference' is a pre-social condition which results in cultural understandings/misunderstandings. Because of this, SSDs should teach their social workers enough about the cultural traits, codes and rules of 'minority cultures' to ensure that white staff can deliver services without giving offence to, or discriminating against, 'ethnic minority' clients. Social work itself does not need to change – its professional knowledges and powers, its understandings of 'ethnicity', etc. – but rather its range of interpretative repertoires by which cultural readings can be made needs to be augmented. To quote from Ely and Denney (1987):

> Ethnic minority institutions are adaptations of the original cultures. Social workers need to know of local ethnic organizations and services. They also need to be familiar with minority systems of cultural preferences and 'rules' (should be) regarded as emphases, cultural preferences, and despite the problem of variation of interpretation from informant to informant, there seems to be no alternative to learning systems of cultural preferences.   (pp. 13–14)

That Denney should be co-author to a piece in which such an emphasis is placed on 'rules' and 'systems of cultural preferences' would seem to indicate a marked shift from his earlier doubt about the possibility and utility of such an interpretative process. It could be argued that his apparent shift exemplifies the ways in which hegemonic conceptualizations become sedimented as a kind of professional common sense. Such common senses will be part of the foundation on which policy and practice is built. Indeed the slippage from this imperative to learn to read and decode 'ethnic minority' cultural codes to that of a form of ethnic absolutism where desires and actions are seen as solely formulated with reference to an 'ethnic community' is demonstrated later in the Ely and Denney book. For instance, in cautioning against applying 'western' notions of ideological freedom and self-determination, the authors quote Roger Ballard favourably:

> Whites often believe South Asian family life to be too constricting. If an Indian or Pakistani woman is in conflict with her parents or husband, an

outsider may assume that the subordinate role which South Asian women are expected to play towards their fathers and husbands . . . is at the root of the problem, such an interpretation may be partially correct, *but the woman would be unlikely to be seeking to alter her situation fundamentally. To do so would be to reject a major part of the cultural values of her own ethnic group.* Her complaint is, in practice, much more likely to be about the particular behaviour of her own husband or father, measured not in terms of her own standards, but of those of her own group.   (p. 86, my emphasis)

Here is a powerful example of the constitutive effects of racialized and gendered common senses on the construction and understanding of both particularized needs and the implementation of welfare policies and practices. Nasir (1996) has made this point well in an article on 'race', gender and social policy. 'The attitude towards Asian females is often patronizing. In terms of their relationships with their families they are seen as being without power, and are sometimes accused of not being able to influence or supervise their children adequately because of this' (p. 28).

We might add that Asian women are constructed as being without individuality and only possessed of 'community'. The quote from Ballard is an example of just such a discursive device in which racialized and gendered power relations are reproduced. First, we have the reinscription of white authority to define and describe cultural 'truths'. Next we have an example of the 'pacification' of the 'South Asian woman' in the sense that she is denied not only any individual agency but even any claim to subjectivity, thus she becomes reinscribed in a dominant, racialized version of gender relations amongst 'South Asians'. Finally, the quote provides an example and validation of the power of the professional to define the 'true' nature of a client's problem.

What is salient about this approach is that whilst its stated aim is to ensure equality of service delivery, it does so in a way which reproduces and strengthens the racial, cultural, gendered and professional hierarchies which are central organizing principles in British welfare institutions and practices. Moreover, even in its own more limited concerns to improve the quality of service delivery in a multi-racial society, a major problem arises because it restricts flexibility in organizational practice. This rigidity arises because once the 'outsiders' have learned the internal 'codes', 'values' and 'standards', no other adaptation is necessary. It is an effect of seeing ethnicity, culture and identity as fixed rather than contingent or relational categories.

Because of the link between professional common senses and social work practice it should be clear that there is more at stake here than a 'mere' conceptual struggle over the meaning and status that is attributed to cultural variation. Indeed any examination of such practice will reveal instances of the damaging effects of cultural translations premised on ethnic absolutism and in Part II of this book I explore some examples of the ways in which practice is shaped by such racializing discourse.

The struggle over how to conceptualize 'race' and ethnicity had as one of its central concerns the delivery of services to racialized sections of the population, especially in the inner cities. As we have seen, many working within the dominant paradigms saw the issue primarily in terms of how to ensure that local authority social services departments had an adequate understanding of 'ethnic minority' or 'immigrant' communities to ensure unbiased and 'ethnically sensitive' service delivery. However, I have argued that such service delivery was often premised on fixed, absolutist conceptions of 'race' and ethnicity with the result that the policies which were developed reinscribed black clients and social workers in racialized and gendered social relations.

Opposites attract: a meeting of minds in the conceptual pool

White policy-makers, managers and practitioners were not alone in viewing 'race' and ethnicity as fixed, essential categories and it is possible to trace a convergence of ethnic absolutist ideas in much of the literature emerging from the radical black critique of social work. This has been most clearly and forcefully presented in the writings and statements of the Association of Black Social Workers and Allied Professionals (ABSWAP) and especially those of the organization's founder and first president, John Small. ABSWAP was founded in 1980 and it is clear from reports of the founding conference that part of the motivation for the organization and its members was to reveal, confront and undermine the explicit and implicit racism in much social work policy and practice. In this sense they were part of a much wider tide of black activism which was aimed at fighting racism and promoting black liberation, part of which had the effect of challenging the existing dominant notions of culture and identity (see, for example, Bryan, Dadzie and Scafe, 1985; and *Feminist Review*, 17, 1984). This was also the moment when a wave of municipal socialism was adding a commitment to fighting numerous forms of discrimination and oppression both outside and, more importantly, inside the town hall and its departments, including social services departments. In this context ABSWAP did some vital and pioneering work in challenging the myth of the pathological black (Caribbean) family. Thus, they continued the political challenge to constructions of black family forms and gender relations as deviant and in need of welfare intervention. Importantly, ABSWAP also drew attention to the practice implications of the discursive underpinnings of policy. For example, Small (1989) writes:

the dominant construct [of the individual in society which operates in social work] excludes the black experience. . . . Consequently, concepts, definitions of situations and descriptions of events are seen purely from a white perspective. . . . Operating within this framework, the social worker uses professional techniques to bring the individual or family into line with the built-in assumptions and values of the dominant constructs. (pp. 280–1)

But this statement is also double-edged, for while it highlights the links between discourse and practice, it also has another effect. For in this enunciation there is an inherent opposition between the cultural forms and experiences of black groups and the primary place accorded the individual in social work knowledge (which here can be seen as being understood as deriving from western philosophical traditions). It is interesting because it repeats the notion identified earlier in Ballard's approach. Both writers uncritically accept the binary 'black/white' in which the one automatically and persistently excludes the other. There are fixed 'black' and 'white' experiences, understandings and perceptions of 'self', and no room is allowed for the possibility of shared understandings, correspondences of experience or fluidity of identity across group boundaries, nor indeed of heterogeneity within groups. Thus, despite quite profound differences between the two authors they are both occupying positions within the same discursive formation.

For Small, as with other authors associated with ABSWAP (see, for example, Maxime, 1986), this notion of fixed, mutually exclusive categories is particularly pronounced in their conception of identity. Basically they work with an explicitly racialized version of the Cartesian subject, which, given the 'right' environment, will grow into an adult able to express her or his unified and stable core. The only difference is that for Small the subject is black and this black subject is a coherent 'me' at ease with themselves and their people (race) only if their social environment is conducive to the development of such a 'raced' self. This is achieved through the

phenomenon of primary identification [which] consists of all the constructs of black people. These constructs are derivative of the conditioning process that they had in *their own* societies and families. They include ideas, the construction of events based on experience, beliefs and practices. In short they represent total being. They constitute a social whole, embodying the basic fabric of character and personality, in an integrated and coherent structure. (p. 280, my emphasis)

In referring to 'their own', Small reproduces the dominant and racializing idea that black is always already 'other' to British society. Moreover, in this formulation Small is silent on the links and disjunctions between processes of primary identification, recognition of a gendered 'other', splitting and the formation of an 'I'. His enunciation is one which posits a fixed and universal racial 'other' while occluding the possibility and place of a gendered 'other' in either psychic or social worlds. It was from a perspective such as this that ABSWAP was to launch a major attack on transracial adoption, and it is within this context that we see their conception of identity and its process of formation brought into play.

This point can be illustrated through a range of comments:

> black children growing up in white families fail to develop a positive black identity. Instead they suffer identity confusion and develop a negative self concept, believing or wishing that they were white, harbouring negative attitudes towards black people.   (Maxime, 1986, quoted in Tizard and Phoenix, 1993)

> The aim of adoption must always be to provide a child without parents a suitable environment to enable the child to develop normally. The commitment must be to the child, not the parents, nor the agency. When we address ourselves to a suitable environment for a black child the issue of the child's identity should be given priority above all other factors. Identity is paramount. [It is] only out of the appropriate integration of the black child's personality that a concrete identity can be formed. If a healthy personality is to be formed, the psychic image of the child must merge with the reality of what the child actually is. That is to say, if the child is black (reality) he must first recognise and accept that he is actually black (psychic image).   (Small, 1984, p. 135–6)

> The most important ingredients that contribute to a full integration of people are all the ways and habits that unify their world and give them a sense of who they are. If this is clear, then a constant picture of what they are and what they ought to be provides guidelines for conduct and behaviour. However, the conception of self by black people and the conception by white society is generally contradictory.   (Small, 1989, p. 288)

It is this purported dissonance between 'black' and 'white' conceptions, which in this view are always absolute and inevitable, that leads to psychic disorientation and subsequent mental ill health. As has already been said, care must be taken not to dismiss the realities of racism in British society which, as one of its effects, has led to an over-representation of African-Caribbean people in mental health statistics and institutions. Evidence of the relationship between racism and psychiatric misdiagnosis on the one hand, and racism and actual mental breakdown on the other, has long been documented (Littlewood and Lipsedge, 1982; Francis, 1993).

There is, however, a long distance between recognizing the effects of racism in both psychiatric and social work practice and arguing that a 'healthy' self-image and an 'integrated' identity are reducible to the single issue of 'race'; or indeed to arguing that 'black' and 'white' are fixed binary opposites. As Tizard and Phoenix (1993) have argued, such a position 'assumes that there is a black culture, quite distinct and different from white culture, shared by all black people, irrespective of age, gender, social class or place of upbringing' (pp. 36–7). In the ABSWAP perspective these other axes have no place either as sites of psychic formation, as sites of domination and power, or as sites of resistance. They are certainly indeterminate in terms of the construction of identities, the formation of which is seen as a once-and-for-all procedure, either of 'success' or of 'failure'.

Notwithstanding the Tizard and Phoenix suggestion of a more complex picture of identity, cultural forms and the politics of 'race', the ABSWAP position was sufficiently influential that by the end of the 1980s a new orthodoxy had emerged regarding the issue of transracial adoption and most local authorities had adopted a 'same-race' placement policy for adoption and fostering (Rhodes, 1992). This represented a triumph for various forms of ethnic absolutism as the basis on which social work policy and practice was to be formulated. General agreement on the part of policy-makers and practitioners about the existence and content of 'racial' or ethnic particularities could be seen as the starting point for ensuring that black staff were employed in social services departments. In this way ethnically determined 'needs' could be recognized and met. The transracial adoption and fostering debate could help bring the black staff model into full fruition. By the time the adoption debate was fully on its contentious way, recruitment of black people to social work courses and social services departments was proceeding in some areas, and the formulation of adoption and fostering good practice as being equivalent to a 'same-race' placements policy was one source of legitimation for such recruitment.

The black staff model

This model also contains essentialist categories but this time 'knowledge', or at least the cultural knowledge which SSDs need to access, is conceptualized as residing in the racialized bodies of particular 'types' of people. Thus, black staff were thought to ensure equality of service provision, free from racist or cultural misunderstandings, because they would be like, indeed replicate, their clients regardless of divisions of class, gender, age, locality or indeed even the professional/client relation. No learning process would be required because in the social worker/client encounter like will meet like. We have already seen this in the previous chapter and in the earlier Manning quotation, and we see it replicated in the following:

> It is hard to overestimate the importance of black staff if statutory agencies are to achieve the kinds of relationships with black communities which are necessary. Whether or not they are employed specifically in specialist or advisory capacities, their roles inevitably are multiple where white staff are uncertain about what changes should be taking place. (Connelly, 1988, p. 29)

Similar arguments for employing black staff in social services departments can be found elsewhere.[1]

Particularity of need is matched by particularity of 'knowledge', both of which are seen as being literally embodied in people constructed as discrete and homogeneous categories. As a result of this correspondence, service delivery to 'ethnic minority' clients will be improved. In addition, black social workers will be able to help undermine racist practice and attitudes within SSDs.

However, as Stubbs (1985) has identified, the extent to which black social workers are able to undermine processes which reproduce racism and be in the forefront of a challenge to existing ideologies of 'professionalism' is not at all clear cut. As he notes, the ability of black social workers to do just this is an open and empirical question, the answer to which must be found in relation to the interstitial positioning of black social workers between equal opportunities policies, ethnic sensitivity models and departmental notions of the 'good black social worker'. The 'good black social worker' is one who 'at best, poses no threat to the reproduction of racist structures or, at worst, actually aids their reproduction' (p. 17). Attempts by management and white social workers to position black colleagues in this way is inevitably a partial and contradictory process according to Stubbs. Thus, whilst the challenge to social work as a state apparatus may be limited, organized challenges by black workers may have more impact on changing both the SSD as an organization and the daily social worker/client interaction.

By considering the question of the employment of black social workers in this way, Stubbs moves considerably beyond the static approaches in the other professional literature considered here. However, what his approach fails to include is any acknowledgement that the black social worker might be a heterogeneous and ambivalent subject. It is only their positioning within discourse and social relations that is recognized as potentially ambiguous. The interiorization of these potential ambivalences and ambiguities as reflected in their subjectivities and identities is occluded in this view. The result is that Stubbs maintains his understanding of the black social worker in structuralist or organizational terms alone and in so doing constructs an idealized and homogeneous black 'community'. This undermines the strengths of his analysis, for it tends to foreclose analysis of division and ambiguity amongst this 'community'.

The limitations of a perspective which inscribes racial or ethnic absolutes and constructs needs as always already predictable should be clear, not least because the everyday dynamics of an SSD are such as to place people in multiple positions which may be in tension or contradiction with one another. For example, Gilroy (1987, p. 66) has suggested that the adoption of an ideology of ethnic absolutism on the part of black social workers and other professionals working in the personal social services provides a partial means by which they can negotiate the contradictions of working within local authorities. The extent to which this is the case is considered in the following chapter. At the theoretical level what is clear is that if the complexity of these fields of social relations is to be captured, so that differential needs may indeed be recognized and met without recourse to absolutes or prescriptive formulae, a reconceptualization is required. It is to this that I now turn.

A reconceptualization

Because the ethnic sensitivity and black staff strategies are underpinned by fixed and essentialist notions of 'race' and ethnicity, all the experience of racialized groups is understood as deriving from these modalities. 'Race'/ethnicity is accorded a foundational status structuring all experience and determining identity/subjectivity. In this view social work practitioners need to understand this so that they can ensure both that needs are met and that identities are stable and healthy. What this formulation misses is the profound sociality of 'race' and ethnicity. How 'race'/ethnicity is deployed to position subjects in relations of power, the contestations over the meanings given to ethnic difference, and the ways in which ethnicity may intersect with racism, gender, class or sexuality to structure experience are issues completely ignored by these orthodox conceptions. As an 'ethnicizing' discourse, 'difference' in the orthodoxy fails to be considered in terms of the complex of power relations within which subjects are constituted and within which ethnicity is inscribed. With the partial exception of Stubbs, the various positions outlined above entirely occlude these points.[2]

To develop an analytical framework which will allow social workers to recognize ethnic difference in all its complexity, but without being reductive or simplistic, we need to reconceptualize ethnicity as a social category which carries a multiplicity of meanings. The meaning attached to 'race'/ethnicity will vary and shift in the process of lived social relations. Brah (1992) has offered a conceptualization of difference which goes a considerable way towards providing an analytical framework which can capture this complexity. She identifies four referents encompassed by the word 'difference'.

1   Difference as experience. This focuses on the individual level of the 'everyday'. Importantly, and in stark contrast to the formulations in the orthodoxy, this is not conceptualized as a 'truth' but rather as a way of making symbolic and personal sense of the daily. It references in part the ways in which we construct 'narratives of the self' in an effort to integrate the multiple and fragmentary people we are.

2   Difference as social relation. This operates at the level of the social structure and collective experience and history. It relates to the way in which meaning is given to the struggles over structural, political and historical commonalities.

3   Difference as subjectivity. This relates to the psychic constitution of 'otherness' and 'self' in its racialized, gendered or sexualized modalities – that form of experience and self-understanding that much of the social work literature on 'race'/ethnicity cannot allow.

4   Difference as identity. This references the struggle over various modes of being in the world, the meanings given to those modes and the identifications of group belonging which are made from them.

To reconceptualize ethnicity or ethnic difference in this way offers social work (as policy and practice) the potential of using the concepts of 'difference' and 'ethnicity' in a way which is neither prescriptive, reductive nor technicist. It allows for the possibility of thinking about ethnicity as constantly in the process of becoming, being constructed within the complex interplay of personal, collective, structural and political experience and location. Our ethnicities – gendered, aged, sexualized and classed – can be seen as always in a state of movement, sometimes with one aspect more to the fore than others. What will be at play in any social worker/client encounter is not only the complex intersection of relations of power along numerous axes within which the client is positioned and which structure her life – but also the set of complexes which position and structure the social worker's life. Within the organization social workers are also constituted as ethnic, gendered, sexual and professional subjects. The factors which act to bring any to the fore in a given circumstance cannot be predicted or reduced to an assumed primary or foundational modality. They will always be inscribed within a set of social and organizational power relations and therefore contingent. Within an ethnically diverse geographic area and with a multi-racial team of social workers, 'ethnicity' is likely to be one of the major factors at play but it may or may not be the primary one at any particular time. As with other 'identities', the ethnic positions we occupy will be historically and, in the context of social services departments, organizationally and professionally contingent. How and when ethnic identities are foregrounded will be the result of the interplay of multiple 'differences' and the sets of power relations in which these are embedded. Moreover, people who are discursively positioned as sharing the same ethnicity may or may not take up this position, as will be illustrated in the chapters which follow. The point is that cultural or ethnic identity

> is not something which already exists, transcending place, time, history and culture. Cultural identities come from somewhere, have histories. But like everything which is historical, they undergo constant transformation. Far from being externally fixed in some essentialized past, they are subject to the continuous 'play' of history, culture and power. Far from being grounded in a mere 'recovery' of the past, which is waiting to be found, and which, when found, will secure our sense of ourselves into eternity, identities are the names we give to the different ways we are positioned by, and position ourselves within, the narratives of the past.   (Hall, 1990, p. 225)

Thus, we are both structurally located and actively occupy a number of subject positions open to us. We will also position those with whom we interact in those spaces we think fitting for them. This triple movement in processes of positioning occurs within the context of the multiple meanings invoked by the concept of 'difference' and serves to establish the terrain on which social relations are lived out. The task is to develop an analytical framework sophisticated enough to deal with this so that policy does not become prescriptive and damaging.

It is not that formal or informal policy and practice can be developed without cognizance of the modality of ethnicity. It is rather that there are no easy or prescriptive answers and that ethnicity is not a property only of racialized populations of colour. Resorting to a form of ethnic absolutism, either in the form of 'matching' social workers and service users, or in the form of identifying the 'real' causes of a service user's problems, only serves to reinscribe black, Asian and other people of colour in racialized social relations. It is precisely this complexity and 'messiness' that both orthodox social work theory and the approach adopted by some radical black professionals fail to address. In contrast, a determined and rapid retreat from the orthodox models of how ethnicity 'works' in social work is required if this complexity is to be grasped and addressed. The starting point for this is to consider the different forms ethnic belonging takes in different contexts, and how these forms intersect with other axes of identification and power *within* the organization. To begin this process is to begin to think about how the experience black women (and men) have of social services, either as employees or as service users, can be irrevocably altered for the better. It is also to lay the ground upon which recognition of differential need can be understood as part of the process for undoing relations of domination, not as part of the process of reproducing these relations.

Part II

Complex Acts of Becoming: Working 'Race' and Gender

In this second part of the book I extend the landscape of encounter be-tween 'race', gender and social welfare by analysing a series of accounts taken from the interviews I conducted during the research period. In particular I explore the complexities of the racialized and gendered world of the social services department that these accounts reveal and so bring into sharp relief the Manichean simplicities of those 'voices' we have already heard.

Writing of the imaginative limits and possibilities faced by the writer of fiction, Toni Morrison has stated:

> I am interested in what prompts and makes possible this process of enter-ing what one is estranged from – and in what disables the foray . . . into corners of the consciousness held off and away from the reach of the writer's imagination. My work requires me to think about how free I can be as an African-American woman writer in my genderized, sexualized, wholly racialized world. To think about . . . the full implications of my sit-uation leads me to consider what happens when other writers work in a highly and historically racialized society. For them, as for me, imagining is not merely looking or looking at; nor is it taking oneself intact into the other. It is, for the purposes of the work, *becoming.* (1992, p. 4, her emphasis)

The chapters that follow tease out some of the contexts and forms that such an act of becoming on the part of women working in social ser-vices takes.

5

'Evidence of Things Not Seen': The Complexities of the 'Everyday' for Black Women Social Workers

Introduction

In the preceding chapter I discussed the dominant professional discourses on 'race' and ethnicity and suggested that whilst these discourses had, in part, arisen as a way of responding to the needs of black client groups they had also had the effect of positioning such clients, and black social workers, in essentialized and fixed categories. This resulted in the reproduction of the 'othering' of these clients and social workers. As discourses they reflect and produce systems of meaning which constitute professional knowledges about racialized populations. In their turn these knowledges intersect with other aspects of social work knowledge. As such, these racializing discourses both influence practice and construct subject positions and systems of representations. In this chapter I consider the link between racialized representations of black clients and social workers and their impact on practice, and the disruptions to these representations which flow from the 'everyday' of social work practice. I discuss a small number of incidents which were recounted to me by different participants and which point to the ossifying tendency of dominant conceptions of 'race' and ethnicity which circulate in the profession of social work. This juxtaposition highlights the complex social relationships which are obscured by professional discourses on 'race' and ethnicity and yet which have to be negotiated in the daily working practice of black social workers.

Analysis and discussion

In this and subsequent chapters where I introduce accounts I have adopted the following method for organizing the participants' enunciations. Each new speaker is first identified by ethnic group, grade and departmental division. 'Ethnic group' as used here corresponds to that used in the 1991 Census and was adopted by the women themselves. The number at the beginning of each sequence of an account (1a, 1b, etc.) is the one referred to in the discussions. Where ellipses (. . .) are used it is to ensure anonymity, to indicate brief reinforcement from me or to indicate where the sequence has been cut for reasons of space. Italicized words or phrases in an account indicate that the participant has emphasized the word(s) or point.

Complex acts of becoming: four accounts

Account 1: Cultural stereotypes / management practice

This first account reports an event that occurred prior to the 1989 Children Act and centres on the effect of rigidly held assumptions on the part of a team manager about familial practices amongst populations whose origin or descent is Caribbean.
[Ethnic group: African-Caribbean. Grade: 'Senior'. Division: Children and Families]

1a

[G. L.] You talked about, or you alluded to I should say, some dissatisfaction around issues to do with staff or managers' attitudes, do you want to elaborate on that at all, especially if these were to do with 'race' or gender issues at all?
[Participant] There were a lot of those! I mean I can do. With my first manager in . . . she was very difficult. She was a white woman who had been a manager in the building for a long, long, long time . . . she was just really difficult and some days she would be OK and other days she'd just be extremely difficult and she had very racist opinions that she covered up, or tried to cover up . . . I can remember one case in particular where there was a particular child whose mother was suffering from domestic violence. The parents weren't married and she assumed the child was black which was an ongoing thing with her. It was something that, you know, I'd be correcting her about all the time. . . . Now on this particular occasion the child was taken on a place-of-safety order on one night by the police because the father had tried to strangle the mother and the child had been caught up in that web and somehow they'd incurred some injuries that were not describable, I mean you weren't able to explain them as being accidental, so the police removed the child and the following day we got the out-of-hours referral . . . after, the child was on the place-of-safety order and was put with a foster carer. Now the child had been placed with a black foster carer, now she [the child] was a white child, blonde hair, blue eyes and one of her questions [i.e. from the manager] the next morning was, I mean prior to this, oh, let me give you some background. Prior to this incident this child had been handled by a black woman

social worker who'd been suffering a lot of problems in the team for many years. She was another black woman whose post I had come into and covered as a locum because she had refused to come back to the team because there was a lot of problems that she'd experienced and she did not want to return there, em, that was part of the history to do with the team.

1b

[G. L.] That was around what year?
[Participant] This was, you're talking around '87, '88, near the beginning of the time when I first came in. . . . So this was the background to it, she had left and, apart from me who had just come in, there was only one other black woman on the team, erm, and what happened was that she [the other black woman social worker still on the team] had gone to this home address of the child and she had made an assessment visit and had recommended that this child be allocated to a black family because there were a lot of concerning issues. The child being left alone, you know, there were untold allegations being made against the mother, whether she was leaving the child alone, there was the violence from the father that had been reported on numerous times and there was a lot of concerns in terms of the child and that some support was needed. Now we never had any notification or confirmation that this child had been injured in any way there was just an awful lot of concern. Well, that can happen. Now this other social worker had gone, made the visit and recommended the child, er, the case, be allocated, meaning a full-time social worker working on the case with the family.

There are two main points I want to draw attention to at this point in the account. Apart from the way in which the participant retraces her steps in order to establish that she is giving an example of the ways in which 'race' and racism enter into case management, the speaker here immediately constructs an intra-group divide between black and white women by foregrounding 'race'. This is despite, or perhaps because, my question is concerned with difficulties arising as a result of 'race' or gender. This foregrounding of the terrain of 'race' and racism is in some senses emphasized by the language she uses to describe the child involved in the case – 'blonde hair, blue eyes' – which could be factual, but also invokes an emblematic representation of whiteness. It is also noticeable that at times the language used by the participant in these sequences evokes a matter of factness about the issues which social workers face – 'there was just an awful lot of concern. Well that can happen.' In the context where she is being interviewed by a black woman who is asking her to discuss her working life as another black woman this is perhaps not surprising but it does have the effect of highlighting the issue of racism that she wants to illustrate. Once she has established the focus of her account, in the next sequence (1c) the participant is able to convey some of the ways in which racializing discourse intrudes into daily work practice for black social workers. For example, she makes it clear that in the context of a 'lack of respect' for the work of another black woman social worker, a meticulous care to record all incidents and concerns arises. This appears to be partly motivated by a concern to pre-empt any undue criticism of her co-worker's work practice but in so doing the participant is also able to establish a high professional standard on the part of her colleague.

The account continues:

1c

[G. L.] This was after this particular out-of-hours incident?

[Participant] No, this was before it, I'm just trying to give you some background to it. Now, erm, another thing that used to happen is on certain cases, if this particular social worker, the black woman social worker, made certain recommendations they weren't always followed through and that was I think because of lack of respect for her work. Or thinking that she made too much fuss about certain things that she didn't need to. But she made notes of these concerns and she'd written them down, she'd made the assessment visit and recommended allocation. The case did not get allocated. Now I was a bit, like, I used to go and argue and say this should happen or that should happen, and on that occasion she'd made three consecutive visits and had recommended the same thing each time. Now I didn't know this and then she came to me and she said this is what's been going on, so I took the case on myself . . . cos I had a big mouth and I wouldn't just leave things if something came up I would try and do something about it. So I took it upon myself and I booked in an assessment visit to myself and I told the team manager this is what's gonna happen. I had to argue with her because she wasn't happy about that because it's supposed to go through the normal process and I said OK I understand what you are saying but she's made these recommendations and you've just totally ignored them. . . .

And I, erm, think, it feels to me too concerning to just be left like that and I'm not happy with what you've done. So I said I'm going to do the visit and, erm, I'll bring the case back to you. Now I went off, did the assessment and I came to the same conclusion – that the case had to be allocated urgently because it was getting, the situation seemed to be just getting worse . . . and she never did anything about it . . . and she made some remark about, erm, saying something, er, 'Oh it's what *they* do you know, it's just normal you know it's what they do.' I asked her what do you mean, what do you mean! She didn't say anything. And then she was talking to somebody else and she said: 'Well you know, West Indian families, you know it's not too unusual and I'm sure she's [the mother] able to put up with it.' That kind of remark! Well, I just flipped a lid and I said what are you talking about! Abuse and violence are not normal patterns of life, it certainly wasn't for me and I know a lot of people, etc., but anyway, so I made the recommendation that the case had to be allocated and, er, it wasn't allocated. Now I was going away, I think I was going to Nigeria or somewhere, I was going on holiday for four weeks, otherwise what I would have done is taken the case on myself and just told her that it had been allocated.

If racializing discourse on the part of the managers acts both to enhance professionalism and to produce a need for meticulous (and more onerous?) recording, this sequence also conveys a sense of combat on the part of the participant ('I used to go and argue and say this should happen or that should happen'), whilst simultaneously showing the urgency of the actual case. This in itself suggests an added level of complexity since the need to guard against racism is superimposed on the need for all social workers to ensure that every aspect of their statutory duty to protect vulnerable children is implemented. This sequence is also the point at which the speaker gives the first strong indication that as far as she is concerned the manager's approach to the case is mediated through a set of ethnicizing assumptions about the behaviour patterns of Caribbean families and the levels of tolerance 'West Indian' women have to violence. It is through this discourse that she constructs the meaning of the manager's (in)actions. In so doing the participant is able to establish that caseload management within her team is structured through forms of absolutist discourse. A more elaborated sense of this is established as the account continues.

1d

[G. L.] So you're saying that this was actually not a Caribbean family?
[Participant] *No! This is this same white family* but she's just assuming that certain patterns
[G. L.] that certain patterns
[Participant] yeah [laughter at the statement made in unison] she's just assuming and this was quite indicative of the way she used to behave. Now what happened was that, erm, I was going away and what I would normally do is just take the case myself and if she's gonna argue with me then we'll have the argument. But on this occasion I was going away the following week . . . and I said it needs to be allocated urgently. Now it was not allocated but she backed down a bit and said she would pend it for a period of time before it goes for allocation. So I said well on your head be it and I just left it at that, there was nothing else I could do. Then while I was away, three days before I got back, this place-of-safety order was taken out on the child with the unidentifiable injuries I described before. The mother had been beaten up and the child had got this bruising . . . The police removed the child and I said like why did this happen, sort of asked around and she [the manager] said: 'Well it's just one of those things', sort of brushed it aside and then there was a phone call that came through, because it was dealt with by the out-of-hours social worker, there was a phone call that came through that said, it was from Fostering and Adoption, that said that this child had to be moved because it was a mixed-race placement, the child was a white child, she'd been placed in emergency care with a black foster carer and so she had to be moved to a white foster carer because it's a same-race placement policy here.
   But I'll never forget her response when I told her about the phone call. At first she said: 'Well why does she have to be moved, you know she's with a black foster carer.' And I said what do you mean, she's got blonde hair and blue eyes just like you, I said you can't, she can't stay there and the shock that came on her face . . . and she went really red and everything, and I said, yeah she is, you

know, and she said, well 'why', because she had this assumption that as well, that because I am a black woman and because I argue certain things, I said I don't really care what colour the child is, I said if there are certain things happening that are wrong . . . it's my job to get certain things sorted out and, erm. But she said 'you were arguing certain things' and I said because there were a lot of concerns about this child and you were just totally ignoring what the other worker had said that is why I was arguing so much. But she thought I was arguing because it's a black child and I wanted the case to be allocated, you know which was dangerous.

Here it is clear that for this participant the daily workplace interactions were played out on 'raced' terrain. The interaction as presented here is overdetermined by the struggle over meanings between people who are positioned within racial discourse and occupy statuses defined by the organizational hierarchy. The participant constructs a narrative in which the senior person in organizational terms is eventually hoist on the petard of her own ethnicizing assumptions and the (apparently) poor practice which this resulted in. Moreover, the participant's triumphalism is carried in the tone of the account and indeed in her refusal to be located in an equally racializing black nationalist discourse – 'I don't really care what colour the child is' and her insistence on her professional concerns – 'there were a lot of concerns about this child'. The paradox is that despite this refusal she uses the 'same race' placement policy tactically in order to achieve her discursive 'victory'. This case demonstrates the implications for service delivery of ethnic absolutist readings or explanations of behaviour. Clearly readings of 'culturally specific' behaviour were being made on the basis of an interpretation of the 'rules' and 'codes' as constructed by a hegemonic discourse on 'race', the result being that such absolutist ideas structured both the quality of service delivery and the way in which the black women social workers were able to perform their jobs. A further example of ways in which racializing discourses structure workplace relations and practices is evident in the case which follows.

Account 2: Ethnicized needs / complicated belongings

This case concerns a young teenage woman of Caribbean descent who was being fostered by a white foster carer. She had previously been fostered by a member of her extended family in a mixed-race household where it was felt that her 'cultural needs' were being met. However, this arrangement was not sustainable over the long term and an alternative had to be found. The new arrangements were fairly complicated because it involved working across two local authority SSDs: the originating

authority, which remained the lead one and which had allocated the case to a black woman social worker (the participant), and a second authority where the foster carer lived. No black worker, female or male, was involved in the case from this second authority. This was experienced as a problem by the lead social worker (the participant) because she felt the interpersonal/interorganizational dynamics to be configured through the prism of racism. As far as she saw it the social workers in the second authority neither recognized nor had any interest in dealing with racially determined identity needs. Furthermore, the participant felt that the white social worker from the second authority who had daily responsibility for the case did not recognize, indeed undermined, her own (i.e. the participant's) professional judgement, mostly because of the latter's concerns about the young woman's identity needs. At the same time the apparent 'matching' in terms of 'race' between the black social worker and the young woman did not make for an easy relationship as becomes clear from the account. The account also shows that in contrast to the previous speaker the participant here constructs a narrative which positions her within an absolutist discourse. However, the two participants do share some factors in common. First, both display an acute awareness of the way in which racism structures their daily workplace interactions. Second, they both explicitly derive meanings about these interactions through racially differentiating discourses. Third, they both use these forms of discourse to position and challenge white colleagues.
[Ethnic group: African-Caribbean. Grade: Basic grade. Division: Children and Families]

2a

[G. L.] So you are the authority, really, you represent . . . [the lead authority]?
[Participant] That's right so . . . [the second authority] are doing it on our behalf, they have to check things out with us and that's the power that they don't like . . . I always have a very hard time, my team manager has accompanied me on a couple of occasions because I had such an awful time. The first time I went there I wanted the case transferred . . . I felt less than less, it was very bad, because I only saw white members of staff up there, there were no black staff in that particular office . . . it was very hard work and to have to tell two white male team managers and a white female placements social worker who represented the family that the child was placed with, and another white female social worker, *all* these white professionals, to try and explain cultural needs and identity, because it's a *black child we're talking about*, to try and explain that to them was very hard work and at the last meeting the situation, because I am the only one talking about identity and talking about cultural issues at the statutory review, the child turned round to me . . . she turned round to me and said: 'What do you want me to do – walk around in an African outfit!'. So this is the level, this is what I'm trying to explain to them, that there are concerns, what input is there for her, because she's currently placed with a white family. I'm not pleased about

that and . . . [the lead authority] has a policy that black children are placed with same-race placements where possible. I don't feel that . . . [the second authority] has made an effort . . . They know that I'm not pleased with her being placed with a white foster parent in an area where there are no black people . . . and because she doesn't know anybody, she's not going to seek them out, so issues of her identity which is coming through, different things that she says, and that was a classic for me. Now for me as a black worker that's ringing alarm bells, for the white workers it was a case of mockery, that's right you know, erm, you're seen as going overboard on this *black* thing, type of thing. So I felt very angry at that because this child is internalizing that all I do is go on about black issues, go on about identity all the time and I'm sort of trying to champion the cause. But it *has* to be prescriptive because she's not going to get it if it's not built into this placement that is *totally* inappropriate, with professionals who she's dealing with who are *all* white . . . if it's not put in a prescriptive way it doesn't happen at all and I have, I'm accountable to make sure that her needs are fully met, so because it's put in a prescriptive way it's seen as if that's *all* I do . . . and I can't convince the white workers, professionals supposedly . . . so how am I then going to convince this young person a long, long distance away, if I have to convince her social workers in the first place that she is in great need.

Here we can see an example of the use of a form of ethnic absolutism as a means to negotiate an extremely difficult work situation which is redolent with contradiction. The case also raises a number of issues related to the adequacy of the black staff model for ensuring equality of service delivery to multi-ethnic client groups. Moreover, it illustrates the contradictory effects of recourse to a discourse of ethnic absolutism. The strength of feelings which imbue this account illustrates sharply the immense difficulties which black social work staff may have to negotiate in their working lives. This in itself is suggestive of the limitations of the black staff model if it is implemented on the basis of a premise that the issues of 'race' and racism begin and end with recruitment of black and 'ethnic minority' staff. However, the participant's awareness of her own feelings and sense that her professional integrity is being undermined does not prevent her from constructing a concern about the client's identity within an absolutist discourse. Indeed, it is precisely the client's apparent hostility to, and distancing from, the speaker that legitimates the latter's identification of an identity crisis. There are very strong echoes in this account of the approach adopted by Small and others associated with the Association of Black Social Workers and Allied Professionals. Yet this notwithstanding, the account also illustrates that positioning within racializing discourse does not mean that the same identities are produced or that a 'raced' positioning cannot be disrupted by other, cross-cutting axes of differentiation and power – 'it's a black child we're talking about [and yet this black child] turned round to me and said: "What do you want me to do – walk round in an African outfit"'.

Here we get the sense that the process of identification with a racial 'same' broke down or was refused by the child in the face of a more powerful process of differentiation around the social worker/client axis.

Despite this, this participant is very aware that in so keenly adhering to the 'same-race' placement policy she is adopting a rigid and prescriptive approach to a job which does not operate with such certainties. Indeed, in some senses she constructs a narrative in which she almost wants to distance herself from any reductive or rigid approach to her work but is prevented from doing so because of the attack on her professional judgement and what she sees as the urgency of the girl's situation. Extreme situations such as this demand extreme responses – 'But it *has* to be prescriptive because she's not going to get it if it's not built into this placement that is *totally* inappropriate'. Having established this, she returns to her concern to validate her own professional authority and legitimacy as a way of resisting being reduced to a one-dimensional ethnic or racial entity – 'if it's not put in a prescriptive way it doesn't happen at all and I have, I'm accountable to make sure that her needs are fully met, so because it's put in a prescriptive way it's seen as if that's *all* I do'. Racial discourse acts both to underwrite her professional concerns and specific knowledges and to deny recognition of her generic social work skills on the part of her white counterparts from another SSD. Prescription arises, then, because of the logistics, professional antagonisms and diagnosis of the girl's needs. Ethnic absolutist discourse provides a way of mediating and surviving the tensions and contradictions of workplace relationships.

It is clear from this that recourse to such discursive terrain comes from the dilemmas arising out of a complex web of workplace relations. More generally, the conceptualization of 'race' and ethnicity embedded in this account raises a number of pressing theoretical and practical issues. First, the approach adopted here reproduces the persistent and damaging idea that black/'ethnic minority' communities are homogeneous and as such its members will share a common identity. Indeed, as I showed in the previous chapter, such an identity is regarded as evidence of mental health and adjustment by those who subscribe to this discourse. This in its turn helps to sustain the production of racializing discourse since the idea of homogeneity is central to the process of racialization and one of the mechanisms by which the 'otherness' of racialized populations is sustained. Thus, heterogeneity is constructed as a property of white people only. Third, the operation of any other axes of power in structuring the nature of the encounter between black social worker and black client is automatically occluded. Finally, at the level of the employment experience of black social workers, one of the consequences of a racialized basis for their employment is their marginalization and ghettoization. Their more generic professional knowledges and skills are denied because they are reduced to a bundle of ethnically derived (and therefore inherent) capacities.

Yet in terms of notions of cultural absolutes and fixed, coherent, if racialized, identities the case highlights the complex character of the social relations between racially differentiated people in the context of social work practice and within which professional identities are formed and reformed. At one level racism is raised as a central structuring feature of black social workers' experiences of the everyday routines of their employment. But it is equally clear that recourse to an ethnic absolutism does not offer any escape from the processes of racialization which worked to position her as a worker who is assumed to have limited professional skills. Indeed, far from undermining racialization the stance she adopted meant that she could only make a claim to professional legitimacy on racialized terrain. Similarly, her claim to 'insider' knowledge of the young woman's needs did not elicit a bond of identification between 'racial' or ethnic 'equivalents' but imposed the power of the local state official over the black client. Moreover, as Phoenix has noted, 'there need be no easy or automatic identification between individuals who share a gender or racial position' (1994), and whilst all the people in this example (white as well as black) were positioned within a racialized discourse and set of institutional practices, that two were black did not result in an automatic understanding or solidarity between the two. This was all played out on terrain mapped by a discursive formation in which 'race' and identity are seen as fixed, immutable categories and which took place in the context of (inter)organizational and professional imperatives. This illustrates well the limitations of a perspective which inscribes racial or ethnic absolutes and constructs needs as always and already predictable. The case illustrates the multiple, shifting and contingent nature of the identities which arise in the context of a social worker's caseload.

Account 3: Social worker / client 'matching'

These last points are further illustrated in the next case which is directly concerned with 'ethnic matching' between social worker and client. It shows 'ethnicity' at work but in a hierarchical organizational setting in which shared ethnic group positioning is fractured by other axes of differentiation and power.

[Ethnic group: African-Caribbean. Grade: 'Senior'. Division: Children and Families]

3a

[G. L.] So are you saying then really that management definitely have a view on 'race' and ethnicity? How would you describe this view?

[Participant] Their view is difficult to pin down and it always strikes me as being convenient because on that level they won't challenge black workers because they don't want to be seen as racist. But on another sort of level, a practice which is common is where white workers are working with black families and the case is complicated and the white workers feel or will say 'I think this family needs a black worker', but it is often convenient to get us to work with black families. The white workers can't cope really in that case. The contradiction is that for black workers they will be working with white families, very complicated cases because of the nature of the work and you get stuck sometimes, it gets difficult, because we can't say we think this family needs a white worker, what I'm saying is that white workers when they are stuck use us as an excuse, their whiteness to get out of work, and then it is said to black workers 'what it needs is a black worker'. Now that is quite convenient for managers, because managers are white yeah? . . . And they often agree with the white worker, that this case, that they are not getting anywhere with them, yeah? Whereas if you have a black worker take it, somehow you are expected to be able to work with them. . . .

White managers, white workers won't acknowledge or are even aware of these sorts of intrinsic sort of issues involved for black workers, professionalism and boundaries, how you negotiate relationships with black families when they see you as a befriending person, you are having to assert that you are a professional person and that it is a professional relationship.

Here we have the first suggestion of a solidarity being formed around whiteness. This indicates a shift from the predominant emphasis in the professional literature where solidarity on the basis of 'race', ethnicity or colour is limited to racialized populations of colour. In effect what the speaker achieves here is a 'racing' of the discursively 'non-racial' by explicitly positioning white workers within such a racial domain. She does this as a way of showing how white colleagues and managers avoid difficult issues by denying any 'racial' or 'ethnic' knowledge on their part. The account also makes visible ways in which being positioned within racial discourse complicates the work for black social workers in ways which are not at all recognized by managers. In her view the entry of black social workers into SSDs has not been accompanied by any understanding of the changed supervisory and managerial needs and demands which may arise. Having established this, the speaker elaborates the point by showing how similarity of position within racialized discourse is disrupted by being differently positioned in the social relations of social services departments.

3b

[G. L.] So there are professional pitfalls for black workers about professional boundaries, it's about . . .
[Participant] It's about how black clients see black workers . . . and how they want to see us, they don't want to see us as part of the establishment that they

see as oppressive. A black worker knocks on the door and they think they are going to get a different service and they do qualitatively but some of their assumptions about the kind of service they are going to get are actually wrong. The two most common things that we have problems with is black clients not expecting black workers to use the authority of the law in a way which challenges the parents because they associate power with white workers and white managers. . . . And what black workers are having to say to white managers is you keep dumping this work on us as in 'birds of a feather so there is going to be no problem'. Whatever comes up we can sort it out, so we don't get decent supervision around those issues because white managers haven't even begun to think about them, so we have to teach them what the issues are, let alone expecting to be supervised. Because of the nature of the work, you know, it is not certainty, there is a lot of uncertainty. . . . You know it's not – you do it like this and you get this result, and it's all about processes and communication. So, to come back to your point, I think it is difficult for us as black workers to pin down what white managers and colleagues think because it is changeable and it is convenient. What they definitely don't want is to be seen to be racist because they are so changeable and that is clear.

For this speaker the issue of non-recognition of professional authority becomes posed as black clients not expecting black social workers to *use* their professional power and status. This is in contrast to the formulation of a similar problem in the previous account where the problem was posed as one in which white social workers would not admit of their black colleagues *having* such professional power and status. Another point of contrast between these two accounts is that here the speaker explicitly highlights the uncertainties attached to social work and so indicates the inappropriateness of prescriptive case handling. Paradoxically it is through this that she is able to refer to the difficulties of working with white colleagues. Thus, mapped onto the prevailing common sense about 'ethnic matching', the lack of certainty and the inappropriateness of prescriptive formulae for handling cases are exactly the means by which white colleagues and managers can avoid confronting issues of 'race' and racism. A thread of commonality between this account and the previous one is that both women construct narratives which show the complexity of the webs of social relations within social work teams. What divides them is the ways in which they use racial discourse to understand these relations.

All the cases discussed so far have had issues of 'race' and ethnicity at their core but not in any simple or static way – a way which simply involves 'correct' cultural readings. Indeed what they indicate is that notions of 'correct' or 'insider' cultural readings provide the terrain on which white colleagues can avoid recognition and confrontation of racial dynamics within the SSD. These cases have illustrated that 'race' and ethnicity are inscribed within relations of grade and professional status which structure the social interactions within the organization. Ethnic identifications become disrupted both by the divide between professional and client and by that between managers and fieldworkers. These complexities are further illustrated in the case which follows.

Account 4: 'Same-race' fostering and adoption

This is also centred on the issue of 'same-race' placements policy in fostering and adoption. It illustrates the intricate web of interests and identifications which are at stake within an organizational setting where wider societal axes of subordination and dominance become articulated to professional and political agenda.
[Ethnic group: African-Carribean. Grade: 'Senior'. Division: Children and Families]

4a

[G. L.] Does the authority have an equal opportunities policy or an ethnic record keeping and monitoring policy?
[Participant] Yes ethnic monitoring . . . but they don't have a race placement policy but the practice and the ethos is same race.
[G. L.] So they have a guidance, so I see what you mean, erm, but no formal statements. Is that what you mean?
[Participant] Yeah, not around same-race placement. In their adverts they always say they are an equal opps employer, I don't actually know if they have got an equal opps policy but the practice is a bit different for example same-race placements for children.
[G. L.] What do you think about that?
[Participant] Well I have mixed feelings about same-race placement, . . . the rationale that the borough gives is that if they have a policy they have to adhere to it, and it is not always the right thing to do, and I actually agree with that, because there has been situations where we would have placed a mixed-race child. . . . There is one example. We had a teenager recently, sixteen, who is mixed race who wanted a white foster family, regardless of what we thought about that, her mother's white and she grew up with, in a lone white parent family, so that is her experience. Under the Children Act she can exercise those choices and that preference, I felt we should have honoured it. Black workers in the department blocked that, but the reason for not having a policy was precisely to allow that, mostly exceptional, practice be possible.
[G. L.] So the reason for not having a stated policy, a written formal policy . . .
[Participant] is because people think they would have to adhere to the rhetoric regardless of the child's entire need, that is the stated reason why they haven't got a policy.

This participant immediately establishes her ambivalence about same-race placement policies because she wants to be able to allow for flexibility in case management. In her account children's needs are constructed as variable and flexible and therefore she recognizes that a departmental policy needs to be able to accommodate this. Interestingly she also establishes a tension between legal entitlements of children looked after by SSDs and a rigid departmental practice. However, she goes on to construct social work (4b) as an occupation and social services departments as organizations, as complex sites in which a same-race policy might be important or useful.

4b

[G. L.] Right, OK, but because the practice is one of same race you are saying that you might feel slightly mixed about it, the case like the one you have just cited, where the desires of that young woman are legitimate and she has the right to say what she wanted?
[Participant] Yes, I think we should have honoured that . . .
[G. L.] and it was the authority-wide Black Workers Group who stopped it, not the local departmental group?
[Participant] Yes, and they have always blocked cases like that, or it has always been very contentious because they adhere to the rhetoric of black children must have black families. And the fear is that if they give in on those sorts of cases it will become common practice, so arguably if you have a policy you would avoid those situations. Do you know what I mean? Where people could feel safe. Because it is not common practice to undermine policy.
[G. L.] Right, right and did it cause divisions at all in the Black Workers Group?
[Participant] Em, no, no, it caused all sorts of feelings in the local black workers group who are mostly women but the Black Workers Group objecting to it was in another place, our adoption and fostering teams are in another building. So it caused divisions amongst – the case worker and manager was white – so it got polarized into 'this is coming to us, this request to us because of the white workers, whereas if you had a black worker she would have worked to get this dealt with, with a black family'. Oversimplified really.

It is clear that here the participant makes the issue of same-race policy more complex by distinguishing between starting points for thinking about such a policy. One view might be formed if the starting point is the complex 'needs' of specific children, whereas another view might emerge if the starting point is developing strategies for disciplining departmental racism in fostering and adoption policy and practice – 'so arguably if you have a policy you would avoid those situations'. However, to some extent the speaker has undermined this argument by referring to the black workers group as adhering to 'the *rhetoric* of black children must have black families' (my emphasis) – a terminology which acts to dismiss or reduce their approach. Moreover, she continues with this line of argument at the end of the sequence where she refers to the representation of the issues in terms only of a black/white split as 'oversimplified really'.

What is notable is that she both presents such a polarization and counters any suggestion of a homogeneous black view by differentiating between the team-specific black workers group and the Black Workers Group in fostering and adoption (to which I have given capital first letters). Again this suggests far more complexity to departmental relations than is allowed for in the dominant representations of 'race' and ethnicity in the professional literature. Moreover, in an earlier part of the interview (4b) where the speaker describes the 'race' and gender composition of the teams to which she refers, she makes it clear that all the members of the team-specific black workers group are women. This takes on a significance in the parts of the account which follow because it is clear that disagreements between black staff are also between black women and men. Thus she continues:

4c

[G. L.] So describe how this form, the practice in the absence of formal policy, affects the work process if you can.
[Participant] Well the process gets into personalities and it gets into who is going to challenge these black workers, white workers shy away from it because they don't want to be racist. And black workers don't want to be seen in open conflict with other [black] workers, so the process is very messy and personalized.
[G. L.] Yeah, um, so the splits that kind of occur . . . are very much along the lines of 'race', ethnicity, colour and so on. How do the managers respond to this?
[Participant] Well it is interesting because in that particular example it went up to the assistant director level, because there were all sorts of other issues that made this girl very, very vulnerable indeed, including environmental health issues, and what happened was that management was stating to the black workers at the adoption and fostering unit that under the Children Act this girl has a right to make these choices, that psychologically she can't cope with what we are saying she needs and therefore we should give her what she can use, yeah, and that we don't have to be shoving therapy down her throat that she is not ready for, it's a life process basically, but nobody would actually block the black workers because nobody was going to take the responsibility, so the Assistant Director wasn't prepared to take on this particular one and only black manager in the foster and adoption unit. So people just shied away from it and the view of black workers is that one day they [i.e. senior management] are going to leave it to a black worker to kick him off his pedestal basically cos white workers they complain about it.
[G. L.] Kick who off the pedestal?
[Participant] This bloke, black worker, yeah, because he is well into rhetoric.
[G. L.] Right, so the black worker, black manager who is responsible, he is the person who is saying that you should put this young woman into a black family?
[Participant] Yeah, and he's saying 'over my dead body will you do anything else'.
[G. L.] And the management said well there is the Children Act already and you have to look at her individual psychic development but nobody would override his authority, basically. Right?

[Participant] And it was an all-white professional network from the Assistant Director down to the basic-grade worker who was the child's social worker. The only black person involved in that process was that black manager, and nobody would actually say to him we are going to override you on this decision.
[G. L.] Messy.
[Participant] *Very* messy.

The constraining effects of forms of racial discourse and the ways in which they position subjects within them becomes very apparent in this part of the account. However, it also establishes that such racial discourse can have the effect of disrupting organizational lines of power and authority as exemplified in the refusal of white managers to negotiate a way through the complex issues of 'race' which were embedded in this case. In this way the speaker here repeats the point made by the participant in account 3 about the ways in which white managers and social workers refuse to tackle issues of 'race' and racism. Finally, in sequence 4d the participant returns to the complexity of such issues and establishes that there is no easy or simple correspondence between positions within discourse and social relations and the subjectivities and identities which get inscribed within them. Moreover, she establishes her own professionalism on the basis of just such a recognition.

4d

[G. L.] Is this common this kind of managerial response?
[Participant] Yes. I have known it happen, it happens always with mixed-race children.
[G. L.] Why is that, do you think?
[Participant] Because parents start saying they don't want their children placed with black families, em, mixed-race children saying they don't want to be placed with black families, and that always brings a certain amount of conflict. Because the practice is that if you are mixed race you go to a black family unless someone objects and says they don't want to, or if say those kids were placed with white families and the social worker thinks they should stay there. It causes conflict if they want to move them into a black family and for me that is where the contradiction is. You place a very, very young child who's black mixed race with a white family who then develops attachment and sees those people as parents and then in three years they want to chuck them out. My own personal, well my own *professional* view is that to a black child that *is* his parents in terms of attachment and that you can't just open this wide just because of the race element. But there are other things you can do to assist that family. I'm looking at the wider context of that child's needs, where they live, how you assess those carers in meeting that child's needs. . . . So arguably we shouldn't place them there in the first place but sometimes it happens that is all there is available at the time when they come into the service, they leave them there for whatever reason, and then we move them when it's too, when it doesn't make sense to the children. And they then spend time grieving the loss rather than accepting a new background.

In broad terms it is clear that this last case was being fought out on two analytically distinct but intersecting terrains. First, there was that of racial divisions between black and white. This divide overdetermined the case and provided for divisions of grade and authority to be subverted or subordinated to the more hegemonic division of 'race'. Second, however, there was the terrain of gender divisions among the black workers in the department. This is where the gender composition of the teams takes on importance since it was from amongst black women who were expressing opposition (albeit muted) to the position being articulated by the male black manager of the fostering and adoption unit. The result was that rather than grade and authority being subordinated to other agendas, they were being reinforced and, in so doing, re-articulating existing gender divisions amongst black staff within the department.

Individually and collectively these cases suggest that the play of 'race' and ethnicity within SSDs is far more complex and multifaceted than is captured by the hegemonic discourses of 'race' which circulate in the profession. The four cases demonstrate the diverse articulations of 'race'/ethnicity with other forms of social and organizational differentiation. All the cases illustrate the way in which issues of 'race'/ethnicity and racism act to structure the everyday of working life for black women social workers. Similarly, they all show that an understanding of this formed a framework through which the participants speaking here gave meaning to their 'experience'. However, what these accounts also illustrate is that whilst each woman was positioned within racializing discourse, their responses to such positioning varied. Thus, whilst some adopted an absolutist position as a means to negotiate the complexities of their working lives, others were more hesitant about such a position and spoke of a more nuanced response to the tensions and contradictions of life in the SSD. Together these accounts demonstrate the impossibility of a foundational or essentialist view of 'race'/ethnicity or one which abstracts these categories from the social and occupational formations in which such differences are enacted.

6

Categories of Exclusion: 'Race' and Gender in the SSD

Introduction

Since the 1970s the question of 'difference' has come to occupy a central place in much theoretical and policy debate. As I indicated at the beginning of this book, this is related to the confluence of two trends. On the one hand, the rise of feminist, black and other 'new social movements' raised important and challenging political questions about the character and effects of sexual, 'racial' and other forms of subordination which were not easily or satisfactorily explained by subsuming them under class analyses. On the other hand, the rise of post-structuralist approaches to social and cultural questions, particularly in their French or French-influenced versions, has also led to a consideration of the meaning and origin of difference. Despite huge variations within and between these various philosophical and political strands, they have provided the frame through which to explore the workings and effects of discursive and material processes that produce the inequalities which articulate 'difference' and within which social groups and individuals are implicated. Challenges to the forms of thinking, knowledges and practices which articulate sexual, 'racial' and other forms of difference have also provided the terrain upon which new political subjects and constituencies have been formed: subjects and constituencies whose status was not primarily determined by, or expressive of, class relations and whose constitution facilitated a more complex understanding of the dynamics and contradictions of the social formation. The constitution of this widened array of political subjects and constituencies also heralded the emergence of new 'experiences', new versions and understandings of the 'lived', which hitherto had been unrecognized, subsumed under class relations, or in other ways marginalized. 'Difference', then, has provided both a terrain of analytical investigation and an enunciatory position from which those who were previously silenced could construct a place from which to speak.

These developments led in their turn to increasing attempts to theorize difference. As might be expected some of this work has drawn on psychoanalytic notions of difference – that is as primarily sexual difference – and have sought to understand the effects of this form of psychological difference on the construction of subjectivity, desire, ambivalence and 'otherness' (Rose, 1996; Alexander, 1994). 'Postcolonial critics' seeking to analyse forms of racial difference (see, for example, Bhabha, 1983; Mercer, 1994) have also drawn on psychoanalytic theorizations of difference and the constitution of the 'other'. Two further strands have helped propel the analysis of difference to the fore of recent intellectual and political debate. At a more philosophical level, there have been attempts to theorize the question of difference in terms of the ambiguities of meaning and the 'excess' of language (see, for example, Lacan, 1977; Lyotard, 1984; Derrida, 1978). At a more directly political level, there have been attempts to theorize difference as social location and experience (see, for example, Mohanty, 1992; Brah, 1992; Weeks, 1996; Scott, 1992; Braidotti, 1989). Lying somewhere between and across these last two strands in the theorization of difference have been attempts to link the construction of difference as social location to normative and normalizing processes and practices in specific institutional and policy arenas (Foucault, 1979; Saraga, ed., 1998).

Within feminism these developments have been accompanied by attempts to theorize the very terms and concepts which lie at the heart of feminist critiques of the social and psychic organization of relations between women and men. Distinctions have been drawn between 'women' as a term referencing the experiences, social locations and political projects of a range of historically constituted and embodied subjects, and 'Woman' as a discursive category connoting binary distinctions between 'the feminine' and 'the masculine' and other signifiers of sexual difference. Similarly, concepts such as 'sex', 'gender' and 'experience' have become subjected to vigorous interrogation as to both their theoretical implications and their empirical referents. In the following chapter I focus on the question of 'experience' as a category for mediating the 'everyday' of black women social workers' working lives. Having begun to explicate the complex deployment of racial discourse in SSDs in the previous chapter, here I want to turn my attention to the categories of 'gender' and 'race', and the 'differences' each connotes. In particular, I explore the ways in which these two categories were deployed in the accounts of participants and situate this exploration within the context of debates within feminism about the status and implications of sexual and 'racial' difference. My aim in linking theoretical

(and political) debate with empirical work is to draw out a mutually productive exchange between attempts to theorize categories of analysis –
such as 'representation', 'meaning' and 'identity' – and analyses of the
ways in which these categories are 'lived' by embodied subjects in specific contexts. In this way I hope to explore further the complexity of the
social relations which were simultaneously constituted and constituting,
and which also provided the vectors through which the 'lived' was articulated at a particular moment in a specific organizational context.

The chapter is structured around a discussion of two accounts – one
from a white, English area manager; the other from a black, Caribbean-
English team manager. In each of the two accounts the woman speaking
uses her 'self' to illustrate some specific aspect of the 'livedness' of her
working life in a social services department. In the course of these
accounts the women carve out a speaking position within which they construct categories of 'gender' and 'race'. Their 'self' becomes the terrain
upon which these categories are constructed and, moreover, they construct their 'selves' in a way which reproduces binary thinking and reinscribes them within mutually exclusive categories. But their enunciatory
positions do not construct a single binary in which sexual or 'racial' difference is signified, but rather both at once. They thus provide us with
useful material through which to consider the extent to which the 'self'
offers fertile soil for the development of critical (and politically committed) analysis: 'Images of the self arise from the "livedness" of the
interaction of individual and social and then return as a critical tool to
analyse and cut into the specificity of the social formation' (Probyn, 1993,
p. 29). Thus, the accounts considered here allow us to explore two questions: those which arise from theoretical debates about the ontological
and epistemological status of 'women', 'Woman' and those of sexual and
'racial' difference; and those which alert us to the complex social
economies which comprise and articulate the everyday of social work
and which show that analysis of this complexity cannot be satisfactorily
achieved if only one axis of differentiation is privileged.

Feminism and sexual and racial difference

I want to begin by tracing out some of the lines of debate about the
meanings and implications of 'difference' for feminist political projects.
Some of these lines have already been signalled above, but I want to
elaborate a little some of the issues which impinge on the focus of this
chapter. Its title, 'Categories of exclusion: "race" and gender in the SSDs',
is meant to convey an ambiguity about its precise content. This is because
the idea of gender and 'race' as categories of exclusion refers to two sets
of overlapping but distinct things. First, it refers to the ways in which

these two terms reflect attempts to capture in language the materiality of the social relations of power organized around differences of sex and colour/ethnicity, etc; that is, that those who are seen as having the characteristics (assumed to flow from biology) of inferiority or lack of some kind are then sutured into positions of social subordination and exclusion. Second, it also refers to the ways in which, as two clusters of social relations, 'gender' and 'race' are, almost without precedence, *talked* about as if they are mutually exclusive categories; that is, most of us act and talk as if when we are talking/thinking about gender we are talking/thinking *only* about relations between men and women, whilst when talking/thinking about 'race' we are talking/thinking only about relations between black people and white people, or people of colour and white people. Constituting the terrain of investigation in this mutually exclusive way then results in a further, though unspoken, exclusion – or rather another level of condensation – in which 'gender' is understood as having something to do with a homogeneous category called (white) 'women', whilst 'race' is assumed to have something to do with an equally homogeneous category called (black) 'men'. The effect of this is that the double binaries of sexual and racial difference become codified into the single divide between (white) women and (black) men. Now, of course, in many ways in saying this I say nothing new, and the fabulous and evocative title of the 1982 edited volume from the USA, *All the Women are White, All the Blacks are Men, But Some of us are Brave* is a clear example of this. That this has been said for some time now neither detracts from the fact that it still needs saying nor, more importantly, that some very hard work is required to undo both the common sense of this position and its re-articulation in analyses of the everyday of social life.

Feminists have responded to the theoretical, empirical and political closures which this type of thinking has led to. These responses have varied in their focus. Some have attempted to widen the empirical and referential horizons of 'womanhood', extending the meanings of the term 'women' beyond the narrow scope of 'white, western women' whilst holding onto a notion of 'Woman' as a social and discursive category which is constructed in binary relation to 'Man'. 'Woman' in this context is comprised of a whole array of 'women's' social condition and experiences – 'She' is produced out of (an ever-growing) assemblage of 'she's'. Sometimes overlapping with, sometimes in opposition to, this orientation, other feminist approaches have wanted to delineate and make explicit the specificity of condition, identity and experience of particular constituencies of women – black women, lesbian and/or queer women, working-class women, Arab women, Jewish women, etc. Despite the variations in their stated projects, each of these approaches carries with it, implicitly or explicitly, a deeper philosophical or theoretical question about the points of connection between the two sets of meaning con-veyed by the categories 'race' and 'gender' outlined above. This, in its turn, raises difficult political questions about how feminists can develop forms of theoretical and strategic interventions into aspects of the social world in a way which exposes and undermines the reproduction of 'dif-ference' as so many forms of inequality. In short, this has required feminists to tackle the thorny questions of difference and inequality *among* women. For example, Rosi Braidotti, who, following Luce Irigaray, understands sexual difference as the 'fundamental theoretical problem of the century' (p. 92), poses the issue in this way:

> 'difference' thus presented refers primarily to differences *between* men and women, [but] this heterosexist frame of reference is not exhaustive. 'Dif-ference' refers much more importantly to differences *among* women: differences of class, race, and sexual preferences for which the signifier 'woman' is inadequate as a blanket term. Furthermore, the problematic of 'difference' points to another layer of related issues: the differences *within* each single woman, meant as the complex interplay of differing levels of experience, which defer indefinitely any fixed notion of identity.   (1989, p. 93, emphasis in original)

Whilst this formulation expresses the complexity of the problematic of difference, it also leaves unresolved precisely those questions Braidotti raises. First, what are the implications of multiple dimensions of difference for the construction of the category 'Woman'?; and, second, what are the implications of the quest for an ontological 'Woman' for dealing with the array of differences among and within women? For Braidotti, it is precisely through the explication and recognition of the latter that the former can be established. That is, through an under-standing of the conditions and experiences of concrete, 'actually exist-ing' and embodied females, 'Woman' can be brought into positive being, rather than constructed through the notion of lack. This is, in part, what Braidotti means by sexual difference being the issue of the century and it is this that lies at the root of her notion of the feminist political project. But she recognizes that there is no necessary correspondence between 'being a woman' and 'thinking as a feminist woman', and that, therefore, the feminist political project will be obstructed unless it rises to the challenge of 'how to connect the "differences within" each woman to political practice which requires mediation of the "differences among" women, so as to enact and implement sexual difference' (p. 95). This, then, is how Braidotti seeks to construct a unified and coherent political project which can be alive to the array of 'differences' among women.

Braidotti clearly offers a sophisticated exposition of the problematic but I still wonder whether her formulation of the issues and the project does not lead to the construction of a primary mode of difference, into which, ultimately, all other forms of difference become assimilated. I am also not clear as to the extent to which her particular vision is made possible by a specific social condition and set of experiences and is thus limited in its capacity to evoke the range of conditions and experiences of women whose embodiment and subjectivity have been produced by the operation of axes of difference other than sexual difference. Finally, questions arise about the correspondences which can be found between this macro-project and the configuration of the issues in micro-contexts. These are the issues I want to try and think about through an examination of the two accounts which follow, and in so doing I want to slightly reformulate the issues. In this sense, then, we need to think about two questions: on the one hand, about how we have constructed the domains of gender and 'race' (and by extension the social relations of inequality they apparently reference) and, on the other hand, about how we might reconstruct these domains/categories in ways which begin to undermine their assumed empirical and methodological mutually exclusive character.

What I would want to argue is that the political and analytical place that we need to move towards is one where we understand the categories of 'race' and gender as *always* mutually constitutive, even when the language of one (or the other) is foregrounded. In other words, that in racially structured capitalist patriarchal societies, *each* of us is always constituted as a racial and a gendered (and classed, etc.) subject and that our analytical categories have to be able to hold and reflect that. The ways in which this process of mutual constitution occurs will, of course, be context specific – and in this case this is the organizational context of the social services department. However, if 'gender' and 'race' are mutu-ally constitutive categories and processes of becoming, their operation must also be implicated in the production of relations of inequality *within* their referential constituencies as well as between their normative protagonists. In this sense I also want to consider the extent to which the enunciatory positions adopted by differentiated categories of women – here understood as empirical subjects – also involve them in the consti-tution of relations of difference among women and therefore reinscribe them in relations of subordination and domination within the single category 'Woman'.

Speaking women

Let me begin to elaborate these points by considering extracts from two accounts. I have given the women the names 'Annie' and 'Shirley'. Annie was an area office manager and so was at the third tier of management within the organization. She was responsible for three teams of social workers. Shirley was manager of one of these teams, placing her in the fourth tier of management, with Annie as her line manager. Most of Shirley's work involved the direction and supervision of her teams' case-loads, with her own caseload being restricted to those cases defined as particularly difficult or sensitive. Both the extracts are taken from sequences of talk which occurred well into the interview, when both of us had relaxed and gained a flow of interaction.

'Annie's' account

[Ethnic origin:[1] White. Grade: Area Manager. Division: Children and Families]

[G. L.] How do you think differences of 'race' and gender reflect themselves in this area office?
[Annie] Well, I have not been here very long, but I think there are issues around gender, certainly, in that there are two female [team] managers – 'Bianca' and 'Shirley', who are both black – and a white, male team manager, and he is acting up into the deputy post, and I certainly would say I like Bianca and Shirley a lot. It is not that I don't like 'Richard', but I feel more comfortable with women anyway and I am conscious that as a group of three women we combine together to somewhat undermine and get at Richard. [She laughs.] I don't know why I am laughing, and it is not funny and not good, shocking really. It's no better, so if you can do that to one person you can do that to another.

Yes, it's not good, but we do it, and within that both those two women are very competent, very good workers, and there is something about this that is very good for me and although this isn't my permanent job, I am able to swan around and be area manager with team managers, um, and although I haven't thought about it until just now, but *there is this sense of it is like having a better posses-sion, a better car* . . . and part of that is of course not about the fact that they are good workers, but it is that added dimension of good workers who are women and are also black, it is like *you have got the icing on the cake.*

'Shirley's' account

[Ethnic origin: Black Caribbean. Grade: Team Manager. Division: Children and Families]

[G. L.] So tell me then, how do, how does 'race' and gender work here?
[Shirley] I was just thinking, um, when I was talking about the qualities in women, it seems what I perceive is that largely speaking that women have the ability to pick up very minute details which sometimes are overlooked by male workers, who might look at something from the way, from a very factual point of view, rather than from an insightful, experiential point of view, er. A woman might well, say, describe how a mother and child had interacted with her, and the details

of the description might be to do with eye contact, voice level, you know, um, I might not necessarily hear that from a male worker, so in terms of overall perception the perspectives are quite different [because] of our experience as carers, um. What I find men are very good at is the dialogue with other professionals and presenting us in court, and with that kind of confidence of working with outside agencies . . .

The other amazing thing is that in my team there is a social worker who is probably nearing fifty, and he has long, grey hair and he wears jeans and denim jacket and he goes to court like this, no black worker, whether woman or man, could go to court like this and not be criticized, however this white worker has this particular style of his that says this is me and I am not going to change, and he is a very good social worker, but he doesn't feel the need to conform . . .

[G. L.] So you are saying that all this refers to women [as carers, as nurturers, etc.]?

[Shirley] No, I was particularly thinking about black women.

[G. L.] But don't white women tell us that they are also brought up to do all those kind of nurturing things, er, so where does 'race' come in?

[Shirley] I was going to say that it is that thing that is missing with them, that added layer to black women's lives that enables us to be much more insightful, I feel, I feel that if anything the one thing we do have in common is the experience of racism, and it is something that affects every aspect of our life, child rearing to professional, and somehow there is this common belief amongst us that is not necessarily explicit in talking and I suppose that is a problem, that we can recognize and be familiar with, and that we can actually be quite undermining [to each other] so that given that I'm a team manager, that my status might well be more powerful than say a social worker, and that is very difficult for them to accept. We have this thing in common, because there is this connecting umbilical cord, we should all be on the same level.

If we deconstruct these extracts I think they suggest some interesting points about the intersection of gender and 'race' as categories of difference through which experience and identity are constructed and, indeed, deployed.

Let us take these in turn.

Annie begins her response by establishing the organizational positions and the gender and 'race' of those she directly manages – i.e. her team leaders. Having done this, she immediately moves on to construct a gender divide between the three women on the one hand and the man on the other, and in so doing she erases the differences of grade between herself and the other two women. She is acutely aware that as a *management* practice the marginalization she refers to is, at the very least, dubious – but she does this in a way which in her narrative establishes a kind of unity among the women. However, in the next paragraph she immediately begins to undermine this unity within 'the gendered same' and she does it, first, by re-establishing the women's respective locations within the organizational structure – thereby establishing the black women's hierarchically subordinate position. This then allows her to invoke a sense of 'ownership' of these women, which, in discursive mode, we can suggest is highly racialized in that it constructs a chain of association back to slavery. In so doing she enacts 'racial difference' and constitutes herself as a white woman without ever explicitly mentioning it. Therefore, we can deconstruct her account in terms of its constitutive effects and how she deploys notions of gender and 'race' which speak to and enact 'difference', which (re)constitutes unequal social and organizational relations. She constructs herself as both a woman and, albeit more implicitly, white.

Let us now turn our attention to Shirley. This speaker does not begin her account by foregrounding structural locations within the organization but rather puts the issue of gender at the front of her opening remarks. She uses the notion of gender as a category through which to 'explain' differences in the style of working amongst men and women in her social work team. However, she quickly moves on to the issue of 'race' and suggests that this has a twofold relevance for our discussion. First, in the context of the work of social work, gender differences are of a secondary order, and, second, whiteness (at least), or white maleness, has an internal and external organizational effect which expresses itself as a kind of 'freedom' denied any black people. The ambiguity about whether it is 'whiteness' *per se*, or more specifically 'white maleness', which is the determining factor raises unresolved questions about how she sees the relative importance of 'gender' as a structuring principle for white people's subjectivity and experiences in comparison to those of black people. Nevertheless, having pushed 'race' to the foreground she then holds onto it in two ways: first, when she specifies that it is *black* women who, for her, have the specific qualities – qualities which derive from the experience of racism; and, second, when she talks about the effects of the construction of black experience as singular and homogeneous. This she says often leads to the expectation on the part of black colleagues that black people in more senior positions within the organization will not, and should not, impose differences of authority which accompany their location within the organizational hierarchy.

I would argue that these extracts are interesting and revealing because they exemplify two things. On the one hand, they illustrate the complex interweaving of 'race' and gender as categories of 'difference' which mediate experience and shape how individuals interpret their experience. On the other hand, they are demonstrations of the way that people often speak *as if* they are just talking about one set of unequal relations – one axis of 'difference' – at the very same moment as they constitute several such relations. Gender and 'race', then, can be thought of as 'metalanguages' (Brooks-Higginbotham, 1992) – i.e. languages which carry, yet mask, the embeddedness of these categories in a variety of axes of differentiation and subordination. The task, therefore, is to think through ways in which we can be alive to this complex interweaving and not generate analyses and/or strategies which reproduce either the common sense that these are discrete or additive categories, or which work to position any one axis of difference as *the* primary one.

Constructing gender / constructing 'race'

The first thing we need to establish is that 'gender' and 'race' are constituted categories which are always in process – that is they are always in the act of becoming; and again feminist work provides a good starting point. In particular two theorists from the USA have provided us with the tools with which to begin disrupting this process of analytical separation and/or primacy.

One, Joan Scott, addresses the definition of gender; while the other, Evelyn Brooks-Higginbotham, addresses the issue of 'race' as a metalanguage. In their distinct ways each of these writers is concerned with the meaning of terms which lie at the very heart of questions of 'difference' and which have provided the nodal points for the articulation of new political subjects and collectivities. They provide useful starting points for my own analysis because they help us to understand 'gender' and 'race' as processes by which fields of intersecting 'difference' are constituted. Let us look at how they frame the issues. Joan Scott (1992) writes of gender in the following terms:

> The core [of my] definition [of gender] rests on an integral connection between two propositions: gender is a constitutive element of social relations based on perceived differences between the sexes, and gender is a primary way of signifying relationships of power . . . [This second part might be] rephrase[d] as gender is a Primary field within which or by means of which power is articulated. . . . Established as an objective set of references, concepts of gender structure perception and the concrete and symbolic organisation of all social life. To the extent that these references establish distributions of power (differential control over and access to material and symbolic resources), gender becomes implicated in the conception and construction of power itself.   (p. 42 and p. 45)

Whilst Evelyn Brooks-Higginbotham (1992) writes of 'race' in this way:

> Like gender and class, then, race must be seen as a social construction predicated upon the recognition of difference and signifying, the simultaneous distinguishing and positioning of groups vis-à-vis one another . . . Race serves as a 'global sign', a 'metalanguage', since it speaks about and lends meaning to a host of terms and expressions, to myriad aspects of life

that would otherwise fall outside the referential domain of race. . . . Race not only tends to subsume other sets of social relations, namely, gender and class, but it blurs and disguises, suppresses and negates its own complex interplay with the very social relations it envelops. It precludes unity within the same gender group but often appears to solidify people of opposing economic classes. Whether race is textually omitted or textually privileged, its totalising effect in obscuring class and gender remains.   (pp. 253 and 255)

It is immediately clear that there is some variation in how these women construct their arguments since Scott tends to reproduce the analytical and methodological separation of gender and 'race', whereas Brooks-Higginbotham wants to show how 'race' as a language of the everyday masks yet *contains* other axes of difference. Yet I think they both begin to provide us with some of the tools we need if we are to enhance our ability to think simultaneously through these categories as we try to explicate the processes by which difference, and the inequalities and subjectivities it constitutes, is reproduced. In similar ways both these authors offer an opportunity for deepening our understanding of the play of both gender and 'race' and in so doing make these categories more conceptually complex. They challenge us to try and hold the complex interplay among diverse axes of differentiation and subordination by suggesting that as categories of analysis 'gender' and 'race' must be understood as vectors through which complex webs of power relations are articulated.

They achieve this precisely because they attribute a multidimensionality to these categories. Thus, for both Scott and Brooks-Higginbotham 'gender' and 'race' are *constitutive* of difference, rather than just reflective of it. As such, these categories are *implicated* within and *expressive* of power: they mask other social relations in the very same moment as they carry and reinflect these other relations, and therefore, in understanding these categories (social and analytical) as relational, we must see this relationality as multifaceted rather than simply binary. This is an approach to sexual and 'racial' 'difference' which captures more of the 'lived' complexity which was expressed in the accounts of Annie and Shirley and in those considered in chapter 5. Indeed, a review of these extracts illustrates why a more complex understanding of the articulation of 'race' and gender and other axes of differentiation and subordination is necessary. It is perhaps within black feminist, and black feminist informed, analyses of the complex operations of intersecting relations of subordination and power that a way of thinking which enables the approach indicated by Scott and Brooks-Higginbotham to be furthered has been developed. This is summed up in the idea of 'simultaneity of oppression'.

In an overview article of black feminist analyses, Rose Brewer (1993) has identified the following propositions as being at the core of what she calls black feminist theorizing:

1   critiquing dichotomous oppositional thinking by employing both/and rather than either/or categorizations;
2   allowing for the simultaneity of oppression and struggle; thus
3   eschewing additive analyses: race + class + gender;
4   which leads to an understanding of the embeddedness and relationality of race, class and gender and the multiplicative nature of these relationships: race × class × gender;
5   reconstructing the lived experiences, historical positioning, cultural perceptions and social construction of black women who are enmeshed in, and whose ideas emerge out of, that experience; and
6   developing a feminism whose organizing principle is the interaction of class, culture, gender and race.

This distillation of the key principles of a particular feminist perspective is helpful in that it begins to provide the schematic shape for analysis of unequal social relations. Moreover, it does so in a way which allows us to hold in view the various dimensions through which these inequalities manifest themselves: as social position, as lived experience, as discursive constitution.

However, where it is more limited is in its suggestion that this approach is and *can only be* limited to a particular group of women, the single defining feature being that of occupying a subordinate *racial* position, albeit one enmeshed with these other axes of subordination. The effect is to suggest that it is only where women are the *targets of* racism that the notion of simultaneity is appropriate and as a consequence reproduces its own Manichean vision.

In contrast to this I would want to argue that an approach rooted in the idea of 'simultaneity' is one which can and should be applied to the analysis of all (in)equalities issues and that indeed this is the logical position which emerges from the extracts we considered from Annie and Shirley – that is, that where white women are the subjects of analysis, issues of 'race' need to be centred as a key category of analysis alongside those of gender, class, etc. Similarly, where black women are centred, issues of gender need to be foregrounded alongside those of 'race', class, etc.

This, in turn, requires an approach in which 'dominance', as well as subordination or oppression, is seen as part of the complex web of social relations in which we are all entangled – that is, we need to see the subjects of oppression/subordination, at least potentially, as also and simultaneously constituted in positions of dominance/power.

Thus, a multiplicatory approach to the intersection of 'race', gender, class, etc. will be understood as meaning that a person or a group can, within specific contexts, at one and the same moment occupy positions of both *subordination and dominance.*

We see examples of this in the extracts from both Annie and Shirley:

- Annie was in a position of dominance both as a white person (in fact she actively so constituted herself) and as an area manager, but in a position of subordination as a woman and as a manager at the third tier of the organizational hierarchy.
- Shirley was in a position of dominance in organizational terms as a team manager (and perhaps in the wider world this would translate into a position of relative dominance in class terms), but she was in a position of subordination in organizational, gender and 'race' terms.

It was this complex interplay of simultaneous *subordination and dominance* that was both evoked and deployed as the means through which these women gave meaning to and negotiated their organizational life. Moreover, their accounts suggest that it was in the dynamics of the everyday interactions within the organization that these contradictory positions were constituted.

It has been my argument that an understanding of this process of mutual and simultaneous constitution of gender and 'race' needs to be incorporated into the analysis of organizations and the development of equalities strategies. In saying this I am not advocating an organizational restructuring in which the specificities of particular forms of differentiation and difference are occluded and merged into one homogeneous and marginalized cluster. I am arguing, however, for a perspective which moves beyond binary thinking (and the closures this leads to) and enables us to hold the idea that processes of differentiation are *mutually* constitutive. Therefore, where we see subordination we must also look for dominance, and this latter may reside in the 'changing same' as well as the 'other'. To succeed in developing this kind of theoretical starting point, the focus of our analytical gaze must be the culture of the organization. For as Janet Newman has reminded us:

> The informal organisation may continue to transmit cultural messages about the 'proper place' for women: and a gendered hierarchy . . . may be sustained and reproduced through cultural messages. . . . Other informal hierarchies are held in place alongside those of gender. Culture is the site where, for example, the wider ideologies of racism and homophobia become lived out in organisational discourses and practices. Interventions which stop at the level of the formal organisation (for example the pro-

duction of new policies and procedures) are, as a result, likely to be limited
in their effectiveness. (1995, p. 11)

Newman is right to point to the ways in which the culture of an organization may produce and sustain a range of inequalities. I would argue
that 'culture' in this context should be understood as the array of policies, practices, representations, structures and customs of interaction
between individuals and units within the organization. Thus, I would
want to argue for an expanded notion of culture operating here so as to
encompass the formal as well as the informal dynamics. I would also
suggest that to think of multiple systems of social hierarchy being reproduced *alongside* each other limits our capacity to grasp the interaction
among forms of social inequality. Instead we should conceive them as
being reproduced *in* and *through* each other in mutually constituting
ways. It is the articulation of different forms of inequality which collectively make up the organizational formation and structure the 'everyday'
of organizational interaction. We are impelled towards this form of conceptualization by the data considered in this and previous chapters. From
the *Hansard* debates down to the accounts of individual women, we have
seen how gender and 'race' are mutually constitutive categories, even
whilst, as metalanguages, their mutual imbrication is obscured. In this
vein, 'race' has circulated as a metalanguage within and across the political, professional and organizational structures and converged to create
the opportunity for black women to enter qualified social work. Connections with other axes of differentiation were occluded in this racial
discourse, which simultaneously positioned its objects/subjects in fixed
and homogenizing categories.

These points take us back to the constitution of 'the other' and the
philosophical and political question raised by Braidotti about how to
create the conditions in which a positive recognition of difference can
be achieved. Braidotti's project is the constitution of an ontological
and political constituency, 'Woman' – a constituency which has as its
foundations the multiple differences of experience and condition of
'women'. The move from 'Woman' to 'women' means that 'difference'
itself becomes an expanded category in two ways. Difference is not conceived as signalling only the boundaries *between* gendered beings, but
also the differences *within* the group positioned on one side of the binary.
Similarly, difference, in this view, also signals the differences within the
individual *self*. As we saw in chapter 2, it is precisely the repudiation
of differences within the self that provides the psychic mechanisms by
which 'the other' is constituted. Through mechanisms of splitting, pro-
jection and displacement, 'the other' within is expelled – made abject –
and so provides the content around which the boundary of self/other is
formed.

The constitution of difference is, then, multiple not just in the range of experiences and relations it signals (gender, 'race', sexuality, disability, age), but also in the sites and processes which produce it. As the feminist psychoanalyst Jessica Benjamin (1995; 1998) has argued, coming to terms with and embracing difference (and 'the other') is both a psychic and a social project: a project of *self* recognition and transformation as well as one of cultural and political transformation. It involves commitment to the challenge of intersubjectivity 'in which one goes beyond identification to appreciate the other subject as being outside the self' (1998, p. xiii).

The accounts considered in this and the previous chapter illustrate well both these dimensions of self and wider cultural transformation. The social services context which structured and mediated the enunciations of gender and 'race' point to the enormity of the task if SSDs (and by extension other local authority departments) are to be able to facilitate the internal and external recognition of difference. It would require an abandonment of the discursive orthodoxies which circulate the department, since these construct stable boundaries around individuals and groups who are assumed to have fixed, coherent and homogeneous identities. At present, the organizational culture precludes reworking of the discursive categories through which 'race' and gender are conceptualized and constituted. As such this culture limits the extent to which individuals and groups can recognize 'the other' in the self, and the self in 'the other'. This suggests that attention must be paid to the micro-social contexts in which 'race' and gender difference is constituted if a more fluid conceptualization of identity is to be achieved. One step towards this is to analyse the ways in which self and 'other', gender and 'race' are mutually constituted within specific contexts, even while their form of enunciation proceeds as if they are mutually exclusive. In its turn, this requires a theorized approach to the category of 'experience' and the ways in which this category is deployed as a way of giving meaning to everyday interaction in specific contexts. It is to this that I turn my attention in the chapter that follows.

7

Situated Voices: 'Black Women's Experience' and Social Work

Introduction

Prior to the emergence of multiple forms of difference becoming a central concern for feminists, the issue of 'experience' was a key concern. In the post-1960s era, white feminists in Britain and the USA discussed how consciousness-raising groups had the effect of historicizing individual circumstance and individual experience (see, for example, Wandor, 1990). By sharing the content of 'everyday life', that which had been understood as individual was gradually and collectively understood as deeply embedded in a web of social and cultural relations which were themselves rooted in historical change. 'Experience', then, was understood as collective and social: 'the personal as political'. This new understanding led to the highly problematic notion of a global sister-hood organized around an appeal to a unified 'woman's identity'. This unified 'woman' was not the 'Woman' Braidotti wants to call up. Unlike Braidotti's 'Woman', the universal 'woman' of this moment of feminism was not comprised of the multifaceted and complex differences which characterized the heterogeneity of women's condition. As a result, black and third-world women, white working-class women and lesbian women protested at this totalizing definition and began to point to differences amongst women. The outcome of these emergent critiques was that the content of 'women's experience' began to be disassembled, which in turn meant that the authority of white middle-class women to construct a singular and hegemonic 'experience' was profoundly challenged (see, for example, Carby, 1982; Parmar, 1982; *Feminist Review*, 17, 1984).

These challenges notwithstanding, the *category* of 'experience' was not rejected by black and other feminists. As a privileged site from which to speak, and so constitute oneself, the category was appropriated for a different content and with an oppositional purpose. As feminist writings by black women on both sides of the Atlantic proliferated (see, for example, Bryan, Dadzie and Scafe, 1985; Grewal et al., 1987; Sulter, ed., 1990; Choong et al., eds, 1991; Smith, ed., 1983; Anzaldua and Moraga, eds, 1983; Lorde, 1984; Jordan, 1986), the constitution of a 'black women's experience' was well under way. Embedded within many of these writings was a notion of claiming a 'voice': a position from which to speak. This 'speaking' was necessary if the specificity of 'black women's experience' was to be articulated and a claim to a self-defined womanhood made. Such a claim had been denied by white feminist texts because of their exclusions and (perhaps unconscious) claims to universality.

At first the category itself remained unchallenged and unproblematized, not least because at this point the explicit turn to post-structuralist theory had not yet exerted its influence on much of black British feminism. However, there is more behind the tenacity of the category 'experience' than the relative impact of theoretical developments. Rather, the endurance of the category is testimony to its tremendous *political* importance and the power of its challenge to dominant epistemologies. For, in creating a legitimacy to speak *from* experience, feminists (black and white) had made it possible to begin to undo established ideas about what it means to 'know'. This, together with the adoption of some post-structuralist insights such as the category of 'the subject', cast new light on, and raised new problems about, the ways in which social categories and the social/psychic selves which inhabit them are constituted. Those who had formerly understood themselves as 'individuals' could now cast new meaning on their lives and think themselves anew as historically constituted 'beings'. They could now become alive to their *gendered* selves as arising from the genesis of individuals and a collectivity. That the formation of individual and collectivity was now understood as deeply interconnected was itself a radical gesture, for dominant epistemologies have tended to separate 'individual' and 'collective' in ways which articulate numerous inequalities. As Patrick Joyce (1994) has pointed out in relation to class:

> In many regards we are still Engels' children, not least the most sophisticated students of the historical formation of subjectivities, [who are] alive to the complexity of textual positioning of subjects, but borne down by the leaden weight of an obsolete view of class *in which 'individual' is the sign of 'middle class', a 'collective self' that of the 'working class'.* (p. 86, my emphasis)

Whilst the divide between self-knowledge as individual or collective is here a result of class, in the twentieth-century feminist context we can add 'race' as the axis along which this divide is organized. As Nell Painter (1995) has commented, when transposed to the black/white binary, this becomes rewritten as white people having psyches while black people have community. So if white middle-class feminists in the USA and Britain discovered through a collective process that they are constituted as individual selves and from there celebrate what they deem to be a universal sisterhood, black feminists (people) are denied any such individuality (which the notion of psyche suggests) from which to so 'discover' themselves. Those with an 'always already' 'community' are denied the very element from which such processes of identification are made. And, as we saw in chapter 4, the construction of racialized groups of colour as without individuality reaches far beyond the domain of the feminist.

Once the issue of what it means 'to know' is established as a site of contestation, the requisite broadening and deepening of the content of 'knowledge' and 'experience' can be seen as only part of the issue. As a result, if in the early years the sociality of 'experience' began to be accepted, some twenty years or more later, feminists (white and black) in these two national formations (Britain and the USA) have begun to problematize and theorize the category 'experience', to examine its ontological and epistemological status, to see, indeed, how it may be used in politically committed intellectual work.

This necessitated consideration about how to theorize the category of 'experience'. Two US-based feminists have turned their attention to this – one white (Joan Scott), the other a woman of colour (Chandra Talpade Mohanty). Beginning with a profound sense of opposition to the foundational status of experience in much academic (and feminist) work, where the category is constituted as 'uncontestable evidence and as an originary point of explanation – as a foundation upon which analysis is based' (1992, p. 24), Joan Scott argues for a historiography which would reveal the connections between the experiences of different groups, repressive mechanisms and the inner logics by which difference is relationally constituted (p. 25). This requires a problematized notion of experience, one in which it is recognized that

> It is not individuals who have experience, but subjects who are constituted through experience. Experience in this definition then becomes not the origin of our explanation, not the authoritative (because seen or felt) evidence that grounds what is known, but rather that which we seek to explain, that about which knowledge is produced. To think about experience in this way is to historicize it as well as to historicize the identities it
> · produces.   (p. 26)

Here, then, the very category of experience is established as in need of examination, so that the web of historical relations in which all experience is inscribed is brought to the fore. In this way, it is possible to reveal not only the binaries, the boundaries, the closures and erasures which are produced, in time and space, but also the subjectivities and identities which it is possible for specific social groups to inhabit in specific places at specific times.

'Experience' is widened, deepened and embedded. While Scott addresses herself to historians and cultural theorists, Mohanty directs her attention principally to white feminists. Writing in a similar vein to Scott, but earlier and with more explicit emphasis on political imperatives, as well as intellectual ones, Mohanty argues that 'experience must be historically interpreted and theorized if it is to become the basis of feminist solidarity and struggle, and it is at this moment that an understanding of the *politics of location* proves crucial' (1992, pp. 88–9, my emphasis).

Inspired by Adrienne Rich's work (1984), Mohanty uses the term location '. . . to refer to the historical, geographical, cultural, psychic and imaginative boundaries which provide ground for political definition and self-definition' (p. 74). Her concern with the 'politics of location' is derived from her project (shared with many black feminists) to challenge the singular and unitary notion of 'experience' such that it is at once constitutive both of the individual *and* of the collective. Strategically it is the key to understanding that '. . . the experience of being woman can create an illusionary unity, for it is not the experience of being woman, but the meanings attached to gender, race, class, and age at various historical moments' (p. 86). Hence the need to 'locate the politics of experience'.

Both Scott and Mohanty suggest that the way to theorize experience is to concentrate on its historical specificity and excavate its embeddedness in webs of social, political and cultural relations which are themselves organized around axes of power and which act to constitute subjectivities and identities. Without such a problematizing of experience, the binaries, exclusions and erasures which are embedded in it cannot be deconstructed and thus challenged and transformed.

Part of this task involves an analysis of when and how the category of 'experience' is mobilized. This entails an excavation of the location of specific speakers within multiple systems of subordination – those of class, 'race', gender and, indeed, sexuality. One writer who has been concerned with explicating the positions black women occupy in multiple and simultaneous systems of oppression is Barbara Smith, the black lesbian feminist literary critic. Indeed, it is from Smith's pioneering work that Brewer (1993) elaborated her components of the 'simultaneity of oppression', referred to in the previous chapter. Smith emphasizes the need to locate the contexts through which fictional texts by black women authors can be read. For her, black women's position was inexplicable in a framework which conceived of systems of oppression as either discrete or hierarchical.

A Black feminist approach to literature that embodies the realization that the politics of sex as well as the politics of race and class are crucially interlocking factors in the works of Black women writers is an absolute necessity.   (1982, p. 159)

And as she was to make clear in another, more polemical piece, the systems of class, 'race', gender and sexuality had to be understood as intersecting and giving rise to a simultaneity of oppression.

More recent work by Mae Gwendolyn Henderson (1992) has adapted Smith's idea of 'simultaneity of oppression' and taken it in new directions. She offers an inspirational approach to the examination of the discourses through which black women constitute their multiple selves, give meaning to the content of their lives and define the parameters within which their experience is produced and lived. As Henderson says: 'black women speak from a multiple and complex social, historical and cultural positionality which, in effect, constitutes black female subjectivity' (1992, p. 147).

Henderson moves from a recognition of the complex embeddedness of 'black women's experience' to a conception about how black women create a position from which to speak (and write), and the discourses which it is possible to discern in their speech (writing). She begins by suggesting that both 'raced' and gendered perspectives, and the interrelations between them, structure the discourse(s) through which black women speak/write. This she refers to as the 'simultaneity of discourse'.

By using this concept, she argues, it is possible to hold onto the notion of black women as at once 'raced', gendered, classed (and sexual) subjects and thus that they are both ' "Other" of the Same, [and] also . . . "other" of the "other(s)" ' (p. 146). The discourses which are simultaneously embedded within – and serve to structure – black women's speech/writing produce relationships of both difference and identification. This means that black women will speak/write 'racial difference within gender identity and gender difference within racial identity' (p. 145).

Whilst this refers to processes of interaction within and between socially constituted groups in which 'othering' plays a central role, Henderson is attempting to get to another dimension as well. This is the constitution of 'self' that occurs through the simultaneity of discourse. Thus, she suggests that the complex multiplicity of black women's positioning results in the discursive production of a 'self' in which 'other[s]' are always present. Black women's selfhood, and the speech/writing through which this is constituted, necessarily contain both a 'generalized "Other" ' and ' "otherness" within the self' (p. 146), and in the accounts which follow we can see these processes at work.

Critical examinations of how black women in Britain use the category 'experience' to give meaning to the web of relations in which they are inscribed and of the multivocality which this produces are scarce. This chapter is based on interviews in which black women social workers talk about experience as a way to make sense of, and give meaning to, their working lives. It discusses some of their views on the links between 'black women's experience' and social work as a practice; and then considers what conclusions might be drawn about the category 'experience' when 'race' and racism are vectors in the constitution and negotiation of power relations. More specifically, their voices arose in response to two inter-connected questions. What, if any, are the particular skills or attributes which black women can bring to social work; and why are these important. There was a high degree of repetition of the major themes around and through which the women constructed their specificity as black women. These themes centred on 'oppression', 'struggle', 'coming through against the odds', all of which were presented as particular to black womanhood and all of which conveyed a sense of 'otherness' within as well as external to the self.

'Sisters chant: I struggle therefore I am'

I want to argue that the meanings which these black women social workers constructed about both themselves and their work were produced on similar discursive terrain to that which Henderson identifies in the works of African-American women writers. The processes of identification and differentiation, the implicit use of historical memory, the acute awareness of diverse and subordinate social positionings, are factors which it is possible to trace in the accounts that follow. All of these are located within the context of what might be termed an 'occupational situatedness' which defined the parameters within which the women were speaking. Their construction of 'self' and meaning is cast within (the ever-present) shadow of their paid employment and as such they draw on professional discourses in which a 'fit' between 'black women's experience' and the 'nature of social work' is posited.

As in chapter 5, the accounts are numbered sequentially, and at the beginning of each one the speaker's ethnic origin and grade is given in brackets. Again 'ethnic origin' follows the women's self-identification within the categories adopted in the 1991 Census.

Account 1

[Ethnic group: African-Caribbean. Grade: Team Manager]

1a

[G. L.] OK, and do you think there are any particular skills or qualities that black women can bring to social work?
[Participant] [a big nod] I think we have the experience in terms of having to survive, in terms of whether it is limited housing, with our parents growing up, the areas we live in because, yes, we can move on after you get into the job situation you know, ... we have got all those experiences of having to cope with those problems repeatedly, whether it is going to school or wherever you go to, and having to speak up for yourself, and be heard and be counted, and I think that in social services that's what we are paid to try and empower.

Already there are a number of interesting factors being brought into play here. There is the *immediate* invocation of 'experience' as the privileged element defining black women's specificity, but importantly this experience is situated in a social and geographical space where having to cope with a variety of problems is foregrounded. Moreover, the necessity of survival is linked to the creation of a speaking position – a struggle to be recognized – and although the speaker acknowledges that social or occupational mobility in adult life can result in an individual moving away from these circumstances, the early experiences are privileged as being formative, and it is these which correspond to the tasks of social work. The purported link between what she sees as black women's experience and the purpose of social work is elaborated and re-emphasized as she continues.

1b

[G. L.] So you are saying that there is an experience?
[Participant] Yeah, that if you stand up and be counted and speak up for yourself and what you need, and don't give up, and I need to keep repeating it, I think that is what you do with a lot of clients, you know, with their poor housing or whatever else ... you know, you are trying to get them not to just accept things if they are not happy with it, and they feel uncomfortable with it, speak up, and a lot of it is also about the experience of grandparents, so we've experienced a wider idea of family, and the fact that it doesn't damage you. You know some people think that if you don't grow up with your mother and father you are damaged for life, a lot of black people have grown up that way and it hasn't damaged them.

Apart from the repetition of the themes concerning empathy with clients which derives from their similarity of experience with black women, the need to 'speak up', and the nature of social work, the speaker also begins to imply a critique of one of the dominant ideas in both psychology and social work about the place of the biological mother and father in the development of the 'healthy child'. This in turn prefaces a challenge to the pathologization of Caribbean family forms in what follows:

1c

[Participant] So it is a different way of thinking being brought into social services, of what they will teach you at the college, and what others at the top, which is white, tend to think and you know, you can actually give those experiences out to people. A lot of clients will come in and say, well, have you got children or whatever, and I say, well even if you don't have children, you have been a part of, whether it is your cousins or whoever, you have been a part of them, whether you take the responsibility to take them to school or whatever. . . . You have had that experience, but when you look on it, a lot of white people don't, because, em, there *are* white people who deal with the extended families and they strive on that, but there are a lot of them that are so sort of, em, just take responsibility for the immediate one and so not that broader sense of responsibility.

Here the speaker is making a claim for a different form of knowledge, thus giving 'black women's experience' an epistemological status born of its location in a specific body of people. Such knowledge can be imparted to clients, thus replaying the idea that part of the function of social work is to 'improve' or strengthen 'needy' or 'deficient' clients. Here she also explicitly racializes 'black women's experience' by foregrounding the opposition to what she purports to be the predominant approach of white people to family relationships and responsibilities. It is also done in such a way that familial experience becomes recoded as an issue of responsibility. In racializing, she also explicitly works with the binary and plays the opposition 'white/black' – a move which is highlighted by the exceptions which she invokes. Moreover, in the opening sentence of what follows, her sense of a need to be cautious about making too broad generalizations is undermined by the emphasis which her disclaimer gives to her main point.

1d

[Participant] I mean I don't think that is putting black people on a pedestal, but I think it's, you know, talking to people irrespective of ages and so on and in terms of caring and sensitivity, again I don't know whether it is because we have cared for so many people, you know whether we know them or not, sort of like, generations gone past, that again we have put out our hands a lot easier than some white people.

This part is important because of the move which is made from individual experience of diverse family forms and differential positioning within contemporary socio-economic relations, to an emphasis on an historical location in modes of caring. This intergenerational location is then used to make the claim that 'we' are more emotionally generous and have a greater propensity to care. The distinction which has been made between caring *for* and caring *about* (see, for example, Grimwood and Popplestone, 1993; Dalley, 1988) is not made here, but the speaker's reference to the intergenerational relation to caring and to the notion of strangers or 'non-kin' ('whether we know them or not') would suggest that here she is highlighting the 'caring for' aspect. Earlier it is clear that both forms are referenced. What is equally noticeable is her invocation of the historicity of black women's experience, a factor which she emphasizes when asked to expand on the issue of intergenerational relations.

1e

[G. L.] Could you expand a bit more on the second thing that you said, about the generations of caring for lots of people? What do you really mean by that? [Participant] It's actually in terms of that we are people, who, whether we have done it through history or through books or whether we have done it through posters or music or whatever, but we have actually to some degree identified with people who have fought for causes, whatever you want to say, and we have identified, some to a lesser degree than others, and we have identified this with people who are not living right in front of us now . . . so you are not blanketed into 'I can only understand what is happening in 1994 on the 3 May', you have this other wider bit, em, it's difficult to say.

Processes of historical discovery, which are also processes of identification, are foregrounded and this has the effect of reworking 'experience' into a kind of consciousness of connection and positionality. In so doing the sociality of experience is emphasized, but it is also politicized since the sense of historical connection and continuity is actively constituted through the process of excavation and reclamation of those who have struggled for 'causes'. Moreover, this sense of historical connection to 'fighters' is important for social work because knowledge of such genealogical connection helps create a key resource for dealing with the stresses associated with the job. Hence:

1f

[G. L.] Why is that important for social work? [Participant] Social work is a *very* stressful job and if you don't have that capacity to sort of, em, for that sort of tension, because the tension builds up, and you can relieve it because you have different ways of drawing in on things, you know, and if you don't have that then you will burn out and it will get to you quite quickly and you need that capacity to come into work, not say: 'Oh I'm going home and never coming back'. It's like hard to say, it's like you can think of a lot of things, but like. [G. L.] No, I understand, but is it something particular to black women, then, these two things that you describe?

[Participant] In terms of my involvement with working with people, whether it is FSU [Family Service Unit], in social work or whatever, in terms of how people react to situations, how they cope with stressful situations, maybe going out to a client who is shouting off, threatening or whatever else, in terms of coping with these things, I see a difference, you know, in the way people come back [to the office] and it's with them for life. I'm not saying you shouldn't be concerned about your personal safety, but that you have to be able to deal with it, and put it in some kind of perspective, otherwise, em, then you just see those people sticking to one thing, and only happy dealing with people they have met before, you know, and you can actually see that happening even in terms of new workers coming in and welcoming and that sort of thing. Again maybe it is because a lot of black people have had to go in situations where they have been the only one, sometimes they can welcome people on the other side like going in and with the white workers, say if I am on a course, and the majority of the time I am the only black manager, we haven't got that many anyway, and you will be there, and you will have to talk to them first. If I go on a course with the majority of black people, or a meeting and a few white people come in, then we make them welcome, and it is the same in teams, that sort of thing, students come in, whoever they are, it is that and that sort of ease will help you with clients.

There are a number of interesting moves here. First, is the way in which the speaker accords to black people a general level of ease with, and civility towards, white people, even whilst she constructs a hard boundary between black/white in her use of the words 'people on the other side'. The divide between black and white is also sharply made in her inference to the invisibility of black people to white people, compared to the visibility of white to black. Such invisibility/visibility can be read as both reflective and constitutive of the organization of social relations along axes of 'race' in which 'black women's experience' is partially embedded. Her talk of visibility is also organized around a notion of 'minority', which though referred to in numerical terms in the examples she cites, is also predicated on an implicit conception of minority as a social position ascribed by some marker of differentiation. To see this more clearly we have to read between sections of the account. Thus, if white people find themselves in a situation where they are a numerical minority, they will be welcomed by black people. In contrast, because black people will often find themselves in the minority position, they will have an aptitude for dealing with difficult situations which is 'with them for life'. The speaker's use of the ungendered term 'black people' is also notable given that she is responding to the question about black *women*, but, as we have seen, Brooks-Higginbothom (1992) notes that 'race'-talk often acts as a metalanguage through which other axes of power, which organize social relations and construct positions, are at once spoken and masked.

The discursive resources our speaker mobilizes to give meaning to various sorts of interactions which social workers might find themselves in are then expanded to suggest that the combined result of 'experience' and historical identification act to produce people with a greater capacity to cope with stressful situations. This differential capacity is exemplified in the ability to place potentially dangerous situations in a wider context. Though not stated, the chains of association which are embedded in all of her account include the potential threat of racial and/or sexual assault, which black women always face. This threat is embedded in the psyches of all black women in Britain, but this does not mean that they are incapacitated by this potential. Understanding these dangers, together with historical consciousness of the struggles waged by predecessors, not least in anti-slavery and civil rights struggles, means that the range of threats one might encounter in the course of a social work day takes on a different dimension. Herein lies the importance and relevance for social work, because having staff with this capacity has implications for how workloads are managed, stress is dealt with, and interpersonal relations organized.

It is clear, then, that the idea of a 'black women's experience', rooted in historical and contemporary relations, acts as a powerful discourse through which the benefits to social work are constructed. It shifts away from any simple idea of ethnic matching between client and social worker as being the way to deal with the requirements of operating within multi-ethnic populations. This shift is achieved because the speaker in this account uses her argument to suggest that the strengths which such 'experience' produces in people who have undergone it are impartable to all clients and other staff. Moreover, the characteristics of the clients of social work are such that it is not just black clients who need these skills, but all or most of them. Employing black social workers can thus act as a resource for the whole department and all its clients.

Having said this, the language in which she gives her account accords to black women's experience an ontological status which is in part undermined by her suggestion that its usefulness for work with clients is racially non-specific. For if such an experience is shared across sections of the black community and across generations, one would expect the survival skills, which she says flow from the experience, to be present amongst black clients. This contradiction arises from her focus on the usefulness that social services departments can derive from *employing* black women as social workers, and thus she seeks to stress their specificity in these terms. That there is an unproblematized category called 'black women's experience' is the ground on which she makes the claim to specificity, a claim which would be undermined if she had to begin to explore its points of discontinuity among black women. Such constructions and contradictions raise interesting issues which I want to return to; here, though, I want to note the slip between 'black women' and 'black people'. Because this slippage is a frequent occurrence throughout the accounts, and indeed sometimes in the formulation of my own questions, from now on I draw attention to it by marking the words 'women' and 'people' in italics. I want now to explore whether similar discourses can be found in the accounts of others.

Account 2

[Ethnic group: African-Caribbean. Grade: Social Worker]

2a

[G. L.] And do you think there are any particular or special qualities or skills that black women can offer social work, specifically black women?
[Participant] Yeah, em, I think [short pause], I think personally because this authority sets up so much things against black *women*, I think for a black *person* to actually reach the level of being a social worker and attaining qualifications, they have demonstrated already the amount they have to offer, because they have had to fight off so much things, you know, to start with. But thinking more of myself, yeah, I think I have a lot of understanding of you know, em, oppression and, you know, and can, my strongest quality I would say, is being able to enhance people, because I think I had to do that myself, and I just like to sort of do that, I just think we are strong. I think black women are strong and we are fighters and we will work with a particular case, we will ultimately want to do the best for them.

2b

[G. L.] So where does this strength come from that you are talking about?
[Participant] I think it's like, sort of like, fighting everything that is against you, you are fighting the sexism, you're fighting and you know you fight a lot of things within our own community as well, in terms of our male partners or whatever, in terms of parents, or children, or whatever, we do a lot of things on top of, our role is not just, you know, it is, even from the social worker, outside of work I have so many other hats that I wear, you know. I just think it is more like the oppressiveness predominantly from the white society and structures and whatever.

Apart from a general repetition of the major themes already encountered in the first account, some of the differences in the language used here are interesting. For example, the structure of address shifts from the detached, second person singular, 'you', to the first person plural, 'we', and in so doing this speaker begins to construct a community. Again the thread which binds this community centres on the experience of oppression, the multiple sites of those oppressions, and the idea that the experience derives from the structural location of black women/people.

In developing the idea of struggle against institutions and structures, the speaker suggests that black social workers are a physical embodiment of this struggle because they are a concrete example of achievement against the odds. It is at this point that she first makes the slip from 'black women' to 'black people'. In constructing black social workers in this way she introduces the link between black women's experience and social work as an institution in a slightly different way from the previous speaker. Thus, although she refers to the empathy which this experience produces between client and black female social worker, she adds to this by saying that the SSD is itself a major locus of the oppression that black women/people suffer ('This authority sets up so much things against black women').

Another shift of emphasis from the previous speaker is that here there are specific references to issues internal to the ethnic community she cites as her own. It is an example of Henderson's contestatory discourse with a group constructed as 'community' but who stand in an ambiguously (non-)hegemonic position in relation to black women. Thus, her contestatory discourse points to the issue of gendered power relations between black women and men, and generational power differentials within families. In so doing she constructs a less 'innocent' picture of black family and 'communal' life. This, together with her indication of the temporary nature of the authority and power she may derive from her occupational status ('even from the social worker, outside of work . . .'), in turn allows her to point to the shifting and multiple subjectivities and identities which black women inhabit. But if sexism and age-related subordination are referenced as partially determining black women's experience, in the end this speaker foregrounds class and racism as the primary modalities structuring that experience.

2c

[G. L.] Why is that important for social work though?
[Participant] I think because social work is a role where unfortunately it targets a community that is, like, you know, under poverty . . . the majority of our clients seem to fit into that category, and I think the understanding of wanting to bring them out of that, or to offer alternatives, I just think it is, em, it is only where we are at, I mean like in this office, I know I am a social worker and everybody knows I am a social worker, but when I walk out, even around this community, nobody really knows until I say or show my identification or whatever . . . I think it is because we are always having to advocate for ourselves, and I think that the role of a social worker is primarily about advocating for our clients. I think it is one of the things we bring to it.

Here again we have the exposition of a social proximity to clients, a construction of social work as an occupation of advocacy on the part of those who, because of poverty, are less able to do it for themselves, and in this way the speaker introduces a notion of class. Her reference to the tenuous nature of the role/status of 'social worker' contrasted with the enduring subject position of 'black person' is how she introduces racism. This, of course, points to one of the principal features of societies structured in 'race' – that is the tenacity and pervasive character of racial ascriptions and identifications. For this woman, it is this which speaks to a core 'self', whilst a 'self' constituted through an occupation is vulnerable because it is invisible in most situations and contexts. Thus, if in some senses black people can be invisible, in others they are never able to be free of this marker of social identification and differentiation. There is a paradox highlighted here, then, in that it is the very visibility of the marker which creates the conditions for invisibility.

Account 3

[Ethnic group: African-Caribbean. Grade: Social Worker]

3a

[G. L.] Now I want to ask you a question specifically about black women social workers and I am wondering if you think there are any special qualities, skills or experiences that black women can offer social work?
[Participant] Yes, there is a variety of skills and knowledge that we can offer, em, I said the majority of us by nature are survivors, and we know how to survive in society, among all the things that we have to face, racism, sexism, disability, whatever it is, em, [pause] em, we feel, I feel when I look at the way we operate with our caselist, we tend to be more logical, and we tend to organize ourselves that much better, and we have a high turnout in our cases, and we don't hold onto them for the sake of holding onto them. As soon as they need closing we just close them and get rid of them.
[G. L.] This is black women you are talking about?
[Participant] Yes, most of the black women social workers that I work with.
[G. L.] And by black women now, do we mean African-Caribbean or do we mean all?
[Participant] African-Caribbean that I have worked with and what I have seen and what I have worked with during my placements and things like that.

This speaker gives a clear and unhesitant affirmation that black women have something special to offer and again this is said to be rooted in the strengths which are deemed to derive from experience of, and resistance to, the oppressive matrix of social relations organized around a variety of axes. This is understood as resulting in a positive approach to work organization and 'getting the job done'. There is also an interesting 'naturalization' of the purported survival skills of African-Caribbean women.

Then, in what follows, she focuses on the office hierarchies and their associated job demarcations and responsibilities and the ways in which black women's 'naturally' confident and methodical approach to the work disorganizes these hierarchies and demarcations.

3b

[Participant] We tend to, the managers say to us, 'I'm the manager, I should have made that decision' and . . . we tend to have to, if you are going along doing our cases, we plan it, I mean, like, most other social workers, I guess, you know, as well you have to plan your case, it's what you are doing anyway, but whereas we will go and start making whatever we need to do to achieve our goals, em, managers, when we come back and sit down in supervision, we'll be told 'well, you should have discussed that with us'. Maybe it is not unique to us but that is the experience that we have had.

Here there is a notable shift between the impersonal 'you' and the communal 'we' when the speaker wants to emphasize the specificity of black women's approach to the work. She marks the boundaries between black women and other social workers in this way and the meanings she attaches to managerial responses in supervision are constructed through the prism of 'race'. Later, her constitution of a racially and sexually bounded community is crystallized.

3c

[G. L.] When you say through our experiences, what sorts of things do you mean?
[Participant] Through growing up, especially, like, say, the way we had to grow up in the system . . . Going into the education system and things like that and the issues that you face in your own home life as well . . .
[G. L.] What sort of things in your own home life?
[Participant] The way you are expected to be a black *person*, and the stereotyping of how a *woman* should behave, and to be challenging that, like quite a few black *workers*, they feel they are going out of their station to be going into the white man's world and be working and . . .
[G. L.] By whom are they seen?
[Participant] By our own, black people. Or you are getting too independent, women are supposed to be here doing this, doing that.

This reference to the fracturing of the African-Caribbean population along axes of gendered power relations disrupts any idea of a harmonious and homogeneous community, and the speaker's intimation that black personhood and black womanhood are constructions is notable because it is the first time that such a suggestion is made in this way. In effect she adopts a multivocality and suggests three forms of differentiation. Thus, she simultaneously indicates that 'black people' are produced in tension and opposition to 'white people', that 'black women' are produced in tension and opposition to 'black men', and that 'black workers' are in tension and opposition to 'white managers/power'. This last point moves the passage onto a slightly different register. The speaker restates a link commonly made by black people between power and white males, with the effect that the gendered nature of social work as a *profession* is submerged under a gendered discourse of a more generalized *power,* and power is conceived as a racialized (not gendered) field (of coercion). She does this by tapping into discourses which construct 'the white *man's* world' as antithetical to black *people's* interests. She assumes that I, as her black woman interlocutor, will be able to read this, hence her later reference to 'our own'. To enter 'the white man's world' means to cross over, to not only 'forget' who you are, but also to enter into roles of control over other black people. The result of this is that it creates a barrier to the processes of identification between black social worker and black client. She continues:

3d

[Participant] . . . but having to work through those kinds of issues, and then being able to transfer the skills into your work environment and into your case-loads as well, and I guess sometimes [pause] sometimes you get frustrated, and you find your mind is rolling ahead, and you are thinking this should be happening, this should be happening, but you tend not to think that the client still has to work through the process, like how you had to work through it, through whatever problem they are going through.

Although in an earlier chapter (chapter 5, account 4) the control aspects of social work were raised, in the context of black women's experience this tended to be downplayed since the main aim has been to emphasize its caring or enabling side as a means of constructing a specificity and legitimacy of presence in the occupation. It is also the first time in this context that the possibility of tensions between black social worker and black client are implied, and the first time the strains that this tension produces for black social workers, as opposed to those between white colleagues, managers or institution, are suggested.

Account 4

[Ethnic group: African. Grade: Senior Social Worker]

4a

[G. L.] OK, let's come back to the issue . . . of why black women staff . . . You have sometimes referred to the ways in which sometimes it is racism, or conceptions of 'race', but there is gender and perhaps sexuality, all at play . . . On the other hand, you have talked about [pause] black people have something to offer social services and I want you to say about what it is they have to offer, whether there is something particular that black women can offer?

[Participant] *I mean I would say so,* people might disagree with me there, because our experiences are different, we experience different things on the whole, you know, but I would say so, I think as a race, or as races, as well as individuals, but also living in this country having experienced the racism, I think we have got a certain amount of resilience, I would say that for most of the social workers, do you know what I mean, so, you know, there *is something extra there.*   (her emphases)

4b

[G. L.] But why is that important potentially for social services and what is it? You say you are resilient, I want to say to you 'so what?'

[Participant] Erm, well, I am thinking now in terms of service users, OK, so I am thinking in terms of what we can, erm, I was gonna to say impart although that's not the right word, but you know, I was gonna say like role models, but no, like being able to support people who have been in, or have experienced, or are experiencing very difficult situations, so on that level . . .

[G. L.] Yes, but why can *you* support them more than a white woman colleague?

[Participant] I think because their experiences have been different. [said very quietly]

[G. L.] So the experience that you say as a black woman you have, gives you something particular? Is it another form of identification? Perhaps with the experiences of black clients, or?

[Participant] Yeah, that is along the lines I was thinking, em, I'm just trying to think of an example to make it clearer.

4c

[G. L.] Yeah, I mean you can talk more generally if you like, it's just that I want you to say a bit more about it, if possible.

[Participant] Well, I suppose from my experience of service users, I have worked with a lot of single parents for one, so in terms of their experiences, whatever they might be or whatever their particular situations might be, there are often issues that come up to do with violence, or abuse, or both; to do with black men leaving; em, to do with their position in society, to do with not having power, you know, all those sorts of issues, and I suppose I feel because I am a black woman and I have experienced some of those things, and the racism as well, I feel empowered to do certain things and make certain changes and I feel that as black women we can impart something, or we can facilitate some sort of change in service users at that level.

4d

[G. L.] So it is common experience that forms the basis of this particular stuff that black women can offer?

[Participant] Either common experience, or experience that is similar and I suppose the effects of racism and challenging racism and all that to me is a similar experience, you might not have exactly the same but you might need similar tools to deal with it and you can transfer those tools.

The more lengthy interaction between myself and this speaker is noticeable in the ways in which I formulate the questions and it is evident that at times this produced a thoughtfulness or hesitancy in some of her reiterations. However, this hesitancy gave way to firmly expressed views when she was asked to expand. Again there is a repetition of a language in which strength, survival, resilience, as products of the experience of racism, are highly profiled. 'Races' are identifiable and bounded communities, but the idea that the term 'black' covers more than one 'race' is implicit in the first section of this account (4a). This 'experience' gives rise to a type of person, but for this speaker this 'person' seems to be one with an *additional* skill or capacity, rather than a person of a completely different 'type' as suggested in some of the other accounts. For example, her formulation of 'something extra there' is in contrast to the formulation by the speaker in account 3 that 'we tend to be more logical'. This 'something extra' acts to demarcate black women from white women.

Similarly, the connection to service users is spoken in language echoing that already heard, although this speaker seems to focus on links to, and empathy with, black service users. This is less clear in other voices. Importantly, in this formulation the changes that social work can effect on clients suggests that they are the objects which are acted upon by a social work subject – 'facilitate some sort of change in service users'. Experience of and against racism is the privileged factor which can produce this ability, but this does not detract from the echoes of beneficent 'improvement' which was the hallmark of so much nineteenth-century charity and early twentieth-century social work discourse. Moreover, such a discourse has a 'professional' version in the form of viewing social workers as major agents of change (personal and, to some extent, social). In this there is a link to the establishment of psychology as the main element in the knowledge base of social work training. Thus, social workers have a key role to play in the moralization or normalization of pathologized individuals and families. What is also interesting about this passage is that the speaker herself seems hesitant about using a language which carries these meanings. There is a suggestion in the way in which she formulates her response that she is struggling to find words which are least laden with precisely these nineteenth-century 'charitable' and twentieth-century 'professional' discourses (see also Rojeck, Peacock and Collins, 1988).

Account 5

[Ethnic origin: South Asian. Grade: Community Social Worker]

5a

[G. L.] Right. Do you think there are any particular or special qualities that black women from diverse communities can offer social work?
[Participant] Qualities?
[G. L.] Or skills, attributes.
[Participant] Well . . . talking about qualities, I think understanding and awareness of the immediate culture that they work with does matter, and language is a skill, and is a special quality. So yes, I do think they are better skills, if utilized and taken into account.
[G. L.] Better skills than? [laughter]
[Participant] Better skills than white people working with ethnic minority background people.

Here the speaker firmly places the advantage of employing black or Asian women social workers in terms of *cultural* understanding and linguistic ability rather than in terms of an historical and contemporary experience. Of course, there has been evidence in earlier accounts about knowledge of, and embeddedness in, particular cultural or 'racial' communities, but, as we have seen, in those this was superimposed upon racism as the central principle organizing black women's experience. As this speaker continues, her construction of cultural knowledge as ungendered is both emphasized *and* undermined as the issue of gender becomes more complexly posed.

5b

[G. L.] And are those skills, you know, language, background, familiarity with culture, etc., the things you described, could men from the black communities also offer that?
[Participant] Men!? [quite sharp intake of breath]
[G. L.] Men, black men in other words.
[Participant] Yes, because they can identify themselves, and they understand, not as much as a woman to a woman could, but they would be much more aware of the tradition.

Her initial surprise at the idea of thinking about the role of men in this context is clarified when her emphasis on cultural knowledge and understanding as the key modality for good practice in social services is remembered. The way in which she puts the relation is such that she does not speak in absolutely ungendered terms, but rather maps a gendered differential onto a white/black binary understood primarily as a cultural divide. And it is this latter one which is fundamental. Once this is established, it is possible for her to elaborate on the ways in which gender enters to structure the relationship between social services and its 'ethnic minority' clients. Thus:

5c

[G. L.] But is there something absolutely particular to black women from all the diverse black communities, that black women from those communities can offer, even more, or over and above that offered by men from those communities? [pause]
[Participant] Oh, I don't think so, because in this profession one has to be supportive and sympathetic, but I mean the majority of our clients are women anyway. And I feel they feel comfortable with a female, rather than a male.
[G. L.] Why?
[Participant] Well, I can speak for the south Asian women, find it much easier to talk about personal issues to a female rather than a man, certain things could be affecting them but they can't come out and that is why I think, yes, a woman would be more approachable than a man. I worked with a social work assistant who was a south Asian male, and my clients still faced a problem, allowing him in the house, they wouldn't want a man to knock on the door and come in and if it was a woman it would have been easier for both. Personally, in my role, I did have a problem in seeing myself as a certain member of a respected community, if I had to go along with my colleague, and it wouldn't be as nice as it would be if I went on my own or with a female colleague. There is a certain reputation about women working in a profession, and then working with male colleagues, and the reception of the community would be different.

This extract is interesting because of the way in which the speaker's opening denial of any gendered specificity immediately moves on to argue the opposite. Her initial denial is premised on a notion of the caring nature of the profession. This means that all social workers should be able to sympathize, if not empathize, with any client. It is, as it were, a professional requirement. But when her focus shifts from the profession to the client base of social work then gender can enter the field. In contrast to earlier speakers who focused on 'raced' experience (and sometimes class) as the basis of a connection between social worker and client, this speaker highlights gender itself. Similarly, while the gender identification must be underwritten by a cultural sameness and understanding, her differentiation between south Asian male and south Asian female social workers tends towards a primacy of gender. Moreover, gender acts to structure her own experience of the *work*. This in turn is linked to specific views about the world of professional labour and its purported erosion of gender boundaries operating within specific ethnic communities.

So here we have some substance given to the suggestion made by other speakers that part of the issue for women from black communities is the hegemonic prescriptions about how a woman from 'their community' should behave. Because the starting point for this speaker was an emphasis on culture, the *intra-communal* dynamics affecting the social worker/client interaction is foregrounded, whereas, for earlier speakers, the emphasis on combating systems of racist oppression meant a focus on the *inter-communal* dynamics structuring the relationship. This speaker's own status is spoken of in similar terms, such that her positioning within both the professional institution and 'the community' is constructed in relation to the tension between them. Again it is not that an awareness of the effects of an interstitial positioning has not been spoken before, but the profound emphasis on something called a 'black women's experience' is absent from this account. Given the small number of participants of south Asian origin, it is hard to offer any convincing explanation of the different emphasis in this account. Certainly one can raise the question about a possible link to the differential racializations between people of African-Caribbean and south Asian origin/descent: for example, the organization of racism directed at south Asian populations in Britain around *cultural* 'othering'. However, the very small numbers of south Asian origin/descent women among the participants make any more definitive suggestions inappropriate. The value in pointing to the difference here is twofold. On the one hand, the difference serves to shed light on the dominant discursive repertoires in the accounts. On the other hand, presentation of an alternative way of constructing the specificity of black women's potential contributions to social work shows what terrain is opened up when the category of 'experience' is foregrounded as the vector through which meaning is constructed.

Boundaries of 'race' / boundaries of gender

Processes by which 'communities' are discursively produced necessarily involve processes of differentiation and exclusion. Recourse to some essentialized characteristic(s) (biological, social, even material) is made in order to construct the foundational elements of the 'us' as against 'them'. In the preceding section that foundational element in the constitution of the 'community of black women' was 'experience'. Experience was seen as giving rise to an internal strength, an ability to empathize with clients, a methodical and unhesitant approach to the work. This was constructed as rooted in historical as much as contemporary social relations, but a key marker was oppression (always racism, but sometimes also oppression deriving from other axes of differentiation and power) and resistance to it. In short, each account gave rise to a harmony of voices in which it was proclaimed that *being* a black woman social worker was *being* a particular 'type' of person. A number of issues arise from this and I consider these below. Before turning my attention to this, however, I briefly consider the ways in which the boundaries of the 'black women's community' were in part established in terms of the limits or connections to white women and black men.

'Us' and white women

Account 6

[Ethnic origin: African-Caribbean. Grade: Social Worker]

6a

[G. L.] But two things I want to ask you, one is that you have talked about how outside of the office situation black women wear lots of hats and do a lot of things in their role as women outside, but doesn't that apply to white women?
[Participant] It does to an extent, but just because of racism, it clouds everything, every area, so it can't be, I just don't think it can be as bad, there is no way it can be as bad, it can be similar to an extent but I think racism tips the scales, you know.

Similarly:

Account 7

[Ethnic origin: African. Grade: Senior Social Worker]

7a

[G. L.] OK, and what about white women? Can they bring those qualities based on their experiences?
[Participant] Some . . . but not, erm, because I think it is different, yeah, I just think that their experiences have been [pause] yeah, maybe I am talking off the top of my head but I do feel that their experiences have been different, I mean I think they tend to look at things from a different perspective, and even if white women have experienced racism in terms of having a link with black people, I think because of our histories, even just talking about some of these difficult things is going to be difficult and the understanding of it, Oh I can't explain it very well, but yeah [pause] I suppose because there is racism in the middle that is going to affect the process.

It is notable that this speaker recognizes that racism can also affect white people (for example, white women with black children, which is perhaps the example most often encountered in social work). However, if they can get a proximity to it, they cannot feel or experience it in the same way. The divide which results from being a white or black person erects an indissoluble boundary which determines experience. Thus, despite the variation between this speaker and the previous one, the way she poses the situation re-establishes the closeness between them because they both see racism as an essentially black experience. The boundaries created by racialized experiences are clearly expressed in the words of the following speaker.

Account 8

[Ethnic origin: African-Caribbean. Grade: Senior Social Worker]

8a

[G. L.] Yeah, but you said they [i.e. black women] can bring in real experience, now your white . . . women, don't they have real experience outside?
[Participant] Yes.
[G. L.] But what are the differences?
[Participant] They bring in real different things, they bring in their real experience as black women, the cultural experience and life experience, which no matter how much you live in England, and no matter how much contact you have with white people – you can live with them, and you can be friends with them, everything – your experience is still different to theirs and that is the bottom line. I mean they have positive real experience, but it is different.

So 'black women's experience' is the factor which authorizes the construction of the boundary between black women and white women. Racism is the modality most emphasized as the factor creating differential experience, with some reference to 'culture'. Moreover, the boundaries between the two constituencies are expressed as fixed and immutable – 'you can be friends with them, everything, your experience is still different to theirs and that is *the bottom line*'.

Having said this, the fact that these discussions were taking place in the context of a specific occupational setting meant that issues of work informed the ways in which the boundaries were constructed. When pushed further, some of the women began to suggest that the boundaries were perhaps more susceptible to manipulation, at least in the work context, than might be expected from things said earlier. For example, the following speaker goes on to say:

Account 9

[Ethnic origin: African. Grade: Senior Social Worker]

9a

[G. L.] Yeah, right, so what I'm thinking is, then, how do we get beyond, how can you envisage us getting beyond a situation where white social workers can take black cases and do it in a way and not be stumped . . . because if it is about experience, well, our experiences in the foreseeable future are going to be quite different . . . yet earlier you were talking about the need for there to be cases allocated on the basis of a number of criteria, not just that you are the same 'race', so how do you match those two things?

[Participant] I suppose it gets down to personalities as well, because I mean even though I say, and I do, that there would be different, you know [pause] like, one service user might get three different people and get different feelings towards them or be able to work in different ways with each of them and I suppose it is not as if to say they are not going to eventually achieve the same goal, but it could be a slower process, it could be a smoother process, those sorts of things . . . But within that you *can* have white people, I hope this doesn't sound patronizing, but you . . . could have white women who could work well with a black family and you could have other people who have no experiences and totally, and I think that this is damaging . . . so I am not saying that nobody can, but I think people need to be aware, self-aware as well, and if you think this is not appropriate for you then you shouldn't take it on, and in terms of moving forward, I think that if people are looking to work in a particular area, then they need to have some training and some decent training, not just any old thing. I remember when I was in Fostering and Adoption and I went on a training course, 'Working With West African Families' . . . and it was a white woman running it, and 90 per cent of the people on the course were white, and they left thinking 'oh, I can work with West African families', and it was a white woman who did it. I think she had been to Nigeria twice or three times, and spent some time with a family and said: 'They are so kind because they will even give you their food, even if they haven't got much, they will give it to you' in a very patronizing sort of way, and I'm not talking about that level of awareness, and, you would be surprised, but you still have people operating in that kind of way and I suppose it is about the degree to which people can actually take on board, you know, and look at interactions and everything . . . There are two forums just within this office that work could take place, plus we have our central training section and social services training section. So they could have a series of days looking at race and culture and all that sort of stuff . . . But the thing is, ever since I have been here, I think we have had one debate on race and as it so happened I was the person who had put it on the agenda.

This long passage makes it clear that the barriers between black and white women were being constructed within the context of a specific organizational setting where the issues of 'race', racism and culture were thought to be continually marginalized and/or reduced to simplistic and patronizing 'culture tours'. This resulted in the discussion of similarities and differences within gender group, quickly moving into a discussion of the institutional approach to issues of 'race', racism and culture, and the organizational practices which authorize this approach. Experience of a white woman's management of a specific training issue is used both to exemplify the problem and to justify the argument that black and white women's experiences are so different as to prevent any meaningful fluidity across the boundaries of 'race' and culture. The field of contestation is racism, but it is spoken through a reification of 'race'. This has been evident throughout the accounts where there has been an emphasis on 'struggle', 'fighters', etc. Thus, implicit in these sequences is the idea that if there was no racialization and racism, then there would be no need for these terms. The situation with black men is slightly different.

'Us' and black men

Henderson has suggested that black women stand in equivalent distance of difference and identification with white women and black men. Black women's simultaneity of discourse delineates the specifics of the relation to one or the other but addresses both these groups as ambiguously (non)hegemonic. We have already seen from the above extracts that the black women speaking here certainly point to their difference from both white women and black men. However, it is less clear that they draw points of different but equidistant identification between the two. Indeed, with regard to white women social workers, identification was at the very best fragile, even if there was variation in the ways in which speakers constructed the boundaries. Let us listen now to how speakers construct relations with black men social workers. The most notable point is that the discursive construction of difference between them and black men was less sharply defined for two reasons. One is because the talk was often more embedded in reflections on the general difficulties facing them as *black* women social workers. The following lengthy extract was a typical formulation.

Account 10

[Ethnic origin: African-Caribbean. Grade: Social Worker]

10a

[Participant] When I say I am a black woman, I know my black male colleagues find that terrible, if we are talking about racism and I talk about sexism, they say why are you talking about sexism, and I say I am oppressed and you oppress me sometimes, and they can't see it . . . but as a woman as well, I experience sexism, and the power issues when I go into certain schools and talk to headmasters and when I am on the phone, and maybe to some headmasters I am speaking, I might speak received English, you know, white English. So they think it is a white person coming in to see them, and when they see you it is like, hey, 'hello'! After that they never return calls ... the one particular headmaster who is working with one of my Asian families, I have been trying to contact that man since December [six months] to talk about work we are doing with this particular child, and I have only just managed to get in touch with him. . . . I said the parents are concerned that you said he needs to go to a residential school, and they feel if that is going to happen they want him to go ['home', i.e. to country of parents' origin]. And he sort of said to me, well the family is the one who said they want him to go ... and anyway we haven't got the resources [needed for] this child ... I said, well if he does need it, what are you going to do? I personally don't feel he needs it, residential, ... but educational psychological work alongside him ... and his family. And he goes, no, because there is no consistency with the family home, and whatever work is done in school, would it be followed up, and he thought there were more severe cases in the school ... And I was so annoyed, I said I will get onto our psychologist and services and I put the phone down, and I spoke to my team manager about it, and ... I asked him to phone the school, that man ... I said to my manager that I cannot prove that it is to do with me being a black woman social worker professional, and he is a white male head teacher ... and I found it really, really offensive.

The speaker here begins by referring to the points of difference between black women and black men social workers which arise because of the power inequalities associated with gender, but then gives far more time and energy in the pace and tenor of her account to the issues which arise from racism and sexism in relation to white men. This is where the speaker 'feels' the strength of the obstacles she encounters during the course of her work. The irony is that the interaction between herself and the headmaster is mediated by another white man (her manager), but this only serves to reinforce the sense embedded in the account that it is in this relation that her gendered 'self' is most acutely felt.

The other reason why boundaries between black women and black men are less sharply delineated arises from the ways in which meanings are conveyed through non-verbal forms of communication, for example tone, facial expression or other bodily signs. It was these which often acted to emphasize the relative strengths or weaknesses of the delineation between themselves and black men in comparison with white women. The reading of these signs was intimately connected to the interaction between two black women: one as interviewer, the other as interviewee. For example:

Account 11

[Ethnic origin: African-Caribbean. Grade: Senior Social Worker]

11a

[G. L.] But then I want to ask you, black men suffer racism too . . . they may not have the same kind of gender issues . . . but they have racism as well. So if the marker between black women and white women is racism, and that is the key issue that makes black women strong, then wouldn't it just make black people strong?

[Participant] Yes, it does make black people strong, but specifically if we are just going to relate it to white women, I would have to say, yeah, that is for me one of the higher dividing things, but yes black men experience racism as well, but I think, black women, we can experience oppression from our black men even in a professional setting as well as in the home or social settings as well. So it is like in a cocoon and we are just fighting everybody, just to get what we want.

This speaker's use of the words 'one of the higher dividing things' in connection to the boundaries racism constructs between black and white women immediately suggests that the points of tension and distinction between black women and black men will be less emphatically enunciated. So while this speaker consistently raises points about the differentiations between black women and black men, she always suggests a more absolute divide between black and white women. Racism is privileged because 'racism tips the scales, you know'.

Brooks-Higginbothom (1992) has argued that 'race acts as a "global sign" or "metalanguage", since it speaks about and lends meaning to myriad aspects of life that would otherwise fall outside the referential domain of race' (p. 253). Acting as a metalanguage it simultaneously provides a resource against racist subordination, whilst occluding problems of power internal to black communities around issues of gender, class or sexuality, and thereby obstructing their resolution (p. 273). This twofold process is in evidence in accounts 10 and 11. The effects of the hegemony of 'race' as a metalanguage are such that these speakers appear less willing or able to construct a harmony of interests within the same gender group, and tend to soften the boundaries of difference between themselves and black men. This does not mean, however, that they do not speak such a boundary at all but rather that we need to be cognizant of the contexts which provide the frame within which their accounts are constructed, and listen to the subtexts which are embedded in their speech.

Colouring the category: 'racing' the experience

In their different ways the authors considered at the beginning of this chapter argued for a reading of 'experience' against the grain of 'common sense'. Rather than taking its ontological status for granted, 'experience' needs to be situated in wider configurations of social, cultural, economic and political relations if the specificities of certain constellations of experience are to be excavated. Only through such a situational reading can the subjectivities and identities produced by experience be understood and analysed. But, added to the 'big' locations along axes of differentiation which organize social formations are the more micro-contexts of, for example, specific families or specific workplaces and occupations. These, too, need to be recognized as the contexts in which archaeological cross-readings such as those proposed by Scott, Mohanty and Henderson occur.

It seems to me that there are three areas which are of particular interest in this cross-reading. First, there is the question of the processes by which concrete historical subjects are created and the place of 'experience' in that. Second, there is the issue deriving from Mohanty's concern about what happens when experience is tied to issues of 'race' and racism (as well as gender, sexuality, class), in other words, what happens when the category is 'coloured'. Third, there is the issue of the relation between multivocality and the fluid positionings black women social workers occupy.

Scott's argument is that 'what counts as experience is neither self-evident nor straightforward; it is always contested, always therefore political' (1992, p. 37), and that to think of it in this way 'does not undercut politics by denying the existence of subjects, it instead interrogates the processes of their creation' (p. 38). This immediately opens up the possibility of thinking about the 'subject of experience' as at once shifting and multiple because she stands at the intersections of complex webs of relations organized around numerous axes of power and differentiation. While rooted in the terrain established by feminist constructions and valorizations of the category, it opens a way out of the totalizing and universalist formulations of 'women's experience' common to early second-wave white (and western) feminists. For whilst it demands that the experience which is spoken is heard, it also demands that the circumstances of that speaking are excavated and analysed.

Most of the speakers considered here proceed in such a way that 'experience' is taken as the starting point of explanation. It is precisely the ontological or foundational status of their collective experience which confirms the importance of employing black women social workers in social services departments. This experience is said to produce an understanding, or form of knowledge, about the dynamics of racism (and class) and oppression both historically and contemporarily, which much of the client base will be familiar with. Experience becomes the connective tissue binding social workers and clients and it is this which is vital for social services departments. Their employment is an occupational and professional necessity based on a perspective of 'who feels it knows it'. At this level the women speaking here reproduce a way of thinking about and using experience which both Scott and Mohanty critique. But I want to argue that, if we take to their logical conclusion their injunctions to interpret and locate experience in light of the web of relations which produce it, then the voices of these women suggest a more complex use of the category. This is precisely because it is a situated use.

The women were attempting to construct their own specificity in the context of a set of questions about their employment. Being asked these questions by a black woman interlocutor ostensibly established an interaction in which the categories 'black woman' and 'black women's experience' needed no preliminary introduction. But even in these conditions, and perhaps because of them, a more complex mobilization of the category 'experience' occurred. For whilst there was a harmony of voices constructing a unitary 'black women's experience', many also spoke as if they had a peripheral vision of the contingent nature of experience and its complex gendered, 'raced' and classed production. One speaker referred to the realization that her institutional location results in her having a different set of experiences from those with whom she had formerly constructed community. This distancing arises because her location in 'race', gender and class relations becomes reconfigured, a process which is both unavoidable and painful to her. This is similar to another speaker, who seeks a 'way out' of this 'dilemma of distance' by privileging early experiences of oppression, relative poverty, etc., and thus creating a legitimacy and specificity for black women social workers.

This would suggest that if we are to adopt the approach urged by both Scott and Mohanty three further questions have to be asked: what is it that speakers are attempting to achieve by the invocation of a particular foundational experience; who is it that is invoking this experience; and to whom are they speaking? When this is done, awareness of the contingent, produced nature of 'experience' may well be implicit in any given sequence of talk, but subordinated to what is seen as a more urgent imperative. It is only by applying Scott and Mohanty's theoretical positions to concrete, but none the less historical, subjects that this can be grasped.

If black women social workers were using a foundational experience to authorize their role and place in social services departments, they were doing so in an environment in which racism within their workplaces was once again coming to the fore. After an initial 'heyday' in the 1980s, when recruitment of black staff to qualified social work positions was a priority in some authorities, the situation in the 1990s was much altered. For example, the 1991 Social Services Inspectorate report, *Women in the Social Services*, noted both that despite a recognition of the need for a multi-ethnic social work corps, black social workers were often viewed as a problem rather than an asset, and that black women seldom achieved managerial positions because of pervasive racism and sexism. As *Community Care* (1993) noted, when black women do enter managerial positions within their departments 'they are particularly exposed and isolated, and the institutions are slow to support them – worse, their performance is expected to be peerless. On the converse, there are many "over-qualified" and experienced black workers, able to perform at higher levels, but discouraged within their organizations which go on to reinforce this perception of "difficult people"' (p. 14). All black workers are affected by the upsurge in racism and one of the measures of this is the decline in the numbers of black people at senior management levels in social services departments.

In this context the 'coloured' or 'raced' nature of the 'experience' constructed by the women speaking here is not at all surprising. It is given a foundational status precisely because it is this which can provide the specificity of the contribution they can offer. They do not become 'good' social workers because of the technical or professional training they receive, but rather because this is mapped onto a subject who understands the client base of social work.

Recourse to a foundational 'experience' also serves another purpose in this context. By constructing an historical continuity between themselves and previous generations of 'fighters' and 'survivors' they find a way through and give meaning to the everyday of their working lives. These speaking subjects are then located in an institutional context in which the intersections of 'race', racism and gender are such that their claims to a professional status and competence are being undermined as departments reorganize in the wake of welfare restructuring and the attack on anti-racism in social work.

If this provides the context for this group of black women's multivocality, still other issues arise. One of these is related to the totalizing effects which result from privileging 'race'. Because of the closures and erasures which the metalanguage of 'race' can impose, we need a way to capture some of the complexities and points of difference which can be at work *within* the dominant binaries which have organized meaning for people's everyday life. Henderson's notions of multivocality or simultaneity of discourse begins this because it enables us to situate the voices which engage multiple interlocutors in one and the same moment.

For her, black women's speech/writing is profoundly and self-consciously relational but it is this in both an *inter*-relational sense and an *intra*-relational one. For the simultaneity of discourse through which black women create themselves, and claim the space from which to speak, is directed to an external and internal same/other. 'What distinguishes black women's writing, then, is the privileging (rather than repressing) of "the other in ourselves"' (p. 147) and in moving into this speaking position she disrupts the '. . . intervention by the other(s) who speak for and about black women' (p. 151). To enable this 'dialogic of difference and dialectic of identity . . . black women must speak in a plurality of voices as well as in a multiplicity of discourses' (p. 149). They must, as she says, 'speak in tongues'. Black women's discourses are both testimonial and contestatory because her interlocutors are comprised of a range of same/other(s) organized across numerous axes of differentiation and power.

> Through the multiple voices that enunciate her complex subjectivity, the black woman . . . not only speaks familiarly in the discourse of other(s), but as Other she is in contestorial dialogue with the hegemonic dominant and subdominant or 'ambiguously (non)hegemonic' discourses. . . . As such, black women . . . enter into testimonial discourse with black men as blacks, with white women as women, and with black women as black women. At the same time, they enter into a competitive discourse with black men as women, with white women as blacks, and with white men as black women. If black women speak a discourse of racial and gendered difference in the dominant or hegemonic discursive order, they speak a discourse of racial and gender identity and difference in the sub-dominant discursive order.   (p. 148)

As 'speaking subjects', then, black women in their multiple selves move within and across discourses as they communicate in modes of identification and differentiation with those who constitute an element of themselves.

The voices of these black women social workers offer a clear example of such multivocality in a specific occupational setting. One aspect of their occupational situatedness is that the audiences to whom they are speaking are predominantly white women – as colleagues, managers and in some cases organizational subordinates. Because social work is such a highly gendered occupation, white (and to some extent black) men will also constitute the audiences to whom these women are speaking, but these men will much less often occupy subordinate organizational positions to them. It is this aspect of social services departments as gendered domains which in part will account for the marked emphasis in the extracts on the differences between black and white women. They do this by drawing on the discursive repertoires available. As we have seen, some of these involve a collective historical and contemporary 'experience' of racist exclusions and marginalizations occurring outside of the employment context. These 'memories' and 'experiences' are invoked to make sense of the work situation but are of course mediated by the occupational situatedness in which they are mobilized.

A second aspect of this occupational situatedness is provided by professional discourses about the nature of social work. For example, the frequent references to social work as being about caring, support, help, imparting life skills. In this sense it is clear that the speakers were drawing on a link between a discursively constituted 'black women's experience' and professional discourses in opposition to the situation they find themselves in organizationally: a situation which they feel undermines and devalues them. The result is that their recourse to a set of professional discourses has to be read in the wider context of their racialized and gendered positioning.

This is part of the 'multivocality' or 'simultaneity of discourse' that these black women adopt. Moreover, in terms of organizational situatedness they do so from a position where, in contrast to Shirley in chapter 6, they are unambiguously subordinate. However, it is also clear that as black women *social workers* they have statutory and organizational power in relation to *clients*, the great majority of whom are white and black women. In this sense they can occupy a position of being ambiguously dominant. It will be remembered that in noting the constituencies to whom black women speak their 'simultaneity of discourse', Henderson always positioned black women as in a relation of either identity or difference but never as in any form of dominance. It is clear that in the case of social workers such a formulation cannot be sustained. And in the accounts given here I would argue that the speakers' claim to professional authority through the mapping of 'black women's experience' onto professional discourse constitutes them as at once organizationally subordinate and ambiguously dominant. This double positioning can only be gleaned by 'locating the politics of experience'.

Conclusion

In this book I have developed an argument about the entry of black and Asian women into professional social work in local authority social services departments. Prior to the 1980s, where women from racialized populations of colour were working in such departments, it tended to be as unqualified social work assistants, often located in the residential sector or in other parts of social care carrying lower status. By the mid-1980s, this situation had begun to change in certain parts of the country and it was this change that I have attempted to analyse.

My argument is framed within a social regulationist perspective and begins with the Foucauldian notion of governmentality. This is concerned with the management of populations and the formation of citizens/subjects who can be incorporated into regimes of power. Central to governmentality is the imposition of identities, but identities which are at once resisted and utilized in the construction of boundaries which differentiate 'types' of people. I adopted this idea in an attempt to understand the link between the formation of a new black subject called 'ethnic minority' and the opening up of professional social work to black and Asian women. From this I argued that state regulated institutions and practices were centrally involved in this process of reconstitution of the racialized subject of colour and I gave some brief consideration to education and policing to illustrate this point. In particular I was concerned to show how Caribbean and Asian families were identified as a key site upon which black populations could be incorporated into the nation on terms which continued to construct them as 'other'.

The identification of the family in this way laid the ground for the inclusion of social work in a project of 'racial formation' in which 'racial time' delineates the historical specificities of articulations of racial discourse. That it is necessary to periodize the specificities of 'race', racism and the black and/or Asian experience as they have evolved in the last half century was identified by people working at the Centre for Contemporary Cultural Studies more than a decade ago (see, for example, *The Empire Strikes Back*, 1982; and Hall et al., 1978). In this, racism was conceptualized as an unstable, shifting and contradictory phenomenon constantly undergoing transformation, alongside and within wider political-economic structures and social relations. As such, the experience of racialized populations of colour in post-Second-World-War Britain was envisaged as being structured in three overlapping but conceptually distinct phases. First was the period of immediate response to what was seen as relatively large numbers of black and Asian migrants coming into Britain: the period from 1948 up to the first Commonwealth Immigrants Act in 1962. The second phase lasted from 1962 up to the early 1970s, when various policy responses were initiated by central and local state agencies which were designed (albeit in an uneven way) to deal with the 'problems' associated with black and Asian settlement. The third phase, identified by the authors of *The Empire Strikes Back*, began in the mid-1970s and continued up to the time of their writing. This period was characterized as a time of crisis management in which the control and containment of forms of black resistance to racist exclusions was given priority. This is the moment, among others, when a discourse of community policing occupies public debate and racialized families of colour are marked out as either compatible with, or resistant to, a project of relegitimation. It is clear from discussions in earlier parts of this book that black and Asian family forms and relations were identified as barriers to processes of assimilation and integration in all three of these periods. But in each of these phases it is a specific black subject which is referenced – i.e. the shift from 'coloured', through 'immigrant', to 'ethnic minority' – and each of these connotes a different dimension of the 'problem' to be solved. What is particularly important about the 'ethnic minority' is that this subject has the status of being citizen/subject whilst simultaneously being constituted as an essentialized 'other' who is now a permanent figure in Britain. The terms of their incorporation into 'the nation' are, then, necessarily distinct from that of the 'coloured' colonial subject, or of the 'immigrant'. It is because of this shift in the type of black subject that I argue that the period between the early 1980s and early 1990s constitutes another moment in racial time. This is also the time when a number of local authorities controlled by left-wing Labour administrations attempted to incorporate many of the demands of those social movements which had contested the terms of their inclusion in the social relations of welfare. Within such local authorities this took the form of equal opportunities policies and structures which were utilized as an alternative way of resolving some of the many tensions which were produced by and reflected the organic crisis.

Periodization of the politics of 'race', racism and black and Asian experience in this way facilitates thinking about the movements and contradictions in the constitution of different racialized subjects and it is in this context that I have argued social work came to occupy a specific place in the process of incorporating racialized populations of colour into the field of governmentality. At a time of organic crisis, in part signified by the increasingly violent contestations between police and sections of the black communities, social work, as a specific, if contradictory, arena of the local state is identified as a key institution in the mediation of this contestation. This is why the riotous rebellions of the early 1980s acted in part to create an impetus for local authority social services departments to seek to recruit and train professional black social workers. But why social work which by its very nature only works with specific families? Precisely because social work is the agency that monitors, surveys and moralizes those families which are constituted as 'deviant', 'pathological' or 'dysfunctional'. As such, social workers could be involved in the project of 'normalizing' and 'moralizing' those black and Asian families and individuals caught within its net, whilst articulating this within a discourse of developing 'ethnically sensitive' services and therefore expressing its professional self-image.

While this has been my general argument, more specifically I have traced the ways in which a process of racial formation occurred in two local authority social services departments. I have argued that several layers provided the context in which this process took place. The first of these layers was produced by the structural relations between central and local government where central government set the legal and financial possibilities and constraints on local authority action in matters 'racial' but the local level was designated the proper location for the immediate management of 'race' and 'ethnic minority' populations. Thus, parliamentary debates on pieces of legislation through which local authorities were able to act on 'race' were saturated by racial discourse but in a way in which this was both seen and not seen. In contrast to this elusive visibility in central government debate, the equal opportunities agenda of the 1980s legitimated explicit discussion and development of policy on 'race' at the local level. This was, of course, a specific and time-limited moment that was eroded by the successive and successful attacks of Thatcher administrations and sections of the media. Moreover, I have argued that the focus on promoting equality of opportunity in employment by local authority social services departments was destabilized by the rise of a discourse of service which accompanied the restructuring of welfare by central government.

Yet another layer framing the entry of women from racialized populations of colour into professional social work was the rise of a discourse of ethnicity within the profession of social work itself. In this sense I have argued that a form of contestatory politics articulated by black welfare professionals intersected with the equal opportunities 'moment' in local authorities expressed in the 'ethnic sensitivity' and 'black social worker' models. Together, these were the mechanisms for the delivery of appropriate services to ethnically diverse client populations.

By charting a set of connections which move from the macro-social, to central/local government relations, to local/professional discourses, I have suggested a framework in which a space was created for the entry of black and Asian women into qualified social work positions. But a framework for such entry is not the same as the everyday experience of such employment and to gain some insights into the complexities of this I have analysed a number of accounts given by interview participants.

My purpose in this was twofold. I wanted to stage a kind of encounter between the racial and racializing discourses circulating in central government, local government and professional circles and those deployed by women employed as professional social workers in their attempt to represent and negotiate their place in the profession and the organization. My second concern, directly linked to the first, was to destabilize the first set of racial discourses by juxtaposing them to a series of accounts that speak of the complexities of the everyday in the racialized, sexualized and gendered world that is the social services department. Chapter 5 begins this process of encounter by offering a number of accounts that contest the Manichean simplicity conveyed in the discourses of parliamentarians, local government policies and professional spokespeople. The complexities expressed in these accounts also raise issues that extend beyond the bounds of local authority departments and touch upon some key feminist issues. Hence, I have used the organizational context of the social services department to explore the analytic utility and limits of certain feminist approaches to an emancipatory project for the category 'woman'. The micro-social context of this 'encounter' brings new inflections to the thorny question of 'differences' among a subordinated social category. The final chapter retains a focus on the intellectual and political challenges to current feminist theories and debates posed by narrative accounts of black and Asian women social workers. In these accounts the implications and specificities of context for the ways in which racialized and gendered positions are inhabited is sharply posed. We see a clear mobilization of a discourse of 'black women's experience' as a means of creating and legitimating the specificity of these women's contributions to their departments. What these accounts show is that 'racial' and ethnic categories are simultaneously occupied and resisted as a way of mediating a set of working lives which are overdetermined by 'race' and gender.

Overall, then, I have presented a deeply textured narrative of the creation of spatially specific employment opportunities in one occupation. I have tried to identify the webs of social and discursive relations which position black and Asian women social workers in ways which constitute them as essential 'racial'/ethnic subjects and which have the paradoxical effect of providing an employment opportunity whilst simultaneously constraining their professional autonomy. It cannot be overstated that this is an argument about employment in *welfare* which articulates with a specific moment of racial formation. It remains for further work to be carried out that explores the applicability of this approach to other sites of state organized welfare, whilst within social work further research on the formation of other racial and gendered subjects is required if the picture presented here is to be broadened.

Notes

Preface

1 Access to participants in the survey was gained by circulating a memorandum within the two social services departments. The memorandum outlined the issues being addressed in the research project and invited volunteers willing to discuss these issues. I was also able to identify myself as a black woman and it is likely that this influenced people's decisions to volunteer.

Introduction

1 The difficulties of which terms to use in relation to people from 'ethnic minority' populations are profound. For reasons which will become clear, I do not believe 'ethnic minority' to be a simple or neutral term denoting a self-evident collection of social groups. Hence, its use in this book is always within inverted commas. I tend to use the term 'black' in its late-1970s–1980s sense to connote a common socio-political location among people of diverse national and ethnic origin and descent. Whilst this usage reflects my own political history, I recognize its limitations even though I persist in deploying it. It is a kind of perversity born of lack of a widely acceptable alternative (and no doubt some personal nostalgia for an earlier political moment, especially amongst black feminists). Intermittently, I substitute the term 'black' with that of 'racialized populations of colour', drawing on a convention found in the USA. This too has its limitations (which are too wide to go into here) but it does serve to convey to the reader the social groups I am referencing at that point in the text. I apologize in advance to any reader 'of colour' who feels vexed by my use of any of these terms and can only hope that we begin a collective debate about what terminology we can adopt which captures both the connections among us, the profound points of divergence and the multiplicity of ways in which we might construct ourselves as 'raced', gendered, classed and sexual beings.

2   This formulation is used when referring to Britain as a cultural construction. I use it as a way of drawing attention to the slippages between England and Britain that are so common in popular (and, at times, official) discourse. The conflation of the three nations of Britain to the one nation of England reflects the dominance of England as a representational and normative force in constructions of Britain as a nation. The conflation also occludes the cultural and national heterogeneity of British peoples – a move partly achieved by constructing these peoples as exclusively and irreducibly white. This itself enables a second move – i.e. to construct all those who are not white as not fully belonging to the nation.

Chapter 1   Configuring the Terrain: Governmentality, Racialized Population and Social Work

1   The following points rely heavily on Stoler's account of the lectures given in chapter 3 of her book (Stoler, 1995).
2   Davidoff and Hall make the point that middle-class women had to fight for their claim to a role as public moralizers. The implication of this is that the struggle in the mid-nineteenth century by women of the Charity Organisation Society was born out of a struggle rooted in gender relations and their re-articulation with wider economic and political relations.
3   Much of what follows in this section on education has been developed from the general argument advanced by Bonnick in her thesis. I use her material to elicit the links to governmentality, although it is clear that our general organizing frameworks differ.
4   John Alderson explicitly refers to the link between the development of community policing and the need to reassert legitimacy in the eyes of the populace at large (Alderson in Cowell, Jones and Young, 1982).

Chpater 2   Now you see it, Now you don't: 'Race', Social Policy and the Blind Eye of Central Government

1   It is important to note that it is only certain immigration that became restricted. Because of the equation between black or 'coloured' people and immigration, other groups of people entering the country were not discursively constituted as immigrants. This had the effect that Britain began to be seen as a country of no immigration (with the exception of some groups speaking from the far Right), hence masking the continued entry of large numbers of migrants into Britain. This is particularly true of Irish migration.
2   I have developed this line of thinking in conversation with Catherine Hall.
3   The psychoanalytic approaches which inform the phraseology used in this quotation are complex and beyond the scope of my enquiry. However, some elucidation may be helpful. It is clear that Steiner is drawing on the work of Melanie Klein as well as Freud here as evidenced by his use of the words 'mourn' and 'reparative processes'. Klein saw the processes of 'mourning' for

the psychic loss which emerged as a result of the Oedipal complex as an important part of psychic health. 'Reparation' for feelings of hatred, ill will, etc., towards the 'rival' parent was also a key part of coming to terms with the illicit inner feelings attached to the complex. However, to reach the stage where such 'reparation' could be made – through what Klein called the 'depressive position' – first they had to be acknowledged (seen). Such acknowledgement facilitates acceptance of the co-existence of 'good' and 'bad' – internally, externally and symbolically. In similar vein, the idea of the 'external couple' is a reference to both the real and the symbolic. In Steiner, the real couple referred to is related to work with a client which he uses to demonstrate his argument about the blind eye mechanism. But the 'external couple' is also symbolic in that it represents the objects of hate and desire (illicit feelings) and that which must be come to terms with.

4   In an article in the *Guardian* (26 June 1995), Ros Coward pointed to the gendered and classed nature of the attack on the welfare state (and the visions which it embodied), which is expressed in this formulation.

Chapter 3   Sites of Condensation: Social Services and Racial Formation at the Local Level

1   In the London authority ('Coolville') there were still some women who had no formal social work qualification but who had formal social work responsibilities. I interviewed only one such woman.

2   With this in mind, approval was won for the establishment of a clinical psychologist service in February 1986. Some three and a half years later, when the service was under threat of closure, a report in defence of the service argued that it 'offer[s] a unique transcultural approach which addresses and caters for the aspirations and needs of the multi-racial and multi-cultural community' (*Report to the Social Services Committee and Finance Sub-Committee – Indicative Cash Limits – Proposal to Abolish Clinical Psychologist Service*, October/November 1990).

3   Janet Newman (1998) has identified two key aspects of managerialism that were effectively absent from the changes that occurred in Coolville at this time. These are new modes of co-ordination within and between departments and agencies, and the construction of new subject positions and identities for all who work within the agency. Despite the absence in Coolville of these shifts, in any fundamental sense, many of the authority's employees believed a shift to managerialism to have occurred.

4   At this time it is still the director who was appointed in 1983 and was, at that time, associated with the foregrounding of issues of racial equality in both employment and service provision. That near to the end of his employment as director he could now be associated with the marked shift in emphasis which I have been outlining is indicative of the ways in which it is the combination of institutional framework and personnel that makes the promotion of equalities work more or less possible.

5   A sustained critique of this and similar positions had been advanced by

Parmar, P. as early as 1981. See her 'Young Asian Women: A Critique of the Pathological Approach', *Multiracial Education*, vol. 9, no. 3 summer.

6 That this was possible is indicative of the way in which the spatial distribution and concentration of 'ethnic minority' populations can give rise to a geographical mapping of 'race'. See, for example, Hall et al. (1978).

7 Interview with ex-member of the Positive Action Unit, 1995.

8 In the Coolville scheme for women middle managers this kind of manipulation was less possible because of the relatively few black women in social services at this level. This suggests that if policy designed to address one area of inequality fails to explore the heterogeneity *within* the category it is very likely to disadvantage black (and other) women.

9 Whether black and Asian women social workers would be encouraged by this increase in recruitment to traditional sectors such as this is more doubtful.

Chapter 4 'The Call of the Wild': Contestatory Professional Discourses on 'Race' and Ethnicity

1 See, for example, Association of Directors of Social Services and Commission for Racial Equality (1978); numerous contributions in Cheetham (ed.) (1982).

2 I would argue that this is true also of the perspective adopted by Dominelli (1988), despite the importance of her work and the fact that she was among the first to argue for an anti-racist social work.

Chapter 6 Categories of Exclusion: 'Race' and Gender in the SSD

1 In keeping with the descriptions used in other sections of account, the ethnic origin categories used here are those used in the 1991 census, hence the slight variations here and on p. 157.

References

Adkins, L. (1995) *Gendered Work: Sexuality, Family and the Labour Market*, Buckingham: Open University Press.

Ahmad, B. (1990) *Black Perspectives in Social Work*, London: Venture Press.

Ahmad, S., Cheetham, J. and Small, J. (1986) *Social Work with Black Children and their Families*, London: Batsford.

Alexander, S. (1994) *Becoming a Woman*, London: Virago.

Anderson, B. (1983) *Imagined Communities*, London: Verso.

Anzaldua, G. and Moraga, C. (eds) (1983) *This Bridge Called My Back*, New York: Kitchen Table: Women of Color Press.

Association of Directors of Social Services/Commission for Racial Equality (1978) *Multi-Racial Britain: The Social Services Response*, London: CRE.

Ball, H. (1988) 'The limits of influence: ethnic minorities and the partnership programme', *New Community*, vol. 15, no. 1.

Ballard, R. (1979) 'Ethnic Minorities and the Social Services: What type of service?', in Khan, V.S. (ed.) *Minority Families in Britain*, Basingstoke: Macmillan.

Baptiste, M. J. (1988) 'The implications of the new immigration bill', *Critical Social Policy*, 23.

The Barclay Report (1982).

Beechey, V. (1987) *Unequal Work*, London: Verso.

Benjamin, J. (1995) 'Sameness and difference: toward an "over-inclusive" theory of gender development', in Elliott, A. and Frosh, S., *Psychoanalysis in Contexts*, London/New York: Routledge.

—— (1998) *Shadow of the Other: Intersubjectivity and Gender in Psychoanalysis*, London/New York: Routledge.

Ben-Tovim, G., Gabriel, J., Law, I. and Stredder, K. (1986) *The Local Politics of Race*, Basingstoke: Macmillan.

Bhabha, H. (1983) 'The other question', in *Screen*, vol. 24, no. 6.

—— (1994) *The Location of Culture*, London: Routledge.

Bhat, A., Carr-Hill, R. and Ohri, S. (eds) (1988) *Britain's Black Population: A New Perspective*, 2nd edn, The Radical Statistics Race Group, Aldershot: Gower.

Bhavnani, K. K. (1983) 'Racist acts', *Spare Rib*, nos 115, 116, 117.

Bonnick, L. (1993) *The Racial Structuring of Educational Marginality 1960–1985* (unpublished Ph.D. thesis), London: University of London, Institute of Education.

Booth, H. (1988) 'Identifying ethnic origin: the past, present and future of official data production', in Bhat, A., Carr-Hill, R. and Ohri, S. (eds) (1988).

Bowlby, J. (1953) *Child Care and the Growth of Love*, Harmondsworth: Penguin.

Brah, A. (1992) 'Difference, diversity and differentiation', in Donald, J. and Rattansi, A. (eds) *'Race', Culture and Difference*, London: Sage.

—— (1996) *Cartographies of Diaspora*, London: Routledge.

Braham, P., Rhodes, E. and Pearn, M. (eds) (1981) *Discrimination and Disadvantage in Employment: The Experience of Black Workers*, London: Harper and Row.

Braidotti, R. (1989) 'The politics of ontological difference', in Brennan, T. (ed.) (1989).

Braidwood, S. J. (1994) *Black Poor and White Philanthropists*, Liverpool: Liverpool University Press.

Brennan, T. (ed.) (1989) *Between Feminism and Psychoanalysis*, London: Routledge.

Brewer, R. M. (1993) 'Theorizing race, class and gender: the new scholarship of Black feminist intellectuals and Black women's labour', in James, S. M. and Busia, A. P. A., *Theorizing Black Feminisms*, London/New York: Routledge.

British Association of Social Workers (1975) *Code of Ethics for Social Work*, London: BASW.

Brooks-Higginbothom, E. (1992) 'The metalanguage of race', *Signs*, 17.

Brown, J. (1981) 'The function of communities in police strategy', *Police Studies*, Spring.

Bryan, B., Dadzie, S. and Scafe, S. (1985) *The Heart of the Race*, London: Virago.

Burr, V. (1995) *An Introduction to Social Constructionism*, London: Routledge.

Butler, J. (1993) *Bodies That Matter*, New York: Routledge.

Cain, H. and Yuval-Davis, N. (1990) 'The "equal opportunities community" and the anti-racist struggle', *Critical Social Policy*, 29.

Carabine, J. (1998) 'New horizons? New insights? Postmodernising social policy and the case of sexuality', in Carter, J. (ed.) (1998).

Carby, H. V. (1982) 'White woman listen! Black feminism and the boundaries of sisterhood', in Centre for Contemporary Cultural Studies (1982).

Carter, J. (ed.) (1998) *Postmodernity and the Fragment of Welfare*, London: Routledge.

Castells, M. (1975) 'Immigrant workers and class struggles in advanced capitalism: the Western European experience', *Politics and Society*, vol. 5, no. 1, pp. 33–66.

Castles, S. and Kosack, G. (1972) 'The function of labour immigration in Western European capitalism', *New Left Review*, 73, pp. 3–21.

—— (1973) *Immigrant Workers and Class Structure in Western Europe*, Oxford: Institute of Race Relations.

Cavendish, R. (1982) *Women On the Line*, London: Routledge and Kegan Paul.

Centre for Contemporary Cultural Studies (1982) *The Empire Strikes Back*, London: Hutchinson.

Cesarani, D. (1996) 'The changing character of citizenship and nationality in Britain', in Cesarani, D. and Fulbrook, M. (eds) *Citizenship, Nationality and Migration in Europe*, London: Routledge.

Cheetham, J. (1972) *Social Work with Immigrants*, London: Routledge and Kegan Paul.

—— (1982) 'Positive discrimination in social work: negotiating the opposition', *New Community*, vol. 5, pp. 27–37.

—— (ed.) (1982) *Social Work and Ethnicity*, London: George Allen and Unwin.

Cheetham, J., James, W., Loney, M., Mayor, B. and Prescott, W. (eds) (1981) *Social and Community Work in a Multi-Racial Society*, London: Harper and Row.

Choong, D., Colewilson, O., Parker, S. and Pearse, G. (eds) (1991) *Don't Ask Me Why: An Anthology of Short Stories by Black Women*, London: Black Women Talk.

Clarke, J. (1998) 'The problem of the state after the welfare state', in M. May (ed.) *Social Policy Review*, 8, London: Social Policy Association.

Clarke, J. and Newman, J. B. (1993) 'The right to manage: a second managerial revolution', *Cultural Studies*, vol. 7, no. 3.

Cockburn, C. (1983) *Brothers: Male Dominance and Technological Change*, London: Pluto.

—— (1991) *In The Way Of Women*, London: Macmillan.

Cohen, B. G. and Jenner, P. J. (1968/9) 'The employment of immigrants: a case study within the wool industry', in Braham, P., Rhodes, E. and Pearn, M. (eds) (1981).

Cohen, S. (1972) *Folk Devils and Moral Panics: Creation of Mods and Rockers*, London: Paladin.

Commission for Racial Equality (1980) *Why Positive Action?* Guidance Paper, London: CRE.

—— (1995) *The Second Review of the Race Relations Act*, London: CRE.

Community Care (1993) 20 May, pp. 14–15.

Connelly, N. (1985) *Social Services Departments and Race: A Discussion Paper*, London: Policy Studies Institute.

—— (1988) *Care in the Multiracial Community*, London: Policy Studies Institute.

—— (1990) 'Social services departments: the process and progress of change', in Ball, W. and Solomos, J. *Race and Local Politics*, Basingstoke: Macmillan.

Coolville, London Borough of (1982) *Report to Social Services Committee* (item G), 15 March.

—— (1982) *Report by the Director of Social Services, Training Opportunities for Black Staff*, 7 September.

—— (1982) *Minute no. 53 agreed at Social Services Committee*, 30 November.

—— (1984) *Bid for Section 11 LGA 66 Resources Progress Report: A Strategy for Race Relations in Social Services*, June.

—— (1984) *Towards the Development of a Transracial/Cultural Model of Service Provision: A Strategy for Race Relations in Social Services*, 20 September.

—— (1984) *Section 11 Proposal – Community Social Workers, Report to Social Services Committee*, 20 September.

——(1986) *Report from the Director of Social Services, Summary of Section 11 Proposals 1984/85*, 20 September.

——(1990) *Social Services Restructure 2nd Phase*, 11 July.

——(1990) *Service Contract 1990/91 – Towards 3-Year Objectives*, 11 July.

——(1990) *Minute of Social Services Committee held on 11 July 1990, no. 28.*

——(1991) *Equal Opportunities and Community Affairs Corporate Review – A Structure for Equality in Service Provision*. Report to Social Services Committee, 9 October.

——(1991) *Progress Report of the 1990/91 Race Relations Work Programme within Social Services Directorate*, 9 October.

——(1992) *Equalities Officers – Social Services.* Report of the Director of Social Services, 14 April.

——(1995) *Developing Equalities Work Within Social Services*. Report to Social Services Committee, 5 July.

Cousins, M. and Hussain, A. (1984) *Michel Foucault*, Basingstoke: Macmillan.

Cowell, D., Jones, T. and Young, J. (1982) *Policing The Riots*, London: Junction Books.

Crompton, R. and Sanderson, K. (1990) *Gendered Jobs and Social Change*, London: Unwin Hyman.

Dalley, G. (1988) *Ideologies of Caring: Rethinking Community and Collectivism*, London: Macmillan.

Davidoff, L. and Hall, C. (1987) *Family Fortunes*, London: Hutchinson.

Denney, D. (1983) 'Some dominant perspectives in the literature relating to multi-racial social work', *British Journal of Social Work*, vol. 13, pp. 149–74.

Denney, D. (1995) 'Hall' in George, V. and Page, R. (eds) *Modern Thinkers on Welfare*, London: Prentice Hall.

Department of Education and Science (1964a) *The Education of Immigrants*, London: HMSO.

——(1964b) *The Second Report of the Commonwealth Immigrants Advisory Council*, London: HMSO.

——(1971) *The Education of Immigrants, Survey 13*, London: HMSO.

Department of the Environment (1977) *Policy for the Inner Cities*, White Paper, Cmnd 6845, London: HMSO.

——(1981) *The Urban Programme: Ministerial Guidelines*, London, HMSO.

Derrida, J. (1978) *Writing and Difference*, London: Routledge and Kegan Paul.

Dominelli, L. (1988) *Anti-Racist Social Work*, London: BASW/Macmillan.

——(1992) 'An uncaring profession? An examination of racism in social work', in Braham, P., Rattansi, A. and Skellington, R. *Racism and AntiRacism*, London: Sage.

Donzelot, J. (1979) *The Policing of Families: Welfare versus the State*, London: Hutchinson.

Doyal, L., Hunt, G. and Mellor, J. (1981) 'Your life in their hands: migrant workers in the health service', *Critical Social Policy*, vol. 1, no. 2.

Dutt, R. (ed.) (1990) *Towards a Black Perspective in Child Protection*, London: Race Equality Unit.

Dummett, A. (1986) *Towards a Just Immigration Policy*, London: Action Against Immigration and Nationality/Cobden Trust.

The Economist (1958) 27 November.

Ely, P. and D. Denney (1987) *Social Work in a Multi-Racial Society*, Aldershot: Gower.

Feminist Review (1984) 'Many voices: one chant', 17.

Foucault, M. (1972) *The Archaeology of Knowledge*, London: Tavistock Publications.

——(1979) *Discipline and Punish*, London: Penguin.

——(1990) *Difendere la società*, Florence: Ponte alle Grazie.

——(1991) 'Governmentality', translated and reprinted in Burchell, G, Gordon, C. and Miller, P., *The Foucault Effect: Studies in Governmentality*, London: Harvester Wheatsheaf.

Francis, E. (1993) 'Psychiatric racism and social policy: black people and the psychiatric services', in James, W. and Harris, C., *Inside Babylon*, London: Verso.

Fryer, P. (1984) *Staying Power: The History of Black People in Britain*, London: Pluto.

Game, A. (1991) *Undoing the Social: Towards a Deconstructive Sociology*, Milton Keynes: Open University Press.

George, V. and Wilding, P. (1976) *Ideology and Social Welfare*, London: Routledge and Kegan Paul.

Gibbon, P. (1990) 'Equal opportunities policy and race equality', *Critical Social Policy*, 28, Summer.

Gilroy, P. (1982) 'The myth of black criminality', *The Socialist Register*, London: The Merlin Press.

——(1987) *There Ain't No Black in the Union Jack*, London: Hutchinson.

——(1990) 'The end of anti-racism', in Ball, W. and Solomos, J., *Race and Local Politics*, Basingstoke: Macmillan.

Ginsburg, N. (1992) *Divisions of Welfare: A Critical Introduction to Comparative Social Policy*, London: Sage.

Glennerster, H. (1991) 'Social Policy since the Second World War', in Hills, J. (ed.) *The State of Welfare*, Oxford: Clarendon Press.

Glennerster, H. and Hills, J. (1998) (eds) *The State of Welfare: The Economics of Social Spending*, 2nd edn, Oxford: Oxford University Press.

Glucksmann, M. (1990) *Women Assemble: Women Workers and the New Industries in Inter-War Britain*, London: Routledge.

Goldberg, D. T. (1993) *Racist Culture: Philosophy and the Politics of Meaning*, Cambridge, Mass./Oxford: Blackwell.

Gordon, P. (1985) *Policing Immigration: Britain's Internal Controls*, London: Pluto.

Grewal, S., Kay, J., Landor, L., Lewis, G. and Parmar, P. (1987) *Charting the Journey*, London: Sheba Feminist Press.

Grimwood, C. and Popplestone, R. (1993) (eds) *Women, Management and Care*, Basingstoke: Macmillan.

The *Guardian* (1995) 2 August.

Guillaumin, C. (1995) *Racism, Sexism, Power and Ideology*, London: Routledge.

Gutzmore, C. (1983) 'Capital, "black youth" and crime', *Race and Class*, vol. xxv, no. 2.

Hall, S. (1978) 'Racism and reaction', in *Five Views of Multi-Racial Britain*, London: CRE and BBC TV Further Education.

——(1990) 'Cultural identity and diaspora', in Rutherford, J. (ed.) *Identity: Community, Culture, Difference*, London: Lawrence and Wishart.

——(1992a) 'New ethnicities', reprinted in Donald, J. and Rattansi, A. *'Race', Culture and Difference*, London: Sage.

——(1992b) 'The west and the rest: discourse and power', in Hall, S. and Gieben, B. (eds) *Formations Of Modernity*, London: Sage.

Hall, S., Critcher, C., Jefferson, T., Clarke, J. and Roberts, B. (1978) *Policing the Crisis: Mugging the State and Law and Order*, Basingstoke: Macmillan.

Hallett, C. (ed.) (1989) *Women and Social Services Departments*, Hemel Hempstead: Harvester Wheatsheaf.

Halsey, A. H. (1992) 'Foreword', in Dennis, N. and Erdos, G., *Families Without Fatherhood*, London: Institute of Economic Affairs.

Hansard Parliamentary Debates (1966) House of Commons, vol. 729, 14 June.

——(1977) House of Commons, vol. 929, 6 April.

——(1994) House of Commons, vol. 246, 5 July.

Henderson, M. G. (1992) 'Speaking in tongues: dialogics, dialectics and the black woman writer's literary tradition', in Butler, J. and Scott, J. (eds) *Feminists Theorize the Political*, New York/London: Routledge; reprinted from Wall, C. A. (ed.) *Changing Our Own Words*, New Brunswick: Rutgers University Press (1991).

Hickman, M. J. (1995) *Religion, Class and Identity*, Aldershot: Avebury.

Hillyard, P. and Watson, S. (1996) 'Postmodern social policy: a contradiction in terms?', *Journal of Social Policy*, vol. 25, no. 3, pp. 321–46.

HMSO (1977) *Policy for the Inner Cities*, White Paper, Cmnd 6845.

——(1981) *Racial Disadvantage*, vol. 1, House of Commons Home Affairs Committee, Session 1980–81, London: HMSO.

Hollway, W. (1989) *Subjectivity and Method in Psychology: Gender, Meaning and Science*, London: Sage.

Hopkins, J. (1996) 'Social work through the looking glass', in Parton, N. (ed.) *Social Theory, Social Change and Social Work*, London: Routledge.

Hughes, G. and Lewis, G. (eds) (1998) *Unsettling Welfare: The Reconstruction of Social Policy*, London: Routledge in association with the Open University.

Hugman, R. (1991) *Power in the Caring Professions*, Basingstoke: Macmillan.

Hull, G., Scott, P. and Smith, B. (eds) (1982) *All the Women are White, All the Blacks are Men, But Some of us are Brave*, Old Westbury: Feminist Press.

Inland City Council (1984) *Bid for Section 11 LGA 66 Resources – Progress Report*.

——(1984) *Strategy for Ethnic Minorities – Report to Social Services Committee – Race Relations and Equal Opportunities Committee, Appendix 1*, 6 June.

——(1985) *Strategy for Services to Ethnic Minorities, Report to Social Services Committee*, 9 October.

——(1986) *Inland City Council Riots Action Plan – First Report*, April.

——(1986) Minute 4818–8 to 9 July Social Services Committee.

——(1986) *Social Worker Trainee Scheme, Committee Paper*. Report of Director of Social Services, 12 November.

——(1987) *Inland City Council Riots Action Plan – Progress, Report by the Director of Social Services*.

——(1991) *Applications Under Section 11 of the LGA 1966*, 10 April.

——(1991) *Race Relations Work Programme in the Social Services Directorate*, 29 January.

——(1991) *The Shape of Things to Come: A New Framework for the Social Services Department*, 15 July.

——(1994) *The Management Structure of the Social Services Department*, 8 June.

——(1995) *Race Equality Service Delivery Strategy, Report to Social Services Committee*, 11 January.

Itzin, C. (1995) 'The gender culture in organisations', in Itzin, C. and Newman, J. *Gender and Organisational Change*, London: Routledge.

Jenkins, R. and Solomos, J. (eds) (1987) *Racism and Equal Opportunity Policies in the 1980s*, Cambridge: Cambridge University Press.

Johnson, M., Cox, B. and Cross, M. (1989) 'Paying for change? Section 11 and local authority social services', *New Community*, vol. 15, no. 3.

Joint Council For The Welfare of Immigrants (1999) *Immigration, Nationality and Refugee Law Handbook: a User's Guide*, London: JCWI.

Jordan, J. (1986) *On Call: Political Essays*, London/Sydney: Pluto.

Joyce, P. (1994) *Democratic Subjects: The Self and The Social in Nineteenth Century England*, Cambridge: Cambridge University Press.

Kay, D. and Miles, R. (1992) *Refugees or Migrant Workers? European Volunteer Workers in Britain, 1946–1951*, London: Routledge.

Knox, R. (1984) Introduction to *'Oedipus The King' by Sophocles*, London: Penguin Classics.

Kovel, J. (1995) 'On racism and psychoanalysis', in Elliott, A. and Frosh, S. (eds) *Psychoanalysis in Contexts*, London: Routledge.

Krikler, J. (1995) 'Social neurosis and hysterical precognition in South Africa, a case and reflections', *Journal of Social History*, Spring, pp. 491–520.

Lane, C. (ed.) (1998) *The Psychoanalysis of Race*, New York: Columbia University Press.

Lacan, J. (1977) *The Four Fundamental Concepts of Psychoanalysis*, New York: Norton.

Leonard, P. (1997) *Postmodern Welfare*, London: Sage.

Lewis, G. (1993) 'Black women's employment and the British economy', in James, W. and Harris, C., *Inside Babylon*, London: Verso.

——(1998a) 'Citizenship', in Hughes, G. (ed.) *Imagining Welfare Futures*, London: Routledge.

——(1998b) 'Welfare and the social construction of "race"', in Saraga, E. (ed.) (1998).

——(1998c) 'Coming apart at the seams': the crises of the welfare state' in Hughes, G. and Lewis, G. (eds) (1998).

——(2000) 'An encounter of strangers? Stuart Hall meets social policy', in Grossberg, L., McRobie, A. and Gilroy, P. (eds) *Without Guarantees*, London: Verso.

Littlewood, R. and Lipsedge, M. (1982) *Aliens and Alienists: Ethnic Minorities and Psychiatry*, Harmondsworth: Penguin.

London Borough of Coolville – *see* Coolville.

Lorde, A. (1984) *Sister Outsider*, New York: The Crossing Press.

Lyotard, J.-F. (1984) *The Postmodern Condition: A Report on Knowledge*, Minneapolis: University of Michigan Press.

MacDonald, I. (1983) *Immigration Law and Practice in the UK*, London: Butterworths.

Mama, A. (1995) *Beyond the Masks: Race, Gender and Subjectivity*, London: Routledge.

Manning, B. (1979) 'The black social worker's role', reprinted in Cheetham et al. (1981).

Martin, L. (1994) 'Power, continuity and change: decoding black and white women managers' experience in local government', in Tanton, M. (ed.) *Women in Management*, London: Routledge.

Maxime, J. E. (1986) 'Some psychological models of black self-concept', in Ahmad, S., Cheetham, J. and Small, J. (eds) (1986).

McNay, L. (1994) *Foucault: A Critical Introduction*, Oxford: Blackwell.

Mercer, K. (1994) '1968: periodising politics and identity' in Mercer, K. (ed.) *Welcome to the Jungle: New Positions in Black Cultural Studies*, London: Routledge.

Mercer, N. and Longman, J. (1992) 'Accounts and the development of shared understanding in employment training interviews', *Text*, vol. 12, no. 1.

Mishra, R. (1984) *The Welfare State in Crisis*, Brighton: Wheatsheaf Books.

Mohanty, C. Talpade (1992) 'Feminist encounters: locating the politics of experience', in Barrett, M. and Phillips, A. (eds) *Destabilising Theory*, Cambridge: Polity Press; reprinted from *Copyright*, 1987, Fall.

Morrison, T. (1992) *Playing in the Dark*, Boston: Harvard University Press.

Mullard, C. (1982) 'Multiracial education in Britain: from assimilation to cultural pluralism', in Tierney, J. (ed.) *Race, Migration and Schooling*, New York: Holt.

Nanton, P. and Fitzgerald, M. (1990) 'Race policies in local government: boundaries or thresholds?', in Ball, W. and Solomos, J. (eds) *Race and Local Politics*, Basingstoke: Macmillan.

Nasir, S. (1996) ' "Race", gender and social policy', in Hallett, C. (ed.) *Women and Social Policy: An Introduction*, Hemel Hempstead: Harvester Wheatsheaf.

National Council for Voluntary Organisations (1995) *Invisible Partners*, Black Training and Enterprise Group, London: NCVO.

Newman, J. (1995) 'Gender and cultural change', in Itzin, C. and Newman, J. (eds) *Gender, Culture and Organisational Change: Putting Theory into Practice*, London: Routledge.

——(1998) 'Managerialism and social welfare', in Hughes, G. and Lewis, G. (eds) (1998).

Newman, J. and Clarke, J. (1994) 'Going about our business? The managerialisation of public services', in Clarke, J., Cochrane, A. and McLaughlin, E. (eds) *Managing Social Policy*, London: Sage.

Newman, K. (1983) 'Policing and social policy in multi-ethnic areas in London', speech to Cambridge Colloquium on Policing and Social Policy in Multi-Ethnic Areas in Europe.

Obeyesekere, G. (1990) *The Work of Culture: Symbolic Transformation in Psychoanalysis and Anthropology*, Chicago/London: University of Chicago Press.

O'Brien, M. and Penna, S. (1998) *Theorising Welfare*, London: Sage.

Omi, M. and Winant, H. (1994) *Racial Formation in the United States: From the 1960s to the 1990s*, New York: Routledge.

Osborn, D. (1980) 'Policing communities', *Police*, journal of the Police Federation.

Ousley, H. (1984) 'Local authority race initiatives', in Boddy, M. and Fudge (eds) *Local Socialism*, Basingstoke: Macmillan.

——(1990) 'Resisting institutional change', in Ball, W. and Solomos, J. (eds) *Race and Local Politics*, Basingstoke: Macmillan.

Painter, N. (1995) 'Soul murder: African-American slave families', paper presented to the XVIIIth Congress of Historical Studies, August, Montreal.

Parmar, P. (1982) 'Gender, race and class: Asian women in resistance', in Centre for Contemporary Cultural Studies (1982).

——(1981) 'Young Asian women: a critique of the pathological approval: *Multiracial Education*, vol. 9, no. 3, Summer.

Patel, N. (1990) *A 'Race' Against Time?: Social Service, Provision to Black Elders*, London: Runnymede Trust.

——(ed.) (1991) *Setting the Context for Change*, London: CCETSW.

Pearson, R. (1998) *Social Services in a Multi-Racial Society*, London: SSI.

Phizacklea, A. (1983) *One Way Ticket*, London: Routledge.

Phizacklea, A. and Miles, R. (1980) *Labour and Racism*, London: Routledge and Kegan Paul.

Phoenix, A. (1987) 'Theories of gender and black families', in Weiner, G. and Arnot, M. (eds) (1987).

——(1994) 'Practising feminist research: the intersection of gender and "race" in the research process', in Maynard, M. and Purvis, J. (eds) *Researching Women's Lives from a Feminist Perspective*, London: Taylor Francis.

Pollitt, C. (1990) *Managerialism and the Public Services*, Oxford: Blackwell.

Poster, M. (1984) *Foucault Reader*, New York: Pantheon.

Pringle, R. (1988) *Secretaries 'Talk': Sexuality, Power and Work*, London: Verso.

Probyn, E. (1993) *Sexing the Self*, London/New York: Routledge.

Ramdin, R. (1987) *The Making of the Black Working Class in Britain*, Aldershot: Wildwood House.

Rattansi, A. (1992) 'Changing the subject? Racism, Culture and Education, in Donald, J. and Rattansi, A. (eds) *'Race', Culture and Difference*, London: Sage.

——(1995) 'Just framing: ethnicities and racisms in a "postmodern" framework', in Nicholson, L. and Seidman, S. (eds) *Social Postmodernism: Beyond Identity Politics*, Cambridge: Cambridge University Press.

Rex, J. (1978) 'Race and the inner city', in *Five Views of Multi-Racial Britain*, London: CRE and BBC TV Further Education.

Rhodes, P. J. (1992) 'The emergence of a new policy: racial matching in fostering and adoption', *New Community*, vol. 18, no. 2.

Rich, A. (1984) 'Notes towards a politics of location', in *Blood, Bread and Poetry: Selected Prose 1979–1985*, New York/London: W. W. Norton and Company.

Riley, D. (1988) *Am I That Name?*, Basingstoke: Macmillan.

Rojek, C., Peacock, G. and Collins, S. (1988) *Social Work and Received Ideas*, London: Routledge.

Rose, J. (1996) *States of Fantasy*, Oxford: Clarendon Press.

Saggar, S. (1993) 'The politics of "race policy" in Britain', *Critical Social Policy*, 37.

Said, E. (1978) *Orientalism*, London: Penguin.

Saraga, E. (ed.) (1998) *Embodying the Social: Constructions of Difference*, London: Routledge, in association with the Open University.

Schwarz, B. (1996) 'The expansion and contraction of England', in Schwarz, B. (ed.) *The Expansion of England: Race, Ethnicity and Cultural History*, London: Routledge.

Scott, J. (1988) *Gender and the Politics of History*, New York: Columbia University Press.

——(1992) 'Experience', in Butler, J. and Scott, J. (eds) *Feminists Theorize the Political*, New York/London: Routledge.

Sherman, A. (1979) The Daily Telegraph, 9 September.

Sim, J. (1982) 'Scarman: the police counter-attack', *The Socialist Register*, London: The Merlin Press.

Sivanandan, A. (1982) *A Different Hunger: Writings on Black Resistance*, London: Pluto.

Small, J. (1984) 'The crisis in adoption', *International Journal of Social Psychiatry*, vol. 30, nos. 1/2.

——(1989) 'Towards a black perspective in social work: a transcultural exploration', in Langan, M. and Lee, P. (eds) *Radical Social Work Today*, London: Routledge.

Smith, B. (1982) 'Towards a black feminist criticism', reprinted in Hull, G., Scott, P. and Smith, B. (eds) *All the Women are White, All the Blacks are Men, But Some of us are Brave*, Old Westbury: Feminist Press.

——(ed.) (1983) *Home Girls: A Black Feminist Anthology*, New York: Kitchen Table: Women of Color Press.

Social Services Inspectorate (1991) *Women in the Social Services*, Department of Health, London: The Stationery Office.

Solomos, J. (1989) *Race and Racism in Contemporary Britain*, Basingstoke: Macmillan.

——(1998) 'Social policy and social movements: "race", racism and social policies', in Ellison, N. and Pierson, C. (eds) *Developments in British Social Policy*, Basingstoke: Macmillan.

Solomos, J. and Back, L. (1995) *Race, Politics and Social Change*, London: Routledge.

Solomos, J. and Ball, W. (1990) 'New initiatives and the possibilities of reform', in Ball, W. and Solomos, J. (eds) *Race and Local Politics*, Basingstoke: Macmillan.

Solomos, J. and Singh, G. (1990) 'Racial equality, housing and the local state', in Ball, W. and Solomos, J. (eds) *Race and Local Politics*, Basingstoke: Macmillan.

Solomos, J., Findlay, B., Jones, S. and Gilroy, P. (1982) 'The organic crisis of British capitalism and race: the experience of the seventies', in Centre for Contemporary Cultural Studies (1982).

Southall Black Sisters (1989) 'Two struggles: challenging male violence and the police', in Dunhill, C. (ed.) *The Boys in Blue: Women's Challenge to the Police*, London: Virago.

Spivak, G. (1987) *In Other Worlds: Essays in Cultural Politics*, New York: Methuen.

The Stationery Office (1998) *A Healthier Nation*, London: The Stationery Office.

The Stationery Office (1998) *A New NHS*, London: The Stationery Office.

Steiner, J. (1985) 'Turning a blind eye: the cover-up for Oedipus', *International Review of Psycho-analysis*, vol. 12.

Stewart, M. B. (1983) 'Racial discrimination and occupational attainment in Britain', *The Economic Journal*, 93, September.

Stoler, A. L. (1995) *Race and the Education of Desire*, Durham, N.C./London: Duke University Press.

Stubbs, P. (1985) 'The employment of black social workers: from "ethnic sensitivity" to antiracism?', *Critical Social Policy*, no. 12.

Sulter, M. (ed.) (1990) *Passion: Discourses on Black Women's Creativity*, Hebden Bridge: Urban Fox Press.

The Times, 18 July 1981.

Tizard, B. and Phoenix, A. (1993) *Black, White or Mixed Race?: Race and Racism in the Lives of Young People of Mixed Parentage*, London: Routledge.

Touraine, A. (1981) *The Voice and the Eye: An Analysis of Social Movements*, Cambridge: Cambridge University Press.

Vellacott, P. (1971) *Sophocles and Oedipus: A Study of Oedipus Tyrannus*, with a new translation, London: Macmillan.

Walker, R. and Ahmad, W. (1994) 'Windows of opportunity in rotting frames? Care providers, perspectives on community care and black communities', *Critical Social Policy*, 40.

Walvin, J. (1973) *Black and White: Negro and English Society*, London: Allen Lane.

Wandor, M. (1990) *Once A Feminist: Stories of a Generation*, London: Virago.

Watt, S. and Cook, J. (1989) 'Another expectation unfulfilled: black women in social services departments', in Hallett, C. (ed.) (1989).

Weedon, C. (1987) *Feminist Practice and Post-Structuralist Theory*, Oxford: Blackwell.

Weeks, J. (1996) 'The idea of a sexual community: in *Soundings*, issue 2.

Weiner, G. and Arnot, M. (eds) (1987) *Gender Under Scrutiny*, London: Hutchinson in association with the Open University.

Williams, F. (1989) *Social Policy: A Critical Introduction*, Cambridge: Polity Press.

——(1992) 'Somewhere over the rainbow: universality and diversity in social policy', in Manning, J. and Page, P. (eds) *Social Policy Review*, 4.

Winant, H. (1994) 'Racial formation and hegemony: global and local developments', in Rattansi, A. and Westwood, S., *Racism, Modernity and Identity: On the Western Front*, Cambridge: Polity Press.

Wright, F. J. (1976) *British Social Services*, 2nd edn, Plymouth: MacDonald and Evans Ltd.

Young, K. (1987) 'The space between words: local authorities and the concept of equal opportunities', in Jenkins, R. and Solomos, J. (eds) (1987).

Young, K. and Connelly, N. (1981) *Policy and Practice in the Multi-racial City*, London: Policy Studies Institute.

Index

Note: Page numbers referring to interviews with social workers are shown in **bold** type.